CYBERBULLYING AND SEXTING

Drawing on two empirical studies and influential theoretical frameworks, this book provides a critical overview of the key regulatory challenges concerning cyber-bullying and sexting behaviours among young people (persons under 18 years).

The author explores issues such as conceptualising the behaviours, examining the prevailing presence of sexism, myths and stereotypes surrounding gender roles and identity, and the limitations of criminal law as an effective regulatory tool. In doing so, identifying peer-based sexting behaviours as part of a continuum of sexual behaviour is promoted alongside the need to consider interventions beyond the legal landscape and in line with the United Nations Convention on the Rights of the Child. In the main, priority is given to non-legal responses and the need for more effective and comprehensive gender-sensitive education programmes. The book therefore provides a more developed conceptual understanding of sexting and cyberbullying behaviours among young people.

Cyberbullying and Sexting

Regulatory Challenges in the Digital Age

Elizabeth Agnew

·HART·

OXFORD · LONDON · NEW YORK · NEW DELHI · SYDNEY

HART PUBLISHING

Bloomsbury Publishing Plc

Kemp House, Chawley Park, Cumnor Hill, Oxford, OX2 9PH, UK

1385 Broadway, New York, NY 10018, USA

29 Earlsfort Terrace, Dublin 2, Ireland

HART PUBLISHING, the Hart/Stag logo, BLOOMSBURY and the Diana logo are
trademarks of Bloomsbury Publishing Plc

First published in Great Britain 2023

Copyright © Elizabeth Agnew, 2023

Elizabeth Agnew has asserted her right under the Copyright, Designs and
Patents Act 1988 to be identified as Author of this work.

A catalogue record for this book is available from the British Library.

A catalogue record for this book is available from the Library of Congress.

Library of Congress Control Number: 2023947464

ISBN: HB: 978-1-50995-134-5
        ePDF: 978-1-50995-136-9
        ePub: 978-1-50995-135-2

Typeset by Compuscript Ltd, Shannon

To find out more about our authors and books visit www.hartpublishing.co.uk.
Here you will find extracts, author information, details of forthcoming events
and the option to sign up for our newsletters.

ACKNOWLEDGEMENTS

First, I am extremely grateful to the professionals and young people who so generously gave up their time to talk to me and share their experiences. Writing this book would not have been possible without their important voices noted throughout, shaping and informing the discussions.

I would also like to thank my colleagues for their constant support and guidance throughout the writing process, in particular, Eithne Dowds, Ciara Hackett, Luke Moffett and Clare Patton. A special word of thanks to Anne-Marie McAlinden and Phil Scraton, who have continued to show me unwavering support and who have always been there for me, especially when I needed some extra guidance and words of encouragement. Their willingness to generously give up their time and share their expertise never goes unnoticed.

Last, but by no means least, my family: my mum and dad who have always been an inspiration to me. Thank you for the countless hours baby-sitting, the dinners and words of encouragement as I finished writing the book. To my lovely sister, Claire, who took Luca on day trips to allow me time to write. To my partner, Noel, who was always there, willing to listen and making lots of cups of tea and hot chocolate – throwing in the odd joke to make me laugh.

To Luca and Leo, who always bring me joy. I write this book for you both and all children and young people, in the hope that your voices are always heard and listened to.

CONTENTS

ACRONYMS

EA	Education Authority
CEOP	Child Exploitation and Online Protection Centre
CSE	Child Sexual Exploitation
DBS	Disclosure and Barring Service
DUP	Democratic Unionist Party
ECHR	European Convention of Human Rights
ESRC	Economic and Social Research Council
HRA	Human Rights Act 1998
HSB	Harmful Sexual Behaviour
ICT	Information and Communication Technology
LGBTQ+	Lesbian, Gay, Bi-sexual, Trans-sexual, Queer +
MACR	Minimum Age of Criminal Responsibility
MP	Member of Parliament
NI	Northern Ireland
NSPCC	National Society for the Prevention of Cruelty to Children
NSW	New South Wales
PDF	Post Doctoral Fellowship
PSNI	Police Service of Northern Ireland
RSE	Relationship and Sexuality Education
STI	Sexually Transmitted Infection
TA-HSB	Technology-Assisted Harmful Sexual Behaviour
UK	United Kingdom
UN	United Nations
UNCRC	United Nations Convention on the Rights of the Child
WHO	World Health Organisation

TABLE OF CASES

TABLE OF LEGISLATION

UK

EU/UN

Reports

International

1

Introduction

As adults we can't go and tell young people this is not normal. You've got to talk to them, listen to them. If they think it is normal, why do they think it's normal? So I think that would be the way to start off. Find out why they accept this. Do they know what could happen because of what they're doing? ... Does it make you feel comfortable or uncomfortable? And I think those questions have to be asked. The dialogue with the young people to see, to get their opinion rather than us dictating what we know. That doesn't work. We have to listen to the younger generation and find out what their stance is.[1]

Young people engaging in harmful sexual behaviours has provoked a great sense of unease within contemporary socio-political and legal landscapes. Yet, young people's engagement in a broad range of harmful behaviours is not new. Several studies have explored youth involvement in gang-associated sexual exploitation and sexual violence, anti-social behaviour, bullying on- and offline, sexually exploitative relationships and contact forms of sexual abuse.[2] The introduction of the internet has added a new dimension to how behaviours are understood and conceptualised, moving beyond the typical offline context and creating new levels of social anxiety. This is mainly due to features including, the speed at which material can be accessed and disseminated, the breadth of information available and limited *effective* regulatory frameworks. While we know that the internet is a crucial medium through which many young people can communicate and positively interact socially with their peers, the online world has also provided a new platform for young people to engage in more coercive and harmful behaviours. This also includes young people themselves being subject to exploitative behaviours.

With the continual growth and advancement in technological developments, a growing fear that modern electronics have led to the 'end of childhood, innocence, traditional values and authority', has thus emerged.[3] While Livingstone

---

[1] Interview 11 (PhD): Victim Support Organisation.
[2] See H Beckett et al, "'It's Wrong ... But You Get Used to It" A Qualitative Study of Gang-Associated Sexual Violence Towards, and Exploitation of, Young People in England', A Report Commissioned by the Office of the Children's Commissioner's Inquiry into Child Sexual Exploitation in Gangs and Groups (University of Bedfordshire and Children's Commissioner, 2013); L Radford et al, 'Child Abuse and Neglect in the UK Today' (NSPCC, 2011).
[3] S Livingstone, *Young People and New Media: Childhood and the Changing Media Environment* (SAGE, 2002) 2.

labels such thinkers as 'pessimists', the internet *has* provided unique opportunities for children to explore a world they would not otherwise have access to offline, or to the same degree and extent. In this respect, the 'different nature of childhood in a digital age' has become more prevalent.[4] Of the different forms of harmful behaviours that increase children's vulnerability online, cyberbullying and sexting rank among some of the most prevalent. Collectively, there has been an increase in research published by children's charities and statutory organisations with a focus on exploring both bullying behaviours and sexting (see below for a summary of key findings).

Drawing on a wealth of interdisciplinary literature and original empirical work conducted by the author, this book will critically examine peer-on-peer bullying and sexting behaviours and the challenges they present for profession-als and practitioners across a range of sectors, including law, policy, education and safeguarding. The central argument is that due to a number of prevailing and problematic interpretations of childhood, sexuality and criminalisation, certain behaviours displayed by young people, in particular sexting behaviours, have been neglected within contemporary social and legal discourses. This book therefore provides new insights and a more conceptual understanding of the behaviours under review.

To achieve this, the book has four key objectives: (i) to outline the develop-ment of bullying and sexting behaviours among young people and locate such debates within childhood and youth sexuality discourses; (ii) highlight any 'new' and complex features of the behaviours and how these impact law and policy in the area; (iii) explore existing tensions within other current regulatory frame-works (beyond the substantive law) and note any notable gaps and limitations; and (iv) consider best approaches moving forward to ensure that future interventions not only recognise the intricate dimensions to the behaviours being displayed, but also reflect the lived experiences of young people.

The book ultimately contends that: (i) *any* form of intervention, at both policy and practice level, *must* account for the complexity of gender roles and the shift-ing power dynamics within youth culture; (ii) current laws are not designed to cater to the breadth of behaviours young people are presenting with and regulatory frameworks must look beyond the legal landscape; and (iii) sexting behaviours in particular must be viewed as part of a continuum of sexual behaviour, one that accounts for *consensual* and *non-consensual* contexts as well as the blurring of boundaries.

Before examining some of the current data available, it is important to provide some contextual information, including introducing some of the key terms that will be referred to throughout the book.

---

[4] J Rallings, *Youth and the Internet: A Guide for Policy Makers* (Barnardo's, 2015) 2.

I. Key Terms and Definitions

While definitional tensions associated with 'cyberbullying' and 'sexting' specifically are teased out in subsequent Chapters 4 and 5, a brief definition will be provided here to situate the book within the broader literature. 'Cyberbullying', also referred to as 'online social cruelty' and 'electronic bullying', in simplistic terms, is bullying using electronic devices such as Smartphones, laptops and computers.[5] There is a growing body of literature and research exploring bullying behaviours and the National Union of Teachers notes that bullying among children and young people is 'one of the most destructive social processes that young people can experience'.[6] In comparison, understanding sexting as a behaviour young people are engaging in, is still very much in its infancy, although gaining scholarly traction. As awareness of the sexual behaviour has grown, understanding has moved from a narrow and limited construction of the behaviour (and the focus primarily being on the sending of naked and semi-naked pictures) to include wider manifestations of 'sexting' behaviour (including text messages and videos).[7] It is generally agreed that peer-based sexting includes the creating and sharing of sexual images, videos or messages with or without consent.[8] While sexting behaviours among young people can include exploitative and coercive elements (discussed further throughout this book), cases which involve an adult perpetrator would always require a higher level of intervention. The focus of this book is therefore on peer-based behaviours, that being behaviours where all parties involved are under 18 years. To extend the scope of the book beyond the peer context would require analysis of a very different set of challenges.

Following on from this, 'child sexual exploitation' or CSE, has been defined as sexual abuse perpetrated against children (persons under 18 years). As noted by Hackett and Walker, CSE is an 'umbrella term' which covers a wide range of contact and non-contact behaviours and can be perpetrated by adults or peers from diverse backgrounds,[9] although the term is often used within an adult/child context. 'Harmful sexual behaviour' (HSB) is the preferred term used by practitioners when dealing with young people under 18 years who engage in sexually coercive or exploitative behaviours. The term encompasses behaviour which is

---

[5] RM Kowalski et al, *Cyberbullying: Bullying in the Digital Age*, 2nd edn (Oxford, Wiley-Blackwell, 2012) 56.

[6] NUT, *NUT Policy Statement on Preventing Sexual Harassment and Bullying* (NUT, 2014) 3.

[7] See Chapter 5.

[8] See J Ringrose et al, *A Qualitative Study of Children, Young People and 'Sexting': A Report Prepared for the NSPCC* (NSPCC LSE, 2012); E Setty, '"Confident" and "Hot" or "Desperate" and "Cowardly"? Meanings of Young Men's Sexting Practices in Youth Sexting Culture' (2020) 23(5) *Journal of Youth Studies* 561; E Agnew, 'Sexting among Young People: Towards a Gender Sensitive Approach' (2021) 29(1) *International Journal of Children's Rights* 3.

[9] H Beckett and J Walker, 'Words Matter: Reconceptualising the Conceptualisation of Child Sexual Exploitation' in H Beckett and J Pearce (eds), *Understanding and Responding to Child Sexual Exploitation* (Routledge, 2018) 11.

sexual in nature, considered to be developmentally inappropriate for the young person's age and stage of development, and often involves a power imbalance (in terms of age, strength and maturity).[10] Finally, 'peer-on-peer abuse' has been defined as 'physical, sexual and emotional abuse in young people's relationships, including their intimate relationships, friendships and wider peer associations'.[11] The abuse can occur in a range of contexts, covering both on- and offline settings.[12] While HSB focuses on sexually harmful behaviours and 'peer-on-peer' abuse is somewhat wider in scope, there is a degree of overlap between what is defined as HSB and what is considered to be peer-on-peer abuse. As a result, these terms can sometimes be used interchangeably within the literature.

The author refers to both 'children' and 'young people' throughout the book. Both terms simply refer to persons under 18 years of age.

II. Measuring 'Extent'

Data on cyberbullying and sexting practices among young people varies greatly depending on sample size, age range, terminology used and methodological approach. To a lesser extent, reliable data on sexting among young people is available which explores the prevalence of the behaviour.

In relation to bullying on- and offline, during the year 2019/20, the main concerns raised by children aged 11–18 years during ChildLine counselling sessions include mental health, family relationships and bullying.[13] According to the ONS, in 2020, approximately one in five children aged 10–15 years had experienced at least one type of online bullying.[14] The Youth Wellbeing and Prevalence Survey for Northern Ireland 2020 notes that 16.8 per cent of young people aged 11–19 years have been subjected to offline bullying and 14.9 per cent have experienced online bullying.[15] In terms of settings, it has been noted that 72 per cent of young people who experience online bullying go on to say that some of the harmful behaviour was perpetrated at school or during school time.[16] Indeed, experiences of bullying have been noted as a key reason why some children are not attending school. A study conducted during 2010 which examined why young people were 'missing' or 'frequently absent' from school since September 2009, estimated that around 16,493 young people aged 11–15 years

---

[10] See E Agnew and A-M McAlinden, 'Addressing Harmful Sexual Behaviours among Children and Young People: Definitional and Regulatory Tensions' in AK Gill and H Begum (eds), *Child Sexual Abuse in Black and Minoritised Communities* (Palgrave Macmillan, 2023).

[11] C Firmin, *Abuse between Young People* (Routledge, 2018) 28.

[12] Agnew and McAlinden (n 10).

[13] H Bentley et al, *How Safe Are Our Children? 2020* (NSPCC, 2020) 57.

[14] Office for National Statistics, *Online Bullying in England and Wales: Year Ending in March 2020* (ONS, 2020).

[15] L Bunting et al, *The Mental Health of Parents and Children in Northern Ireland* (Youth Wellbeing NI, 2020) 5.

[16] Agnew and McAlinden (n 10).

were not attending state school due to exposure to 'severe' bullying behaviours.[17] The UK Beatbullying project also note that 44 per cent of young people said their victimisation started offline but then continued online.[18] The same survey also explains that one in thirteen children of secondary school age suffer 'persistent' online bullying – this would account for approximately 350,222 children.[19]

Similarly, sexting estimates are extremely varied. For example, one study, which surveyed a sample of young people aged 14–16 years, noted that approximately 40 per cent of young people surveyed knew someone who had sent a 'sext', while 27 per cent of respondents said sexting happens 'regularly or all the time'.[20] Another study notes that one third of children surveyed had received a sexual message and one quarter had received a sexual image – with the majority of senders being the young person's peer.[21] The EU Kids Online study was conducted across 25 countries including the UK, demonstrating that 15 per cent of young people surveyed (11–16 year olds) had received sexual messages, while 3 per cent said they had sent one.[22] In an updated EU Kids Online report for 2020, involving 19 countries of which the UK was not one, a much broader range was noted. It was reported that between 8 per cent (Italy) and 39 per cent (Flanders) of young people aged 12–16 years had received a sexual message in the past year.[23] Wood and colleagues also conducted a survey which involved young people aged 14–17 years across five countries in Europe. In the report young people in England were noted as being more likely to send 'sexts' to a partner (38 per cent), compared to other countries in the study including Norway (30 per cent) and Italy (22 per cent).[24] Finally, Hollis and Belton explain that 68 per cent of young males who participated in their study had engaged in multiple forms of 'technology-assisted harmful sexual behaviour' (TA-HSB), including sexting, sexual harassment and grooming.[25] Importantly, it was also recognised in Hollis and Belton's study that there was 'a level of overlap' regarding sexual behaviours displayed on- and offline among children and young people.[26]

---

[17] V Brown et al, *Estimating the Prevalence of Young People Absent from School Due to Bullying* (Red Balloon Learner Centre Group, 2011) 5–6.

[18] E-J Cross et al, *Virtual Violence II: Progress and Challenges in the Fight against Cyberbullying* (Beatbullying, 2012) 25.

[19] ibid 6.

[20] A Phippen and D Wright, *Sharing Personal Images and Videos among Young People* (UKCCIS, 2011) 1.

[21] Cross et al (n 18) 27.

[22] S Livingstone et al, *EU Kids Online: Final Report* (EU Kids Online, London School of Economics & Political Science, 2011) 22.

[23] D Smahel et al, *EU Kids Online 2020: Survey Results from 19 Countries* (EU Kids Online, 2020) 7.

[24] M Wood et al, 'Images across Europe: The Sending and Receiving of Sexual Images and Associations with Interpersonal Violence in Young People's Relationships' (2015) 59 *Children and Youth Services Review* 149, 153.

[25] V Hollis and E Belton, *Children and Young People Who Engage in Technology-Assisted Harmful Sexual Behaviour – A Study of Their Behaviours, Backgrounds and Characteristics* (Impact and Evidence Series, NSPCC, 2017) 11–12.

[26] ibid 18.

In light of the above reports on peer-based cyberbullying and sexting behaviours, despite some fluctuating figures, the behaviours are growing issues of concern for professionals and practitioners in law, safeguarding and child welfare. Further to this, while the above studies provide significant insights regarding the nature – and to some degree the extent – of cyberbullying and sexting behaviours among young people, determining the *full* nature and extent of the behaviours is becoming increasingly difficult, and in some circumstances, impossible. This is mostly due to the normative nature attached to some aspects of the behaviours displayed, as well as prevailing and problematic assumptions surrounding consent, gender roles and blame culture.[27]

III. Northern Ireland as a Research Site

Following the Government of Ireland Act 1920, the island of Ireland was partitioned into two separate regions: Northern Ireland and the Republic of Ireland. The 1920 Act resulted in a division, a division between those who wished to remain part of the 'Irish Free State' and those who wished to stay part of the United Kingdom.[28] While pockets of unrest were visible, it was not until 1968 that it reached a critical point and tensions erupted. A 30-year conflict (known colloquially as 'The Troubles') ensued between 1968 and 1998. In very simplistic terms, it was a political conflict which centred on the constitutional status and future of the island. The conflict ended with the enactment of the Belfast/Good Friday Agreement in 1998, which saw Westminster devolve powers to a newly established Parliament of Northern Ireland. Yet, despite significant moves forward, Northern Ireland has been in a period of transition ever since as the generational impact of the conflict has been significant. Scholars note how the conflict has gone beyond a territorial or constitutional conflict to one which has been 'far reaching' and impacting many other aspects of community life.[29] Indeed, Stormont (Parliament of Northern Ireland) has been subject to prolonged periods of suspension, mostly due to tensions around power-sharing. The idea of power-sharing requires that there be unionist and nationalist representatives in Parliament. Yet, notable tensions have arisen, particularly over the past few years in relation to Brexit (no working assembly from 2017–2020), and most recently, over the Northern Ireland Protocol.[30] In fact, while writing this book, there has been no

---

[27] Discussed throughout the book but in particular in Chapters 4, 5 and 6.

[28] See R Perry, 'Revising Irish History: The Northern Ireland Conflict and the War of Ideas' (2010) 40(4) *Journal of European Studies* 329.

[29] See S McAlister et al, 'Childhood in Transition: Growing up in "Post-Conflict" Northern Ireland' (2014) 12(3) *Children's Geographies* 297.

[30] J Sargeant, 'Northern Ireland: Functioning of Government without Ministers' (Institute for Government, 14 November 2022) https://www.instituteforgovernment.org.uk/article/explainer/northern-ireland-functioning-government-without-ministers, last accessed 16 July 2023.

functioning Executive in Northern Ireland since February 2022. The absence of a stable assembly and the historical context of the island, reinforces the existence of a set of prevailing tensions surrounding religion, territory and the constitutional status within Northern Ireland – which still very much live on within the socio-political and legal domain.[31]

The history of the island is important as the devolved nature of government means that the Northern Ireland Executive has legislative control over 'transferred matters' including education, justice and policing, health and social services.[32] Yet, the 'legacy' of the conflict continues to limit progressive policies and practices, especially within youth justice and education as young people particularly 'feel undervalued and negatively stereotyped'.[33] In addition, the role of religion within the conflict is an important dimension, as Catholic and Protestant communities were segregated with Catholics mostly associated with Nationalism and Protestants with Unionism. Indeed, Wilkinson notes that the education system within Northern Ireland 'is structured around the widespread segregation of students by religion'.[34] Consequently, a strong morally conservative strain within the region has been commented on, often stagnating progressive laws and policies, particularly associated with female sexual agency and autonomy.[35] The Northern Ireland context is therefore particularly important when discussing youth engagement in harmful behaviours alongside education, gender and morality. The research site is therefore considered throughout the book when placing data in context, at appropriate junctures.

IV. Framing the Analysis: Childhood, Agency and Youth Sexuality

The main focus of theoretical analysis includes social and critical theories on childhood and contemporary discourses on youth sexuality. The literature documents the early 'discovery of childhood' around the seventeenth century, charting the movement from a period where children were economically valued to the conceptualisation of children as weak and vulnerable.[36] It is the continual construction

---

[31] See eg P Moss, 'Northern Ireland: A Year without Devolved Government' (BBC, 9 January 2018) https://www.bbc.co.uk/news/uk-northern-ireland-politics-42608322, last accessed 16 July 2023.
[32] B Dickson, *Law in Northern Ireland*, 3rd edn (Oxford, Hart Publishing, 2018).
[33] D Haydon et al, 'Young People, Conflict and Regulation' (2012) 51(5) *The Howard Journal* 503.
[34] DC Wilkinson, 'Sex and Relationships Education: A Comparison of Variation in Northern Ireland's and England's Policy-Making Processes' (2017) 17(6) *Sex Education* 607.
[35] See eg G Ellison, 'Criminalizing the Payment for Sex in Northern Ireland: Sketching the Contours of a Moral Panic' (2017) 57(1) *The British Journal of Criminology* 194; see also Chapter 3 of this book.
[36] P Ariés, *Centuries of Childhood*, translated from the French by Robert Baldick (London, Cape, 1962) 33; A James and A James, *Constructing Childhood Theory, Policy and Social Practice* (Palgrave Macmillan, 2004).

and reconstruction of childhood which plays a pivotal role in understanding current conceptions and misconceptions of cyberbullying and sexting among young people. In fact, the framing and historical paradigms of childhood have been central to regulatory tensions associated with youth sexuality and a prevailing desire to conform children to the 'romantic' notion of childhood.[37] As Rubin comments: 'great nineteenth century moral paroxysms are still with us. They have left a deep imprint on attitudes about sex.'[38]

Theoretical tensions have thus led to confusing and conflicting messages surrounding young people, childhood and sexuality. These issues have contributed towards a contemporary hypersensitive culture regarding youth sexuality and sexual exploration among children and young people.[39] This can lead to over-regulatory frameworks being engaged for behaviour that is developmentally normal for a young person's age and stage of development, within the technologically advanced world in which we live. Despite this notable concern, there is also a considerable literature base suggesting that early access to overly sexualised material and content can have a detrimental impact on children and young people.[40] Consequently, a careful balance is required between recognising young people's sexual agency while also ensuring they are protected from sexually exploitative and coercive behaviours. Yet, in the context of peer-based sexting, it can sometimes be difficult to disentangle the explorative from the exploitative, as the behaviours very much lie on a continuum of sexual behaviour (discussed further below and in Chapter 7).

Increasing attention to cyberbullying and sexting behaviours among young people has mostly been prompted due to a number of high-profile cases, including Jesse Logan and Amanda Todd. For context, in July 2008, 18-year-old Jesse took her own life after her ex-boyfriend circulated images of her to school peers.[41] In 2012, 15-year-old Amanda Todd took her own life after being groomed online by an adult male to 'flash' her breasts online. The recipient at the other end of the webcam screen shot the image and posted it online, leading to several years of peer-based bullying both on- and offline.[42] While the cases have distinct features relating to the scope of power differentials – Amanda was groomed by an adult, whereas it was Jesse's peer (her ex-boyfriend) who shared the image – both examples bring to the fore two main issues: first, some of the problematic dimensions to youth culture including the prevalence of bullying on- and offline; and, second,

---

[37] P Scraton (ed), '*Childhood*' in '*Crisis*'? (UCL Press, 1997).
[38] GS Rubin, 'Thinking Sex: Notes for a Radical Theory of the Politics of Sexuality' in K Plummer (ed), *Sexualities: Critical Concepts in Sociology* (first published 1984, Routledge, 2002) 189.
[39] See eg Scraton (n 37).
[40] See L Ashurst and A-M McAlinden, 'Young People, Peer-to-Peer Grooming and Sexual Offending' (2015) 62(4) *Probation Journal* 374.
[41] S Hinduja, 'Sexting, the Jesse Logan Case, and What Schools Can Do' (Cyberbullying Research Centre, 2009).
[42] K Dufour, 'Amanda Todd Case Highlights Issue of Online Bullying' (*The Telegraph*, 16 October 2012).

the entrenched stigma associated with youth sexuality. As an illustration, Amanda flashing her breasts was seen to be a 'catalyst of her demise' which significantly influenced the form and content of the media reporting.[43] The act of flashing her breasts therefore became the focus of reporting rather than the grooming and exploitation by an *adult male* and the peer bullying that ensued. Indeed, the 'oppositional images' of children as either innocent or deviant often results in children being framed as actors in their own victimisation, if they do not neatly fit into 'ideal' victim status or traditional childhood narratives.[44] This analysis becomes significant when examining peer-based sexting behaviours.

In recent times, consideration of the wider tensions within sexual crime discourses and the corresponding response to children and young people who display harmful sexual behaviour amongst their peers, has been brought into sharp focus. The literature demonstrates that the child as 'sexual deviant' contradicts established victim and offender models while also calling into question children's 'natural' innocence,[45] the stereotypical image of the sex offender as 'homo sacer' and a 'non-citizen'[46] and the 'sexualisation of risk'.[47] At the same time, central to social and political discourses on harmful and exploitative behaviour, is the notion of the 'outsider' and 'other'.[48] A 'moral panic' often results in the labelling of 'rule-breakers' and the crisis is recognised as a 'key moment'.[49] As Chapters 2 and 3 will illustrate, it can be argued that cyberbullying and sexting among young people is identified as a 'crisis' and a 'key moment' in redefining childhood, youth sexuality and conceptualising harmful sexual behaviours among young people. Whether this 'crisis' is justified will be explored throughout the book at appropriate junctures.

Drawing on the body of scholarship dedicated to childhood, youth sexuality and sexual crime, alongside empirical data, two additional themes emerge which require analysis: (i) the role of consent; and (ii) sexting as part of a continuum of sexual behaviour. First, the role of consent and the blurred boundaries surrounding the parameters of consent will be framed within the context of peer-on-peer

---

[43] R Penney, 'The Rhetoric of the Mistake in Adult Narratives of Youth Sexuality: The Case of Amanda Todd' (2016) 16(4) *Feminist Media Studies* 710.

[44] B Franklin, 'Children's Rights and Media Wrongs: Changing Representations of Children and the Developing Rights Agenda' in B Franklin (ed), *The New Handbook of Children's Rights: Comparative Policy and Practice* (London, Routledge, 2022) Chapter 1; A-M McAlinden, 'Deconstructing Victim and Offender Identities in Discourses on Child Sexual Abuse: Hierarchies, Blame and the Good/Evil Dialectic' (2014) 54(4) *British Journal of Criminology* 180.

[45] A Taylor, 'Troubling Childhood Innocence: Reframing the Debate over the Media Sexualisation of Children' (2010) 35(1) *Australasian Journal of Early Childhood* 48.

[46] 'Homo-sacer', as defined by Spencer is described as 'life without form and value' in D Spencer, 'Sex Offender as Homo Sacer' (2009) 11(2) *Punishment and Society* 220.

[47] S Scott et al, 'Swings and Roundabouts: Risk Anxiety and the Everyday Worlds of Children' (1998) 32(4) *Sociology* 689.

[48] HS Becker, *Outsiders: Studies in the Sociology of Deviance* (The Free Press, 1963); E Goffman, *Stigma: Notes on the Management of Spoiled Identity* (Penguin, 1963).

[49] S Cohen, *Folk Devils and Moral Panics*, 3rd edn (Routledge, 2002) 4; E Carrabine et al, *Criminology: A Sociological Introduction*, 2nd edn (Routledge, 2009) 96.

sexting behaviours. Consent has been noted as central to the debate on peer-based sexting and a key factor in understanding the cultural normalisation of the practice.[50] Youth culture and the socio-cultural context surrounding the peer-based interactions will therefore be carefully examined. In this vein, the complexity of sexting behaviours young people are engaging in, ranging from consensual to exploitative, will become apparent. Second, recognising that sexting is part of a continuum of sexual behaviour will help situate the behaviours within the broader framework of 'normal' and 'healthy' behaviour and 'unhealthy' and potentially 'problematic' sexual behaviour. Because peer-based sexting can range from explorative to more coercive and harmful, as Kelly explains, using a continuum allows the 'similarities with other forms of sexual violence' to be identified while also ensuring that the unique features of the behaviour under review are still central to analysis.[51] Not surprisingly, the influential work of Liz Kelly will therefore be introduced to inform analysis of peer-on-peer sexting, as well as the seminal work of Simon Hackett on harmful sexual behaviours among young people.[52]

Finally, concerns surrounding the current regulation of harmful behaviours was an emerging key theme within the literature and empirical findings. In particular, the disparity in age limits and the over-criminalisation of young people became a focus. As Day notes, due to the complexity of behaviours being displayed, it is extremely difficult to place sexting among young people into 'a legally defined category'.[53] Due to the increasing attention afforded to legal reforms, the strengths and limitations of current organisational and regulatory frameworks in Northern Ireland became another focal point within the research.

Drawing on empirical data collected by the author, this book will therefore contribute to ongoing discussions in the area of peer-on-peer behaviours, within the context of bullying and sexting behaviours specifically. In doing so, the book will provide new critical insights into the emergence, evolving nature and impact of peer-based cyberbullying and sexting, as well as strengthen some ongoing debates in the area.

V. Methodological Design: A Brief Outline

Article 12 of the UN Convention on the Rights of the Child reinforces the importance of including young people's voices on issues that directly impact their lives

---

[50] See K Albury and K Crawford, 'Sexting, Consent and Young People's Ethics: Beyond Megan's Story' (2012) 26(3) *Continuum: Journal of Media & Cultural Studies* 463.

[51] L Kelly, *Surviving Sexual Violence* (Cambridge, Polity, 1988) 137.

[52] See S Hackett, 'Children and Young People with Harmful Sexual Behaviours' in C Barter and B David (eds), *Children Behaving Badly? Peer Violence between Children and Young People* (John Wiley and Sons, 2010).

[53] T Day, 'The New Digital Dating Behaviour – Sexting: Teens' Explicit Love Letters: Criminal Justice or Civil Liability' (2010) 33(1) *Hastings Communications and Entertainment Law Journal* 71.

(see also the quotation set out at the beginning of the chapter). From the outset of this research, it was therefore a priority to include youth voices and to recognise young people's experiences of the behaviours being examined.

This book is based on two empirical pieces of work conducted by the author in Northern Ireland. The first was a doctoral thesis on 'cyberbullying' and 'sexting' behaviours among young people. The research took the form of focus groups and interviews with 15 young people aged 13–17 years and semi-structured interviews with 28 professionals across a range of sectors (eg education, criminal justice; children's charities, safeguarding organisations) (March 2015–May 2016). The second piece of research was an Economic and Social Research Council (ESRC) Post-Doctoral Fellowship (PDF)[54] project which explored issues of consent among young people, in the context of sexual behaviours (October 2019–May 2021).[55] A similar mixed-methods approach was taken, which included semi-structured interviews with 10 key professionals in the area and an attitudinal survey completed by 61 young people aged between 14–18 years (see Appendices 1–4 for a breakdown of professional and youth participants for the two pieces of research).

During both studies, consideration was given to the complexity of the primary research which involved interviewing professionals and young people on a topic which is not only both convoluted and sensitive, but where understanding is still evolving. When it came to recruiting participants, the author was alert to the broader sensitivities and vulnerabilities surrounding this topic and those who may engage in the behaviour (whether consensually or in more coercive settings). Children were therefore recruited using 'gatekeepers' – a children's charity and a local school. This provided a safety mechanism by determining whether it was in the best interests of the child or young person to participate in the project. Professional interviewees were selected using 'purposeful sampling'. A sampling criterion was used based on the knowledge and experience needed to fulfil the research aims and objectives.

Due to resourcing and time constraints, the primary research was never intended to be representative. It was always intended to be a piece of research which aimed to grapple with some of the more challenging dimensions associated with cyberbullying and sexting behaviours. This included noting the limitations within regulatory frameworks as well as making recommendations moving forward. The studies also present a range of complex and interesting insights which are unique to the research site (Northern Ireland) while also linking in with broader tensions and debates internationally.

---

[54] Grant Reference: ES/T005750/1.
[55] This project was initially designed to be a one-year study but due to Covid-19 and lockdown restrictions, there were delays in gathering data. The author received a short extension from ESRC to finish data collection.

VI. Overview of the Book

Having introduced the research, the remaining chapters include seven substantive chapters and a conclusion. Chapter 2 provides an overview of the key social and critical theories on childhood. Examining the theoretical construction and reconstruction of childhood makes clear why cyberbullying and sexting among young people have come to be understood as 'harmful' behaviours. Chapter 3 explores contemporary discourses on youth sexuality, looking more closely at the conceptual frameworks influencing youth sexuality and the modernisation of youth sexuality. The two theoretical chapters situate the research within the existing body of literature and provide a sound framework for analysing empirical findings outlined in subsequent chapters.

Chapter 4 steps back from the theoretical context and introduces the author's empirical research by critically evaluating current perspectives on bullying behaviours. It combines theory with the data by providing an overview of the key themes identified including definitional issues and trivialisation of harm. Chapter 5 charts the development of sexting among young people and analyses a wide range of emerging themes, including gendered dimensions attached to the sexual behaviour alongside exposure to a range of pressures (both at a micro and macro level). Chapter 6 considers the key role of consent and how it is framed and applied in practice. It therefore provides a critical exploration of the main challenges facing young people when negotiating consent within interpersonal relationships, with a focus on sexting behaviours.

Chapter 7, reflecting primarily on Chapter 6, situates empirical and theoretical findings within a continuum. Focusing on the seminal work of Liz Kelly and Simon Hackett, this chapter proposes that peer-based sexting be considered as part of a continuum of sexual behaviour. Chapter 8 is the final empirical chapter and specifically focuses on the current regulatory frameworks governing cyberbullying and sexting behaviours. Drawing on the findings from the preceding chapters, Chapter 8 outlines significant challenges for legal and other professionals in terms of managing these online harmful behaviours, including the limitations of criminal law. There is also a comparative element to this chapter which briefly considers legislative frameworks beyond Northern Ireland within the context of peer-based sexting behaviours. Extending the scope in this way allows the author to consider the diverse legal frameworks engaged in the area. Chapter 9 concludes the research study by providing an overview of the main findings and how data tests theoretical debates, drawing out the broader implications for law and policy and situating the findings within the context of Northern Ireland and beyond.

2

Young People who Display Harmful Behaviours

Theoretical and Empirical Perspectives

Harmful behaviours among young people have consistently been a topic of intense debate among academics and practitioners in the field of children's rights and child protection. In recent years, discussions have heightened due to the diverse range of behaviours young people can and do engage with, both on- and offline. In this chapter, the theoretical tensions surrounding young people and constructions of childhood will be examined. This analysis will provide a contextual account of why certain behaviours between young people are framed as 'harmful' or 'risky', including bullying and sexting behaviours. This theoretical context will also inform future chapters which are tasked with examining why certain regulatory frameworks are ineffective and what preventative measures should be prioritised.

Behaviours including bullying and sexting have raised significant child safety concerns with professionals who work with young people, child protection policymakers and legislators. A key challenge is ensuring that children and young people are protected from harm (sexual and otherwise), while also recognising the dangers associated with the over-regulation of childhood and, in particular, over-regulation of youth sexuality. Indeed, there is a growing tension among professionals regarding what behaviours can be categorised and understood as 'exploration' and a 'normal' part of childhood; and what behaviours are becoming more 'problematic', 'harmful' or 'abusive'.[1] As a matter of course, how such behaviours are defined and understood influences regulatory policies and frameworks.

In order to appropriately consider the implications of current regulatory responses to such behaviours,[2] the persistent conceptual and theoretical frameworks which influence and feed into the social and political debates on youth-based

---

[1] S Hackett, 'Children and Young People with Harmful Sexual Behaviours' in C Barter and B David (eds), *Children Behaving Badly? Peer Violence between Children and Young People* (John Wiley and Sons, 2010); A-M McAlinden, *Children as 'Risk': Sexual Exploitation and Abuse by Children and Young People* (Cambridge University Press, 2018).

[2] Regulatory legislative and policy responses will be examined more thoroughly in Chapters 7 and 8.

behaviours must be examined. It is argued that while many corners of academic thought feed into such debates, the two main theoretical concepts, through which this book will explore the topics of sexting and cyberbullying, are constructions of 'childhood' and the 'youth offender'. Exploring how these concepts have come to be understood will help explain why certain online behaviours among young people have been labelled as problematic and in need of regulation. Further, theoretical analysis will provide a valuable opportunity to consider *why* current regulatory responses to certain youth behaviours, particularly legal sanctions, are often *over-reactive* and fail to capture the complexity of peer-based behaviours.

The chapter will therefore be broken into two main sections. The first section will examine popular social and political framings of 'harmful' behaviour through the conceptual framework of 'childhood'. In doing so, this section will consider how childhood, a significant and fundamental life stage in a child's development, has been constructed and reconstructed within key social, political, legal and academic discourses. Providing a brief examination of the competing paradigms of 'childhood'[3] will help identify parallels between how this important life stage was understood 'then' and 'now'. Exploring these key junctures within childhood debates will further illustrate how the popular assumption of a 'lost' childhood still very much exists. In fact, due to the prevalence and evolution of a range of harmful behaviours displayed by young people (both on- and offline), it *could* be argued that this assumption of a 'lost childhood' has been amplified to new levels of concern within contemporary youth discourses, in particular those relating to digital landscapes.

Next, and building on the childhood debate, the second section of this chapter will consider how the social imaging of the 'young offender' has influenced popular and contemporary rhetoric on youth crime. This examination will be important in understanding the conceptualisation of different 'types' of harm alongside prevailing and persistent constructions of 'victim' and 'offender'. Exploring the development of these key terms will be significant for two main reasons. First, testing the limitations and boundaries of these key concepts will provide a deeper understanding of why certain online behaviours have been labelled as harmful. Second, children and young people who engage in certain forms of online behaviour challenge persistent paradigms of deviance.[4] Consequently, how regulatory bodies have responded to such behaviours has a significant influence over how children view themselves – that is, as either worthy of victim status and/or deserving of help.[5] This imaging impacts on how effective regulatory frameworks are in adequately addressing the complexity of such behaviours.

---

[3] See B Goldson, '"Childhood": An Introduction to Historical and Theoretical Analyses' in P Scraton (ed), *'Childhood' in 'Crisis'* (UCL Press, 1997).

[4] A-M McAlinden, 'Sexting and Cyberbullying' in R Atkinson (ed), *Shades of Deviance: A Primer on Crime, Deviance and Social Harm* (London, Routledge, 2014) 99.

[5] A-M McAlinden, 'Deconstructing Victim and Offender Identities in Discourses on Child Sexual Abuse: Hierarchies, Blame and the Good/Evil Dialectic' (2014) 54(4) *British Journal of Criminology* 180.

Critically engaging with and challenging favoured and prominent socio-cultural and political constructions of children, childhood and the young offender, will therefore provide a solid foundation for subsequent chapters which will be tasked with unpacking regulatory tensions and critically analysing the complexity of bullying and sexting behaviours among young people.

I. Key Terms: Children, Childhood and Adolescence

Before exploring the 'lost' childhood debate, there are a number of important terms which should be defined for context. First, despite a range of vocabulary and phrasing used to describe the different life stages, the two main junctures in a person's life are presented as 'childhood' and 'adulthood'. These two life stages are often presented as distinct and how they are understood and conceptualised is central to the reasoning behind the division of key fundamental rights among children and adults.[6] Second, and interrelated to the previous point, as scholars including Cunningham[7] and James and James[8] note, it is also important to differentiate between 'children' and 'childhood', as both terms are often used interchangeably within childhood discourses. Third, and importantly, the 'bridge' between childhood and adulthood is defined as 'adolescence'.[9] This is a significant period of growth and development for a young person and how this chapter in a young person's life is understood and defined is crucial in understanding currently regulatory responses to peer-based forms of behaviour, including sexual behaviours.

Considering the first two points, children are human beings and should be 'viewed as historical, cultural, political, economic, and social productions'[10] whereas childhood is 'the life-space which our culture limits it to be'.[11] That is, children (as human beings) operate within adult-generated socio-cultural, political, economic, educational and legal structures. These adult-produced systems not only define childhood but also control and regulate children's experiences of childhood. While childhood has been viewed as distinct and separate from adulthood, adolescence has been known as the 'transitional'[12] stage between childhood and adulthood. Interestingly, it has been noted that while the term 'child'

---

[6] See JC Holt, *Escape from Childhood: The Needs and Rights of Children* (Medford, HoltGWS LLC, 2013).

[7] H Cunningham, *Children and Childhood in Western Society Since 1500*, 2nd edn (Pearson Education, 2005).

[8] A James and A James, *Constructing Childhood Theory, Policy and Social Practice* (Palgrave Macmillan, 2004).

[9] See E Ahmed Zaky, 'Adolescence: A Crucial Transitional Stage in Human Life' (2017) 4(6) *Journal of Child and Adolescent Behavior* 1–2.

[10] NK Denzin, *Childhood Socialization*, 2nd edn (New York, Routledge, 2010) 2.

[11] J Qvortrup, 'Childhood Matters: An Introduction' in J Qvortrup et al (eds), *Childhood Matters: Social Theory, Practice and Politics* (Vienna, Avebury, 1994) 3.

[12] Ahmed Zaky (n 9).

is often viewed as a fairly achromous word, 'adolescence' is often viewed more negatively – as a time of heightened risk-taking and disobedience.[13] As discussed further below, this common perception of adolescence feeds into how certain behaviours are framed and conceptualised as 'harmful'. While there is no definitive age at which a child enters adolescence, the life stage is often broken up into three separate phases with approximate age ranges including: early adolescence (10–13 years), middle adolescence (14–17 years) and late adolescence or young adulthood (18–21 years).[14] These age ranges will become significant as legal frameworks and other regulatory mechanisms are analysed, including legal age limits.[15]

When a person experiences a transition in their life, it is expected that the person will go through a certain amount of change. It is well known that throughout adolescence, young people go through a significant developmental period, both physically, psychologically and socially. One specific and crucial transition is the gradual shift from parental dependence to independence.[16] In doing so, young people *should* be supported and encouraged by their parents/guardians/ care providers, to take greater responsibility and become more involved in the decision-making processes which impact their lives.[17] Yet, while there is a wider recognition of greater accountability and responsibility within adolescence, due to deeply entrenched traditional notions of childhood, the support and guidance adolescents receive is often targeted to certain areas of physical, psychologically and social development. For example, most parents/guardians encourage young people to take greater responsibility for smaller tasks such as increasing independence within the home (including carrying out small errands) and providing children with more social independence (outside of the home and within social spaces with their friends).[18] Strikingly, (although not surprisingly), little is often done to support young people to make healthy sexual choices, to understand the more complex issues associated with puberty or to have conversations with young people about their right to sexual autonomy and expression. As one professional explains:

> I've had young people … who are 16, 17, and nobody has ever spoken to them about puberty, about periods, about the body, how they should feel, how they should interact, like nothing.[19]

---

[13] J Muncie, *Youth and Crime*, 3rd edn (SAGE, 2009).

[14] JP Cuna, 'What Are the Three Stages of Adolescence?' (Childrens Health Centre, 2021) https://www.emedicinehealth.com/what_are_the_three_stages_of_adolescence/article_em.htm, last accessed 16 July 2023.

[15] See Chapters 6 and 7.

[16] BJ Casey et al, 'Adolescence: What Do Transmission, Transition and Translation Have to Do With It?' (2010) 67(5) *Neuron* 749.

[17] Y Kao et al, 'Preparation for Adulthood: Shifting Responsibility for Management of Daily Tasks from Parents to Their Children' (2021) 75(2) *The American Journal of Occupational Therapy* 1.

[18] ibid.

[19] Professional Interview 2 (PDF): Sexual Health Charity.

Discussed further in Chapter 3, this is mainly due to a fear that certain knowledge and/or sexual freedoms could be harmful to young people. As Powell states, 'certainly there is a fine line to tread between recognising and allowing young people's sexual autonomy while protecting them from sexual exploitation'.[20] While this is, of course, true, there is also an inherent danger in failing to properly educate young people on issues that are directly impacting their lives, including healthy sexual expression (both on- and offline).

II. Constructions of Childhood

Over the centuries, there have been multiple constructions and reconstructions of childhood. From the 'romantic' and innocent perception of childhood, evident in the writings of Rousseau, on the one hand, to the evil, corrupt and wicked nature of childhood,[21] on the other. While there have been many developments within childhood debates over the years, noting in particular how childhood has been manufactured and influenced by the social, political and economic landscape of that time, one thing that has remained constant is the idea that adults shape popular conceptualisations of childhood: ie, childhood has been written about and understood almost completely by adults and without any or very limited consultation with children and young people.[22] This results in the voices of young people being 'silenced'[23] and policies and agendas being framed around 'adult imaginaries' of childhood,[24] rather than speaking to the real needs and lived experiences of young people. Further, the exclusion of children and young people is often reflected within social, political and legal policies by the imposition of age limits. As outlined by Cipriani, the presence of varying age limits worldwide and the complex and debated notion of children's competency 'depend most heavily upon fluctuating social constructions of childhood, and not on children themselves'.[25]

Within Northern Ireland, significant age limits include 10 years old as being the minimum age of criminal responsibility (MACR), the age of sexual consent at 16 years old and the current age limit placed on the practice of 'sexting' (sending naked or semi-naked images), which is 18 years old. As a result, young people's

---

[20] A Powell, *Sex, Power and Consent: Youth Culture and the Unwritten Rules* (Cambridge University Press, 2010) 116.

[21] See J Da Costa Nunes, 'The Naughty Child in Nineteenth-Century American Art' (1987) 21(2) *Journal of American Studies* 225; J Muncie, *Youth and Crime*, 5th edn (SAGE, 2021).

[22] S Fishman, 'The History of Childhood Sexuality' (1982) 17(2) *Journal of Contemporary History* 269; P Scraton (ed), *'Childhood' in 'Crisis'?* (UCL Press, 1997).

[23] K Corteen and P Scraton, 'Prolonging "Childhood", Manufacturing Innocence and Regulating Sexuality' in P Scraton (ed), *'Childhood' in 'Crisis'?* (UCL Press, 1997).

[24] A Taylor, 'Reconceptualising the "Nature" of Childhood' (2011) 18(4) *Childhood* 420.

[25] D Cipriani, *Children's Rights and the Minimum Age of Criminal Responsibility: A Global Perspective* (Routledge, 2009) 4.

sexual agency is not fully devolved at 16 years. Gillespie poignantly notes, 'the law thus creates a situation where a photograph is considered more serious than actual sexual activity'.[26] Consequently, a debate emerges concerning childhood, sexual agency, criminalisation of young people and 'deviant' sexual behaviour. This conversation among legal and other professionals is not specific to Northern Ireland, as dialogue surrounding youth sexuality and sexual 'risk' continues to emerge internationally. In Australia, for example, scholars including Albury and Crawford also note a disparity in the law referring to the legal parameters as 'clearly out of step' with criminalisation and youth sexual agency.[27]

James and James[28] further argue that care needs to be taken when regulating youth activity that it is for the purposes of child protection and welfare rather than conformity to a particular ideal of how a child should behave and/or what childhood should look like. For example, Henry and Powell note that laws around sexting should be applied carefully so that young people are not criminalised for sexual exploration simply because society fails to acknowledge young people's sexual agency.[29] This is especially important when distinguishing between 'consensual' and 'coercive' sexual behaviours among young people, discussed further in Chapters 5 and 6.

In addition and importantly, the 'romantic' perception of childhood neglects the reality that children and young people can and do present a 'risk' to others.[30] Consequently, stereotypes and myths around 'imagined risk' become embedded within public consciousness and when young people do participate in harmful behaviour, they are demonised and labelled as 'other'.[31] Yet, within contemporary thinking on childhood, there is a notable move towards appreciating the 'plurality' of childhood,[32] an acknowledgement that a 'universal' experience of childhood does not exist[33] and a recognition of the powerful influence of 'social processes' in the construction of childhood.[34] Further, scholars such as Phoenix consider how social constructionism can impact the regulation of 'social problems' such as child sexual exploitation.[35] Literature

---

[26] AA Gillespie, 'Child Pornography' (2018) 27(1) *Information and Communications Technology Law* 32.

[27] K Albury and K Crawford, 'Sexting, Consent and Young People's Ethics: Beyond Megan's Story' (2012) 26(3) *Continuum: Journal of Media and Cultural Studies* 464.

[28] James and James (n 8).

[29] N Henry and A Powell, 'Beyond the "Sext": Technology-Facilitated Sexual Violence and Harassment against Adult Women' (2015) 48(1) *Australian and New Zealand Journal of Criminology* 104.

[30] See J Ringrose et al, *A Qualitative Study of Children, Young People and 'Sexting': A Report Prepared for the NSPCC* (NSPCC LSE, 2012).

[31] See C Greer, *Sex, Crime and the Media: Sex Offending and the Press in a Divided Society* (Routledge, 2003); See also McAlinden (n 5).

[32] Qvortrup (n 11) 5.

[33] C Jenks, *Childhood* (London, Routledge, 1996).

[34] A James and A Prout (eds), *Constructing and Reconstructing Childhood: Contemporary Issues in the Sociological Study of Childhood* (Falmer Press, 1997) x.

[35] J Phoenix, 'Child Sexual Exploitation, Discourse Analysis and Why We Still Need to Talk about Prostitution' in J Pearce (ed), *Child Sexual Exploitation: Why Theory Matters* (Policy Press, 2019) 44.

in the area is therefore illustrating how children and young people *can be* and *are* socialised by a range of factors and agents including gender, schools and peer groups. What is interesting (and indeed important) to note is how the social landscape impacts young people's engagement in certain behaviours, in particular, sexting.

Social factors such as peer socialisation and peer influence were mentioned by professionals and their impact on a range of peer-based sexual behaviours. For example:

> Their peers are going to have an influence on their understanding of sexual behaviour, and the peer influence ... and the conversations that are occurring between those contemporaries, will have a significant impact on that young person's perceptions of particular sexual behaviours.[36]

Consequently, paying attention to the socio-cultural context of childhood is significant when exploring the gendered and power dynamics which lie at the heart of bullying and sexting among young people. Professionals also commented on the significance of family engagement and the weight attached to the daily messaging young people are exposed to within a particular family setting/network. Such interactions can greatly influence and shape a young person's understanding of what is 'healthy' and 'unhealthy' behaviour. As one professional explains:

> Having an understanding of the rights or wrongs of sexual behaviour ... we can have a concrete view of it, but unless it's being modelled, for example, in the home, unless you're seeing the tos and fros within relationships from the primary carers, because it doesn't sit outside of that.[37]

The diversity and complexity of children's childhood experiences means that professionals and practitioners will never *truly* understand the exact nature and extent of peer-based behaviours, including sexual behaviours. Every situation will be highly dependent on a range of social processes and factors that are relevant to that moment in time. This must be remembered when responding to youth-based behaviours, as a 'one size fits all' approach *will not* and *cannot* work.

Furthermore, popular 'framings' of key actors including 'victim' and 'offender' influence how young people perceive the behaviour they are being subjected to (or indeed displaying). This in turn impacts on young people's understanding and awareness of the different types of interventions and supports available to them. Are they worthy of receiving such support? The next section will therefore examine some of the problematic dimensions to current socio-legal constructions of 'victim' and 'offender' and how such perceptions can distort the reality of peer-on-peer harmful behaviours.

---

[36] Professional Interview 1 (PDF): Independent Social Work Consultant.
[37] ibid.

III. Childhood and the Social Construction of 'Victim' and 'Offender'

Centred on previous discussions on popular constructions of childhood, children are often portrayed as the 'ideal victim', the ones in need of protection from a range of dangers, some genuine and others influenced by intense (and often hyperbolic) media reporting on a particular issue.[38] For example, child exploitation, including grooming, presents very real risks to children.[39] In fact, recorded data on child sexual exploitation crimes committed in the UK show that it has increased by 10 per cent during 2021/22.[40] Yet, distorted or exaggerated threats include the often-inflated threat of the 'stranger' who is a sexual predator, waiting outside school playgrounds to prey on young children,[41] and not the teenage girl or boy sitting next to your child in the classroom.

A range of literature has explored the notion of an 'ideal victim' within varying national and international contexts. Common presumptions emerge, including that an 'ideal victim' correlates with 'human vulnerability',[42] is someone who 'demands innocence',[43] and is 'deserving of help'.[44] Indeed, popular conceptualisations of the 'innocence' of victims and the 'evil' of offenders have resulted in a favoured social belief that victims are 'the mirror opposite of perpetrators of crime'.[45] The spurious and highly restrictive perception of victims and offenders perpetuates a dangerous narrative: a narrative which fails to account for the person who can be a victim of crime while also playing a role in the commission of another or similar crime. These blurred boundaries are what McAlinden has termed the 'the continuum of offending'.[46] Street or localised grooming is a good illustration of how distinct victim and offender categories are often contrived and inconsistent with the lived experiences of many children and young people. For example, the Child Exploitation and Online Protection Centre identified how perpetrators of street or localised grooming would use manipulative and pre-meditated methods to exercise control over a young person and then use that power to encourage the victim to unsuspectingly

---

[38] S Jackson, *Childhood and Sexuality* (Oxford, Basil Blackwell, 1982) 1.

[39] A-M McAlinden, *'Grooming' and the Sexual Abuse of Children* (Clarendon Studies in Criminology, 2012).

[40] NSPCC 'Child Sexual Exploitation Crimes up 10% in the Last Year' https://www.nspcc.org.uk/about-us/news-opinion/2022/child-sexual-exploitation-crimes-up-10-in-the-last-year/, last accessed 16 July 2023.

[41] See A-M McAlinden, '"Setting 'Em Up": Personal, Familial and Institutional Grooming in the Sexual Abuse of Children' (2006) 15(3) *Social and Legal Studies* 339.

[42] S Walklate, 'Reframing Criminal Vicitmisation: Finding a Place for Vulnerability and Resilience' (2011) 15(2) *Theoretical Criminology* 179.

[43] K McEvoy and K McConnachie, 'Victimology in Transitional Justice: Victimhood, Innocence and Hierarchy' (2012) 9(5) *European Journal of Criminology* 532.

[44] McAlinden (n 5) 184.

[45] McEvoy and McConnachie (n 43) 527.

[46] McAlinden (n 5) 191.

introduce their friends to men and women who would eventually go on to exploit and abuse them.[47]

Additionally, the Office of the Children's Commissioner in England conducted research on child sexual abuse and exploitation within gangs and groups; the 'CSEGG Inquiry'. The CSEGG final report documented the grooming of young boys (often aged 14–15 years) within gangs to sexually abuse and exploit girls. For example, the report noted how members of gangs would develop close bonds with the boys by picking them up from school and buying them gifts, including trainers and/or phones. Once control was gained, the boys would be told to recruit girls from their schools/communities.[48] Montgomery-Devlin also notes that within gang-related contexts, drugs, alcohol and cigarettes are often given to the young person in a deceitful manner. That is, the young person presumes the drugs and alcohol are gifts, however, once the young person has built up a 'bill' which they cannot afford to pay back, they are told they must pay back 'in kind'.[49] Professionals interviewed also commented on the difficulties in identifying and categorising certain behaviours because the young person's involvement is quite convoluted:

> [a young person] may be engaging in sexual exploitation of another, or precuring other children in the context of a peer gang association as well, and they're involved in the facilitation of that abuse. So, there's a wide, wide range, and it's very, very difficult to get a real sense of it, even to get any assessment framework around young people who engage in, you know, young females who engage in both TA[50] or contact sexual abuse, [it] is incredibly difficult to have any certainty around categories of risk.[51]

Further, the use of coercion/manipulation and young people failing to identify the behaviour as harmful and abusive was noted by a range of professionals. For example, one professional commented on a young person who was given vodka in exchange for having sex with two older males. In response the young person said: 'I got a bottle of vodka out of it and that's what I wanted. So really, I'm the winner.'[52]

Drawing on such findings, the image of the sex offender as *always* being an older male predator within popular discourses on sex offending is therefore becoming increasingly 'undermined'.[53] Despite the above evidence and literature documenting that grooming and other sexually abusive and exploitative behaviours

---

[47] Child Exploitation and Online Protection Centre, *Out of Mind, Out of Sight: Breaking Down the Barriers to Understanding Child Sexual Exploitation* (CEOP, 2011) 10, 11.

[48] S Berelowitz et al, *If Only Someone Had Listened*, final report (London, Office of the Children's Commissioner Inquiry, 2013) 104.

[49] J Montgomery-Devlin, 'The Sexual Exploitation of Children and Young People in Northern Ireland: Overview from the Barnardo's Beyond the Shadows Service' (2008) 14(4) *Child Care in Practice* 390.

[50] Technology Assisted.

[51] Professional Interview 1 (PDF): Independent Social Work Consultant.

[52] Professional Interview 4 (PDF): Children's Charity.

[53] McAlinden (n 39) 48.

extend beyond the socially constructed adult-child paradigm, public and official discourses on sex offending are still fixed on the older male adult predator as the 'offender' and the younger victimised innocent child as the 'victim'.

Moreover, the narrative surrounding grooming and sexual exploitation can often have racial and ethnic undertones. A contributing and significant factor is the reporting of a number of high-profile cases of child sexual exploitation and grooming of children and young people by older men, often from ethnic minority groups. One of the most significant and highly documented cases in the last decade was the Rochdale sexual abuse and grooming scandal.[54] In 2012, nine South Asian men from Rochdale and Oldham were convicted of a range of child sex offences including engaging in sexual activity with minors and rape. The case raised a number of interesting insights. First, while the failure of child protection services – including social services and the police – lay at the heart of the scandal,[55] the Rochdale case also contested the popular attitude that if it 'is not visible on the streets it is not happening'.[56]

Second, and alluded to above, much of the reporting on these cases focused on the ethnic origin of the men in question. The British media often commented on the fact that the perpetrators were from a marginalised group (South Asian men) and were preying on young white females. This created a moral panic surrounding sexual exploitation, race, gender and crime.[57] While this narrative can have many implications, including perpetuating fears and concerns surrounding racial stereotypes associated with grooming,[58] 'stranger danger' as well as the 'problem of multiculturalism',[59] for the purposes of this book, the distorted view of sexual abuse and exploitation is most significant. Focusing on the 'stranger' and marginalised groups of men dilutes the *reality* of sexual crimes – that most victims of crime know their perpetrator and the prevalence of intra and extra familial abuse and exploitation.[60]

Third and finally, despite the identification of adult-led grooming gangs who target and manipulate children and young people now being an objective within many criminal justice agendas,[61] very little research has been dedicated to exploring the full remit of grooming and other sexually exploitative behaviours. In fact, it is only in recent years that an adult could be prosecuted for an offence of 'sexual communication with a child' – now a codified offence

---

[54] See eg F Perraudin, 'Offenders in Rochdale Child Sexual Abuse Scandal "Remain at Large"' (*The Guardian*, 16 May 2017).

[55] BBC News, 'Police "Sorry" over Rochdale Child Sex Abuse Failures' (BBC, 13 March 2015).

[56] Montgomery-Devlin (n 49) 389.

[57] AK Gill and K Harrison, 'Child Grooming and Sexual Exploitation: Are South Asian Men the UK Media's Folk Devils?' (2015) 4(2) *International Journal for Crime, Justice and Social Democracy* 34. Also commented on by McAlinden (n 1).

[58] See E Cockbain and W Tufail, 'Failing Victims, Fuelling Hate: Challenging the Harms of the "Muslim Grooming Gangs" Narrative' (2020) 61(3) *Race and Class* 3.

[59] ibid. See also Gill and Harrison (n 57).

[60] McAlinden (n 39).

[61] For example, see Berelowitz et al (n 48).

in England and Wales under the Serious Crime Act 2015, section 67 and in Northern Ireland under section 90 of the Justice Act (Northern Ireland) 2015.[62] Additional gaps in knowledge include peer-to-peer grooming and, more specifically, grooming and sexting behaviour among young people.[63] Regarding the latter, while legislative provisions have advanced relating to some adult-based digital harms such as 'revenge pornography'[64] and 'upskirting',[65] the law is still lagging behind when it comes to peer-based digital harms, including sexting. This includes underdeveloped legislative provisions as well as sentencing guidelines (particularly around rehabilitation for young people who engage in sexual based harms).[66]

If peer-based harms, including digital harms, are to be responded to effectively, then diluting the prevailing and prevalent misconceptions associated with 'idealised' victims and offenders is required. This will allow young people to understand 'harm' and 'risk' beyond the 'stranger' and adult-child model. In doing so, young people may more easily identify when they are displaying 'harmful' behaviour and/or are being subjected to harm. Further and significantly, challenging victim/offender typologies *should* reduce problematic reporting on young people and participation in 'risky' and 'harmful' behaviours. For example, and noted in Chapter 1, in 2012 the case of Amanda Todd was widely reported on, both nationally and internationally. While Amanda had been groomed and exploited by an older male to expose her breasts online, it was extremely concerning that some reporting of the case suggested that Amanda was partly responsible for her victimisation, as showing her breasts on a webcam challenged popular rhetoric on childhood and youth sexuality.[67] A professional also commented on the complexity of online offences and victimhood, such that very often with online offences (which can exacerbate the harm caused to the victim) the perpetrators 'make the victims do their own abuse. So, they coerce the victim to touch themselves', for example.[68] Young people, referred to here by the professional and those in similar situations to Amanda above, are therefore not seen as 'the "ideal victim" of "real child abuse" – young, pure, passive and blameless'.[69] This misinformed and troubling narrative of what an 'ideal' victim looks like, or

---

[62] If convicted, the defendant can receive up to a two-year term of imprisonment.

[63] See L Ashurst and A-M McAlinden, 'Young People, Peer-to-Peer Grooming and Sexual Offending' (2015) 62(4) *Probation Journal* 374.

[64] The Criminal Justice and Courts Act 2015, s 33 'Disclosing private sexual photographs and films with intent to cause distress'.

[65] The offence can be found in the Sexual Offences Act 2003, s 67A 'Additional Offences' for England and Wales. The Justice (Sexual Offences and Trafficking Victims) Act (Northern Ireland) 2022 amends the Sexual Offences (Northern Ireland) Order 2008 to include Art 71A 'Voyeurism: additional offences (genitals and buttocks)'.

[66] Discussed further in Chapter 7 of this book.

[67] R Penney, 'The Rhetoric of the Mistake in Adult Narratives of Youth Sexuality: the Case of Amanda Todd' (2016) 16(4) *Feminist Media Studies* 710.

[68] Professional Interview 3 (PDF): Independent Social Work Consultant.

[69] McAlinden (n 5) 189.

how an 'ideal' victim behaves, can create immeasurable problems when it comes to disclosure by young people.

IV. Framing of 'Childhood', 'Deviance' and the 'Young Offender'

While the socio-cultural construction of 'deviance' and the 'young offender' has changed and shifted over time, the media and how it reports on cases involving young people powerfully influences and informs public perceptions on youth crime. A principal case which decisively shaped public perceptions on youth criminality and consequently influenced considerable dialogue on youth, crime and justice within the UK (and indeed further afield), was the murder of two-year-old James Bulger by two ten-year-old children in February 1993. Despite the commission of serious crimes by children as being uncommon, the killing of the toddler resurrected evangelical perceptions of the innately 'evil' child[70] as a 'breach' of traditional perceptions of childhood.[71] Many asked the question: 'how was it that two boys still at primary school could be capable of such a wicked crime?'[72] What ensued was a belief that childhood was in 'crisis' and this narrative fuelled public policy debates on the protection and control of children and young people where an 'authoritarian shift in youth justice' was witnessed.[73] A 'more punitive response' to children who break the law was called for.[74] In the aftermath of their conviction, the children were also subjected to 'a sustained level of hostile publicity' and while in custody received hate mail and death threats.[75] The murder had therefore politicised youth crime;[76] re-examined the role of the family in monitoring and controlling children;[77] led to the 'vilification' of social institutions designed to protect children;[78] and resulted in the 'othering' of children who commit serious crimes.[79]

---

[70] D Buckingham, *After the Death of Childhood* (Polity Press, 2000).

[71] A James and C Jenks, 'Public Perceptions of Childhood Criminality' (1996) 47(2) *The British Journal of Sociology* 315.

[72] *Venables v News Group Newspapers Ltd* [2019] EWHC 241 (QB) [2].

[73] Scraton (n 22) 170.

[74] E Delmage, 'The Minimum Age of Criminal Responsibility: A Medico-Legal Perspective' (2013) 13(2) *Youth Justice* 103; P Scraton, 'Whose "Childhood"? What "Crisis"?' in P Scraton (ed) '*Childhood' in 'Crisis*?' (UCL Press, 1997) Chapter 8.

[75] *Venables v News Group Newspapers Ltd* (n 72) [5].

[76] Muncie (n 13).

[77] See H Davis and M Bourhill '"Crisis": The Demonization of Children and Young People' in P Scraton (ed), '*Childhood' in 'Crisis*'? (UCL Press, 1997) – in particular the authors' comparison of William Golding's work, *Lord of the Flies* and the novel's interpretation of how 'deviant children' can become engaged in 'evil and anarchy' in the absence of adult supervision.

[78] ibid 39.

[79] Y Jewkes, *Media and Crime*, 2nd edn (SAGE, 2010).

Following a call to improve youth justice, two audits were commissioned in 1996 and 1998 titled *Misspent Youth' 96: Young People and Crime* and *Misspent Youth' 98: The Challenge for Youth Justice*. In addition, the White Paper titled, *No More Excuses: A New Approach to Tackling Youth Crime in England and Wales* was released. Consequently, what resulted was the enactment of the Crime and Disorder Act 1998 (the 1998 Act). One of the most significant changes within the 1998 Act was noted within section 34: 'the rebuttable presumption of criminal law that a child aged 10 or over is incapable of committing an offence is hereby abolished'.[80] While some developments within the Crime and Disorder Act 1998 have been received positively, including reparation orders and a move towards a restorative justice model, other scholars heavily criticised New Labour's agenda on tackling youth deviancy, in particular section 34.[81] For example, Bandalli argues that the changes in legislation only serve to 'increase the criminalisation of children' resulting in the systematic erosion of the widespread conceptualisation and socio-political construction of childhood as innocence enshrined.[82] Indeed, the James Bulger case was frequently referenced during key social and political debates during the 1990s and the early part of the twenty-first century, which very much centred on 'dangerous children' and 'lawless youth'.[83]

Indicative of its powerful influence on law and policy, the James Bulger case continues to shape childhood and 'shame a nation' 25 years later.[84] One of the boys, Venables, has been in and out of prison since his original conviction for the murder, including a conviction for downloading child pornography in 2010.[85] Most recently, in February 2018, Venables pleaded guilty to a number of child pornography offences. During sentencing, Justice Edis commented on the 1993 murder, saying that the actions of the two boys 'revolted the nation' and 'continues to do so' despite the 25 years that had since passed.[86]

Significantly, Venable's reoffending behaviour all these years later *still* raises questions in relation to juvenile justice and whether the two boys had been properly treated at the time of the murder. While some believe that the boys should have faced a greater punishment, others argue that Venables and Thompson were too young to be processed through the criminal court and a greater focus should

---

[80] See s 3 of The Criminal Justice (Children) (Northern Ireland) Order 1998.

[81] See T Newburn 'Tackling Youth Grime and Reforming Youth Justice: The Origins and Nature of "New Labour" Policy' (1998) 19(3–4) *Policy Studies* 199.

[82] S Bandalli, 'Children, Responsibility, and the New Youth Justice' in B Goldson (ed), *The New Youth Justice* (Russell House Publishing, 2000) 81.

[83] D Haydon and P Scraton, '"Condemn a Little More, Understand a Little Less": The Political Context and Rights' Implications of the Domestic and European Rulings in the Venables-Thompson Case' (2000) 27(3) *Journal of Law and Society* 426.

[84] A Lusher, 'James Bulger Murder: How Failure to Deal with Killer Jon Venables Became Latest Episode in Tragedy that Shames a Nation' (*Independent*, 9 February 2018).

[85] N Khomami, 'James Bulger Killer Back in Jail after Being Caught with Abuse Images Again' (*The Guardian*, 23 November 2017).

[86] Cited in J Grierson, 'Bulger Killer Jailed over Indecent Images of Children' (*The Guardian*, 7 February 2018).

have been placed on rehabilitation rather than retribution. Concerning the former, the MACR was a key feature in the narrative associated with the case. In fact, the Lord Chief Justice in 2019 commented on the age of the boys, noting:

> almost any other country in Europe, these appalling events could not have led to a prosecution. Venables and Thompson would have been dealt with in the care environment, as indeed they would have been if they had been six months or more younger.[87]

Although Venables is now an adult, sensationalist media reporting still refers to the 'evil' child all those years ago. In response to the recent charges, Detective Phil Roberts, who was on duty the day James Bulger was murdered, states, '20 years ago – I stared evil in the face … A freak of nature … Pure evil'.[88] It appears that the 'carefully nurtured' moral indignation and outrage ignited in 1993 still lives on and is continuing to shape contemporary constructions of childhood and youth deviancy.[89]

Other cases which depict childhood as in a period of 'crisis' include the case of the Edlington brothers in April 2009. In this case, two brothers aged 10 and 11 years attacked two young boys. In January 2010 the two brothers were charged with grievous bodily harm with intent. During sentencing, Mr Justice Keith described their crimes as 'truly exceptional'.[90] This case raised interesting questions relating to child safeguarding and welfare failures, as it was said that Doncaster Council were not amply discharging their statutory duties.[91] Indeed, in this particular case there were a number of trigger warnings missed by local authorities regarding the two brothers. This included a number of attacks on teachers and pupils.[92] The outcome was that the Secretary of State for Education at that time requested an independent review of the case.[93] The review considered the implementation and effectiveness of the 'Troubled Families Programme'[94] and the roles of key youth health services. It is important to emphasise that while young people who have been exposed to adverse childhood experiences can go on to engage in behaviours that are harmful and may also be illegal, this is not always the case.[95]

---

[87] *Venables v News Group Newspapers Ltd* (n 72) [3].

[88] A Devlin, 'Where is Robert Thompson Now, When Did the James Bulger Killer Come Out as Gay and Was He the Ringleader in the Murder?' (*The Sun*, 19 March 2018).

[89] B Franklin and J Horwath, 'The Media Abuse of Children: Jake's Progress from Demonic Icon to Restored Childhood Innocent' (1996) 5 *Child Abuse Review* 310.

[90] As cited in 'The Edlington Case: A Review by Lord Carlile of Berriew CBE QC at the Request of The Rt Hon Michael Gove MP, Secretary of State for Education' (Crown Copyright, 2012) 6.

[91] See M Lagaay and L Courtney, 'Time to Listen: Independent Advocacy within the Child Protection Process' (London, The National Children's Bureau, 2013).

[92] 'The Edlington Case' (n 90) 6.

[93] ibid.

[94] The programme was designed to help families in need of extra support while also working alongside local authorities/services.

[95] See CG Malvaso et al, 'Associations between Adverse Childhood Experiences and Trauma among Young People Who Offend: A Systematic Literature Review' (2022) 23(5) *Trauma, Violence and Abuse* 1677.

The Bulger and Edlington cases were both within an offline context. Not surprisingly, a significant amount of contemporary commentary on childhood and youth deviance is now situated within online settings, or there is at least an online element to the harm caused. For example, in 2014 Angela Wrightson was attacked and killed in her home by two teenage girls (13 and 14 years respectively). The girls posted a picture of themselves and Ms Wrightson on social media (Snapchat) just before the victim died of her injuries. This resulted in the defendants being referred to as the 'Snapchat killers'.[96] In the wake of a public outcry, similar questions were asked relating to youth deviancy, childhood and offender typologies. That is, – how could two young girls commit such violent acts?

The use of coercion and abuse of power by some young people both within on- and offline settings greatly contradicts the romantic view of the child as 'weak' and 'innocent' – an image which, as noted previously, dominates a wealth of literature on childhood.[97] Further, as illustrated by reporting associated with the Bulger, Edlington brothers and Wrightson cases, children who commit serious crimes online or offline represent a 'symbol of national malaise and social breakdown' within contemporary deviancy discourses.[98] It is therefore not surprising that a 'moral panic' can often follow such high-profile reporting of cases, as a certain amount of hysteria and perturbation is associated with 'rule-breakers'.[99]

In addition, any child who participates in harmful behaviour, including harmful sexual behaviour,[100] undermines popular understanding on *who* presents a 'risk' to children and young people and the *origins* of 'risk' and 'harm'.[101] That is, for example, the prevailing socio-cultural messaging associated with 'stranger danger' – the notion that adult male strangers pose the greatest threat to children and young people. Yet, reports are continually showing that intra and extra familial abuse[102] and a wide range of peer-on-peer abuse, including bullying and sexting behaviours, present a significant risk to young people.[103]

V. Childhood and the Emergence of the 'Online' Offender: Sexting and Cyberbullying

Public concerns associated with young people and the internet are not new. Indeed, as early as 2008, the Bryon Review was published which focused on exploring the range of potential risks children and young people can be exposed

---

[96] *D v Persons Unknown; F v Persons Unknown* [2021] EWHC 157 (QB) [4], [5].
[97] See Jenks (n 33); James and James (n 8).
[98] Davis and Bourhill (n 77) 45, 46.
[99] S Cohen, *Folk Devils and Moral Panics*, 3rd edn (Routledge, 2002) 4.
[100] Discussed further in Chapter 3 of this book.
[101] Davis and Bourhill (n 77) 45, 46; see also McAlinden (n 4).
[102] McAlinden (n 39); also discussed further in Chapter 3.
[103] See Ringrose et al (n 30); see also Chapters 4 and 5.

to online. The review was led by Dr Tanya Bryon, a clinical psychologist, and a number of recommendations were put forward to enhance children's safety and welfare online. Some recommendations included the establishment of an agency to prioritise child internet safety (UK Council for Child Internet Safety); continued work and engagement with parents/carers/guardians and young people on internet safety to ensure that evidence on risks and harms is current and up to date; public education and awareness relating to online safety (specifically for children and their parents/carers/guardians) and better links with hosting sites, service providers and key charities/agencies, to name a few.[104]

In 2012, another inquiry was led by Claire Perry MP into child online safety, protection and welfare. The Parliamentary inquiry explored young people's exposure to pornography and the associated risks and harms that can stem from viewing such sexualised material and content. In the findings and recommendations report, it was noted that children often have 'unfiltered' access to the internet and are 'easily' viewing pornography.[105] This exposure is having an adverse impact on young people's interpersonal relationships and how they conceptualise and understand sex, sexuality and their bodies.[106] The inquiry also acknowledged that parents often feel ill-equipped to properly protect their children online and require safety education.[107] Notably, the inquiry was criticised for being too 'narrow' in focus and failing to consider the complexity of young people's engagement online.[108]

In fact, studies are continually highlighting young people's reliance on a range of technological tools and advancements as a learning source, to communicate and/or express themselves. The endless access to information and the ability to interface with other young people in a split second is creating a whole new medium for 'risk'-taking behaviours (beyond access to pornography) including cyberbullying and sexting.[109] The next section will therefore tease out these tensions (with specific reference to bullying and sexting), illustrating how socio-legal responses to such behaviours are highly influenced by childhood narratives alongside the growing social fear associated with ongoing technological advancements.

A. Bullying and Childhood

A prevailing myth is that bullying is a 'normal' part of childhood, and this misconception has translated into online contexts, often leading to a common perception

---

[104] Byron Review, *Safer Children in a Digital World: The Report of the Byron Review* (DCSF Publications, 2008).
[105] C Perry, *Independent Inquiry into Online Child Protection* (London, 2012) 3, 14.
[106] ibid 14.
[107] ibid 19.
[108] A Phippen, *Children's Online Behaviour and Safety: Policy and Rights Challenges* (Palgrave Macmillan, 2017) 21.
[109] GS O'Keeffe and K Clarke-Pearson, 'The Impact of Social Media on Children, Adolescents, and Families' (2011) 127(4) *Pediatrics* 800.

that the behaviour is not 'harmful' but simply 'a bit of fun'. This was noted by professionals who explain:

> And sometimes if you go and approach people, they go, well I didn't mean anything by that, you know, it was just a bit of fun.[110]

> It was probably something that wasn't necessarily taken seriously, and it's a wee bit of fun.[111]

> It is a problem, it's definitely a problem but I don't think we are made aware of it ... as much as we could be because I think its just part and parcel for most young people. It's part and parcel of being online. It's seen as .... as just normal you know it's seen as something that happens on Facebook and Twitter.[112]

The persuasiveness of these myths and how they can trivialise the harm caused to the young people who are being subjected to the online bullying behaviour was also expressed by the young people:

> I think a lot of people too don't realise that stuff counts as bullying anymore because like if you see like, you find like a funny photo of like somebody from your school on Facebook and like you like put it on a group chat and people laugh at it like you don't really think that's bullying.[113]

> The person who feels like they're getting bullied and the person actually doing it [thinks] oh that's just banter.[114]

Interviewee excerpts from both professionals and the young people highlight a concerning broader cultural attitude surrounding cyberbullying behaviours – the presence of a flippant attitude and a misplaced belief that some bullying behaviours are 'just a bit of fun'. A failure to challenge this misconception that bullying is simply a normal part of childhood has led to a societal attitude that the behaviour is somehow inconsequential. Yet, as will be discussed in Chapter 4, the impact of bullying behaviours, both on- and offline, can have far-reaching and severe consequences and should not be accepted as a 'normal' part of childhood or adolescence.

Existing literature illustrates how online bullying can be 'a more convenient' option for young people to display harmful behaviour due to the speed at which content can be shared but also the lack of physical contact with the person being subjected to the harm.[115] In support, many professional participants interviewed believe the internet has created a platform for children and young people, who may be perceived as less 'powerful' within a face-to-face context, to become more fearless online due to the absence of physical confrontation: 'those people who would have made really bad face-to-face bullies are actually psychologically

---

[110] Professional Interview 19 (PhD): Criminal Justice Sector.
[111] Professional Interview 14 (PhD): Children's Voluntary Organisation. Participant A.
[112] Professional Interview 2 (PhD): Children's Voluntary Organisation.
[113] Young Person Focus Group (PhD): Female.
[114] Young Person Interview (PhD): Male.
[115] N Antoniadou and CM Kokkinos, 'Cyber and School Bullying: Same or Different Phenomena?' (2015) 25 *Aggression and Violent Behaviour* 364.

brilliant on the internet'[116] as some young people hone in on 'manipulating'[117] their victim. The removal of physical confrontation can empower young people to display harmful behaviours online, behaviours they would not necessarily engage in within an offline context – known as the online disinhibition effect.[118] Consequently, a socio-cultural desire to maintain bullying behaviours as simply 'a bit of fun' relates to a social reluctance to accept that *some* young people engage in conduct online which contradicts long-standing notions of perpetrators of 'online' harmful and coercive behaviours (typical offender moulds) and the romanticised view of children as vulnerable, weak and innocent.

B. Sexting and Childhood

As noted in the Introduction to this book and discussed further in Chapters 5 and 6, sexting among young people can include exploitation and coercion but it can also be 'consensual' and be considered a form of contemporary sexual explora-tion. A reluctance to accept this reality is evident within childhood discourses, resulting in the labelling of *all* youth sexual expression as 'deviant' or 'risky' and leading to the over-regulation of youth sexual agency.[119] Regulatory tensions are heightened where they involve young people who send 'sexts' who are over the age of sexual consent (16 years) but under the legal age for sending a 'nude' image of themselves (18 years). Scholars, including Albury and Crawford, demonstrate how the current narrow definition of sexting behaviour among young people as *always* being a criminal offence fails to make the distinction between 'risky' behaviour through coercion and 'risky' behaviour through consent.[120] For exam-ple, young people who use exploitative methods to receive an image and then maliciously distribute the image should be differentiated from the young people who freely chose and 'consented' to send and receive the image. Whilst in both cases 'risky' behaviour is displayed, the motive and intention behind the harm is significantly different. Yet due to prevailing trends within childhood discourses regarding 'sexual purity' and 'innocence', any child who deviates from this social norm is automatically labelled as participating in 'harmful' and 'problematic' sexual behaviour.

Thus, a similar and inter-related issue emerges between the scenarios outlined above (that is, the 'risky' and 'coercive' case compared to the 'risky' but 'consen-sual' case): the issue of consent. An important consideration around the issue of consent and sexting is the cultural normalisation of the practice among young people alongside gendered power dynamics. One professional commented on the

---

[116] Professional Interview 3 (PhD): Forensic Psychologist.
[117] Professional Interview 20 (PhD): Education Sector.
[118] J Suler, 'The Online Disinhibition Effect' (2004) 7(3) *CyberPsychology and Behaviour* 321.
[119] M Lee and T Crofts, 'Gender, Pressure, Coercion and Pleasure: Untangling Motivations for Sexting between Young People' (2015) 55(3) *British Journal of Criminology* 454.
[120] Albury and Crawford (n 27); Henry and Powell (n 29).

frequency with which young people they work with receive naked images and the nonchalant reaction that can follow:

> I said if you're sitting having your breakfast or your dinner and somebody is invading your life and sending you [an image] and she said, but that's what happens, sometimes I don't open them and sometimes I do and it's just completely normalised for some of the young people we work with.[121]

However, within contemporary childhood discourses there is a reluctance to accept the potential for children to use coercion or manipulation. This refusal to accept the ranging use and abuse of power within youth interactions and relationships has also led to young people themselves not being able to identify coercion:[122]

> I would definitely say struggling with identifying coerc[ion] in all the young people I've worked with and even when they've been quite significant, they've shown me messages on their phone or they've shown me all their messenger interactions or whatever it might be and you're like, but then he said that to you, that looks really bad, that's a bad thing to say to someone ... they'll have missed it.[123]

Sexting (including coercive practices) among young people is challenging Rousseau's romantic image of childhood as a time of innocence. This makes it extremely difficult for the public to understand that children and young people can not only be sexual beings but they can also display harmful sexual and exploitative behaviours. Yet, children and young people who *knowingly* use coercion and manipulation to receive sexting images present different challenges within childhood discourses compared to those children who are simply expressing their sexuality (albeit some of the issues are interrelated).[124]

VI. Conclusion

This chapter has provided an historical and critical overview of the varying debates on the constructions and reconstructions of 'childhood.' Exploration of the critical theories on childhood have highlighted the notion that criminal behaviour and deviance among children and young people is 'part of a broader context of social construction in which images reflect shared and persistent ideologies'.[125] Theoretical analysis has also poignantly shown how the persistent image of the child as innocent, portrayed by Rousseau, has 'retained a powerful and persuasive hold upon the public imagination, reappearing in different guises and with different consequences for children themselves'.[126]

---

[121] Professional Interview 4 (PDF): Children's Charity.
[122] See also Chapter 6.
[123] Professional Interview 4 (PDF): Children's Charity.
[124] Discussed further in Chapter 5.
[125] Scraton (n 22) 172.
[126] Jenks (n 33) 124.

Technology is also playing a significant role in the daily risk-taking experiences of young people, including cyberbullying and sexting, consequently reshaping childhood. Indeed, a significant amount of policy has focused on protecting children from a range of online harms. Yet, despite similar themes emerging relating to better protection for children online and more social education (in particular for children and parents) – laws and policies are still lagging behind when it comes to child safety and welfare. Why might this be? Primarily, there is a failure to *truly* listen to young people on the issues impacting *their* lives and a lack of understanding around the more nuanced dimensions to online behaviours. A reason for this notable gap in emerging policies in the area can be directly linked to childhood discourses and a misplaced belief that 'adults know best' alongside a fear of a 'lost' childhood.

Yet, literature and empirical evidence continually demonstrate that what is truly 'lost' is an unrealistic and utopian interpretation and understanding of what childhood is.[127] Therefore, if we continue to uphold the idealised view of childhood and place greater emphasis on adult expectations of childhood, children's voices will continue to be silenced.[128] If real and effective policies are to be implemented, the perpetuating and dangerous narrative associated with traditional childhood discourses must be challenged.

---

[127] See Scraton (n 22).
[128] C Heywood, *A History of Childhood: Children and Childhood in the West from Medieval to Modern Times* (Polity Press, 2001) 9; see also James and Prout (n 34).

3

Young People who Display Harmful Sexual Behaviour: A Review

The overarching purpose of this chapter is to examine the principal theories of thought within the discipline of sex and sexuality, specifically related to youth, gender and power. Some of the power dynamics at play within modern discourses when addressing youth sexual cultures and 'deviant' sexual behaviour will be better understood. Modern perceptions of childhood and youth sexuality have been influenced heavily by historical narratives on sexuality. The first part of this chapter, therefore, will examine some of the key conceptual frameworks influencing youth sexuality. The broader concerns involving young people and sexually exploitative behaviours on- and offline will be probed.

Indeed, sexting and sexual bullying as behaviours in which young people are engaging are not restricted to childhood and sexuality debates. They also require consideration of the historical context in which we have come to understand young people and sexual exploitation. The second part of this chapter will therefore analyse the emergence of sexual abuse and exploitation as a prominent concern within official and public discourses and provide an important contextual foundation for future empirical analysis. An in-depth analysis of the evolving terrain of sexual exploitation and how tensions and complexities have surfaced will help explain why research into young people who display harmful sexual or other exploitative behaviour often has been either neglected completely or caused an over-reactive and restrictive response via regulatory reform.

Within this broader context, the final part of the chapter will explore the theoretical influences which govern and shape contemporary policies on young people who engage in harmful sexual behaviour. The voluminous nature of political discourses concerning youth sexuality, commercialisation of sex and 'risky' premature sexualisation, has resulted in the implementation of constant new agendas, often nuanced in content. While this analysis was touched on in Chapter 2 within the context of childhood debates, the focus within this chapter will be specifically on the evolving tensions between dominant theories addressing sexuality, teasing out the prevailing power dimensions in negotiating youth sexual identity.

I. Conceptual Frameworks Influencing Youth Sexuality: The Northern Ireland Context

In the Introductory chapter, the unique context of Northern Ireland and its political history was discussed. Given Northern Ireland's staunchly religious political landscape, consideration of religious teaching and how it facilitates dominant thinking in broader terms on sexual agency, sex and sexuality, is important. Indeed, Northern Irish policy remains heavily influenced by Christian thinking and morality. For example, the Abortion Act 1967 decriminalised terminating pregnancies in England, Wales and Scotland under certain circumstances. This included, for example, if the pregnant woman's life was at risk and/or there was a 'substantial risk' that the baby would be born with physical or mental abnormalities.[1] The geographical remit of the legislation did not include Northern Ireland, resulting in women having to travel to England and other parts of the UK to access legal abortion services. While many activists fought hard for women's rights, 'The Troubles' in Northern Ireland overshadowed any attempt to reform the law in this area, creating an 'air of silence' on the issue.[2] Activism began to regain momentum in the twenty-first century, with some key moments propelling the decriminalisation of abortion campaign into the public domain. For example, the Belfast High Court in 2015 ruled that current abortion laws were inconsistent with Article 8 of the European Convention on Human Rights.[3] This was specifically in relation to current laws failing to account for two exceptions: (i) fatal foetal abnormality; and (ii) pregnancy due to sexual crime.[4] Two years later, in 2017, the Republic of Ireland voted to legalise abortion and thus repeal the 8th amendment.[5] This was in the wake of the widely-reported death of Savita Halappanavar, who was denied an abortion even though she was miscarrying. Ms Halappanavar was told that she could not have a termination because Ireland was a 'Catholic country' and while there was still a heartbeat the baby was still alive.[6] A few days later Ms Halappanavar died of sepsis. The case caused a public outcry not only nationally but internationally as many pro-choice campaigners voiced concerns that current abortion laws were leaving pregnant women extremely vulnerable and, at times, in life-threatening situations.[7] Despite significant reforms evolving in neighbouring jurisdictions, it was not until 2019, some 50 years after

---

[1] Abortion Act 1967, s 1(1).

[2] See E Weiderud and K Gillum, 'The Meaning and Impact of International Solidarity for Abortion Rights in NI' in F Bloomer and E Campbell (eds), *Decriminalising Abortion in Northern Ireland* (Bloomsbury, 2022) 31.

[3] *The Northern Ireland Human Rights Commission Application* [2015] NIQB 96.

[4] ibid [184].

[5] See Health (Regulation of Termination of Pregnancy) Act 2018.

[6] BBC News, 'Woman Dies after Abortion Request "Refused" at Galway Hospital' (BBC, 14 November 2012).

[7] M Specia, 'How Savita Halappanavar's Death Spurred Ireland's Abortion Rights Campaign' (*The New York Times*, 27 May 2018).

the Abortion Act 1967, that abortion laws in Northern Ireland eventually were updated to align with other parts of the UK and Ireland.

What is significant to note is that abortion laws were reformed by the Westminster Government and *not* the Northern Irish Executive (as the Northern Ireland Assembly was not sitting at that time). A question therefore arises, would the Northern Ireland Executive have approved the change in law? The DUP said that their party would 'vigorously oppose' any intervention by the UK Government to implement abortion services in Northern Ireland.[8] A reluctance to introduce progressive policies on similar issues has arisen in Northern Ireland, over a comparable time frame. Reforming laws relating to sex work has caused considerable tension. It is clear that the legalisation of sex work is a polarised debate. On the one hand, issues associated with sexual agency and freedom are argued by 'sex positive' feminists.[9] On the other, radical feminists (such as Catherine MacKinnon and Andrea Dworkin) argue that *all* sex work is a gendered base form of sexual violence and a manifestation of patriarchal power.[10] Within Northern Ireland specifically, an unwillingness to accept the complex parameters of sex work alongside a failure to recognise that certain legislative provisions can simply displace behaviours rather than regulate, has been noted.[11] This has been due mainly to a prevailing moral framework which depicts all sex work as 'sinful' and 'immoral'.[12] In fact, Ellison argues that a significant factor influencing the social and political reluctance to *effectively* reform sex work legislation within Northern Ireland is the prevailing 'socially and culturally conservative society'.[13]

The focus has been on abortion and sex work laws; however, the messaging and tensions regarding sexuality (in particular female sexuality) and autonomy resonate strongly with discourses on youth sexuality and agency. While empirical analysis is taken from a different perspective due to the nature of sexting behaviours and the age of the parties involved,[14] similar themes emerge. Further, despite a somewhat diluted Christian presence within policy and practice over the past few years in Northern Ireland, a 'conservative ideology' prevails within schools, especially on topics relating to sex and sexuality.[15] Consequently, the

---

[8] J Elgot, 'DUP Will "Vigorously Oppose" UK Intervention to Speed up NI Abortion Services' (*The Guardian*, 18 March 2021).

[9] See L Gerassi, 'A Heated Debate: Theoretical Perspectives of Sexual Exploitation and Sex Work' (2015) 42(4) *Journal of Sociology and Social Welfare* 79.

[10] See K Miriam, 'Stopping the Traffic in Women: Power, Agency and Abolition in Feminist Debates over Sex-Trafficking' (2005) 36(1) *Journal of Social Philosophy* 1; S Green, *Criminalizing Sex: A Unified Liberal Theory* (Oxford University Press, 2020).

[11] G Ellison et al, *A Review of the Criminalisation of Paying for Sexual Services in Northern Ireland* (Department of Justice, 2019).

[12] ibid 205.

[13] ibid 195.

[14] See Chapter 5, which unpacks empirical findings on sexting among young people and explores issues associated with youth sexuality and agency.

[15] B Rolston et al, 'Sex Education in Northern Ireland Schools: A Critical Evaluation' (2005) 5(3) *Sex Education* 219.

conservative socio-political context in which these behaviours are understood is significant in discerning why sexting among young people has come to be understood solely within a 'risk' and 'dangerous' framework.

II. Theoretical Influences

There are a plethora of writings on what is considered to be 'normal' and 'healthy' sexual development, especially among children and young people.[16] Two key schools of thought influencing much thinking on male/female sexuality, are biological essentialism and social constructivism. In basic terms, a bedrock assumption within biological essentialism is that genetic factors determine human identity and influence sexual behaviour which, in turn, regulates human experiences.[17] Within this context, sexuality is understood as a 'product of inbuilt sex drive' or 'sexual instinct'.[18] In contrast, a key focus within the roots of social constructionism is knowledge. Knowledge is viewed as a social construct, shaped by interactions and relationships with others.[19] In relation to sexuality specifically, social constructionism theory argues that sexual desire is socially constructed and heavily influenced by culture.[20] Therefore, advocates of social constructionism explore the cultural fabric and its influence on sexuality.

These two principal theories become important when considering institutionalised stereotypes on masculinity and femininity – the presumption that men are dominant and have an uncontrollable sex drive and women are unassertive and submissive.[21] Heteronormative ideologies impact on contemporary social, political and legal structures. This is represented powerfully in sexual violence cases where the primary focus within contemporary discourses is placed on the woman's sexual behaviour, leading to victim blaming and shaming.[22] In addition, easy access to pornography has been noted as a key concern as the imaging and construction of gender roles within this context often feed into dangerous stereotypes and myths. A number of professional interviewees commented on

---

[16] See S Hackett, 'Children and Young People with Harmful Sexual Behaviours' in C Barter and B David (eds), *Children Behaving Badly? Peer Violence between Children and Young People* (John Wiley and Sons, 2010).

[17] J DeLamater and J Hyde, 'Essentialism vs Social Constructionism in the Study of Human Sexuality' (1998) 35(1) *The Journal of Sex Research* 10.

[18] V Coppock et al, *The Illusions of 'Post-Feminism': New Women, Old Myths* (Routledge, Taylor and Francis, 1995) 19.

[19] J Giles, 'Social Constructionism and Sexual Desire' (2006) 36(3) *Journal for the Theory of Social Behaviour* 225.

[20] DeLamater and Hyde (n 17); V Burr and P Dick, *Social Constructionism in The Palgrave Handbook of Critical Social Psychology* (Palgrave Macmillan, 2017).

[21] A Oakley, *Sex, Gender and Society* (Maurice Temple Smith Ltd, 1972); E Stanko, *Intimate Intrusions: Women's Experience of Male Violence* (London, Routledge, 1985).

[22] See Chapter 6 for an analysis of the highly publicised 'Rugby Rape Trial' in Northern Ireland.

pornography, raising concerns associated with gender and sexual identity and agency:

> A lot has and can be influenced by pornography. It can be influenced by the way their gender ... that's around where young males are seen to be, they have to act in a particular way to be masculine, and young females have to act in a demure way in order to be feminine.[23]

> Access to porn, proliferation [of] porn, how then that projects a specific body type, and a specific action, that sex should be a specific thing.[24]

Among young people, a pressure to mirror gender stereotypes is having a consequential impact on their understanding of their body, sexual identity and agency.[25] The highly gendered sexual imagery and messaging contained within pornography is shaping young people's sexual attitudes and how they engage and interact with their partners. Professionals also referred to a relationship between viewing pornography and an expectation (particularly among young males) of engaging in more risky sexual practices:

> You can see an incredible increase in anal intercourse, or attempts at anal intercourse, as part and parcel of the young person's introduction into sexual relationships and sexual behaviours, as a direct consequence of what they're viewing ... Young males have an expectation of their sexual partners to engage.[26]

This issue is not new and other studies have shown concerning parallels between viewing pornography and problematic behaviours and attitudes among young people. In particular, the use of coercion to engage in anal sex practices has been examined.[27] The confusing and blurred messages young people are receiving due to daily exposure to sexualised material is clear. Such problematic messaging is putting young people's health at risk, both physically and psychologically, as they struggle to navigate their own sexuality in a world where overly sexualised content is so easily and readily available.

III. Feminist Narratives: A Brief Introduction

Feminist narratives are an interrelated and important topic to discuss. A key moment in historical discourses on human sexuality was the initiation of the feminist movement. While the feminist movement as a form of activism is continuous, scholars have noted three main 'waves'. The first wave was during the nineteenth to early twentieth century and centred on women's fight for political and

---

[23] Professional Interview 1 (PDF): Independent Social Work Consultant.
[24] Professional Interview 2 (PDF): Sexual Health Charity.
[25] See also L Papadopoulos, *Sexualisation of Young People Review* (Home Office, 2010).
[26] Professional Interview 1 (PDF): Independent Social Work Consultant.
[27] C Marston and R Lewis, 'Anal Heterosex among Young People and Implications for Health Promotion: A Qualitative Study in the UK' (2014) 4 *British Medical Journal Open* 1.

economic agency free from patriarchal control.[28] The first wave is mostly known for advocating for women's right to vote and is therefore primarily associated with the Suffragettes movement. The second wave came during the latter part of the twentieth century (1960s–1980s) and focused on liberating women further by highlighting the social structures which continually constrain women and fighting for their right to sexual and reproductive freedom.[29] The third and ongoing wave of feminism came during the 1990s and challenges further gender stereotypes and 'cultural production and critique' – that being primarily on media and pop culture.[30] Further, third-wave feminism has been described as 'more inclusive and racially diverse.'[31] The middle-class white woman was no longer representing the voices of *all* women and greater emphasis was being placed on race and intersectionality.[32] With the introduction and prevalence of the internet and online activism, some scholars have argued that a fourth wave of feminism has emerged which challenges misogyny and sexism.[33] A gendered dimension to online harmful behaviours *is* present online, especially in relation to peer-based sexting behaviours (discussed in Chapter 5). Moreover, evidence suggests that access to online content, including pornography, among young people has influenced the nature of the gendered practice.

Linking feminism to theoretical disciplines of thought on human sexuality and pornography, an early cause within the feminist movement was the anti-pornography movement. Feminists Catherine MacKinnon and Andrea Dworkin were central figures within this debate. Catherine MacKinnon argued that viewing pornography normalised violence against women and was an expression of 'distinctive power of men over women.'[34] Andrea Dworkin referred to pornography as 'sexual terrorism' and believed that pornography actively encourages violence against and contempt for women.[35] On the other side of the debate, pro-sex feminists would contend that pornography can be a form of sexual expression and liberation.[36] While interesting debates have been and continue to be held on this topic, it cannot be ignored that easy access to pornography is having a detrimental impact on young people's knowledge and understanding of sex and

---

[28] A Heilmann, *New Woman Fiction: Women Writing First-Wave Feminism* (Macmillan Press, 2000).

[29] E Munro, 'Feminism: A Fourth Wave?' (2013) 4(2) *Political Insight* 22.

[30] R Snyder, 'What is Third-Wave Feminism? A New Directions Essay' (2008) 34(1) *Journal of Women and Culture in Society* 178.

[31] ibid 180.

[32] See R Clark Mane, 'Transmuting Grammars of Whiteness in Third-Wave Feminism: Interrogating Postrace Histories, Postmodern Abstraction, and the Proliferation of Difference in Third-Wave Texts' (2012) 38(1) *The University of Chicago Press* 71.

[33] K Cochrane, *All the Rebel Women: The Rise of the Fourth Wave of Feminism* (Guardian Books, 2013).

[34] C MacKinnon, 'Sexuality, Pornography and Method: Pleasure under Patriarchy' (1989) 99(2) *Ethics* 315.

[35] A Dworkin, 'Pornography: The New Rerrorism' (1977) 8 *Review of Law and Social Change* 217.

[36] See GS Rubin, 'Thinking Sex: Notes for a Radical Theory of the Politics of Sexuality' in R Parker and P Aggleton (eds), *Culture, Society and Sexuality: A Reader* (Routledge, 2006).

sexuality, in particular, exposure to prevailing heteronormative discourses and gender stereotypes.

Not surprisingly, another key priority within the feminist movement was challenging masculine and feminine stereotypes and myths by disputing the misplaced belief that sexuality and behaviours are rooted in nature – ie, as noted previously, that men have an uncontrollable biological sexual drive and, in contrast, women by nature have and crave caring roles.[37] The professional interviewees tapped in on some of these issues. For example, the instinct for men to have and want sex and the pressure on boys to emulate this gender role:

> Boys are under as much pressure, maybe their first sexual experience as well. They may not want to engage in it but feel that they have to, to prove their manliness.[38]

Discussed further in Chapter 5, while pressures are felt by both boys and girls, the prevailing gender stereotypes have led to an institutionalised 'hierarchy of sexuality' resulting in men's needs being prioritised over women's as well as a long-standing dismissive attitude towards concerning and problematic sexual behaviours.[39] As one professional interviewee notes:

> I even remember from my own school days boys grabbing girls between the legs when the teachers aren't looking and just all of that and it being written off as 'boys will be boys'.[40]

Empirical evidence is showing that sexual stereotypes are shaping how young people view their sexuality, intimate relationships, sexual violence and other harmful and exploitative behaviours. This has been illustrated powerfully in a few recent high-profile cases (discussed below).

There have been pockets of intense feminist activism nationally and internationally promoting legal and policy reform, especially surrounding sexual offences. While law and policy in the area is discussed further in Chapter 6 (specifically in relation to legal frameworks on consent) and Chapter 8 (recourse to laws on bullying and sexting), for the purposes of this chapter, a key area of contention was the prevailing social and political acceptance of gender-based forms of sexual harm. The 'Rugby Rape Trial' in Northern Ireland and other international cases involving well-known figures such as Harvey Weinstein in the US, have dominated news coverage over the past few years.[41] Women and girls being encouraged to remain 'silent' and conditioned to accept that sexual harassment in the workplace and other daily settings is expected, was strongly contested.[42]

---

[37] Stanko (n 21) Chapter 2; M Coy, 'The Impact of the Sexualisation on Young People's Attitudes and Relationships' in *Premature Sexualisation: Understanding the Risks: Outcomes of the NSPCC's Expert Seminar Series* (NSPCC, 2011).

[38] Professional Interview 2 (PDF): Sexual Health Charity.

[39] Coppock et al (n 18) 19.

[40] Professional Interview 4 (PDF): Children's Charity.

[41] For more on the Rugby Rape Trial, see Chapter 6; J Chandra, 'Celebrities Open Up about Shocking Sexual Harassment and Assault Experiences' (*Elle Australia*, 18 October 2017).

[42] ibid.

Indeed, it was the #metoo movement that instigated important conversations around issues of consent and brought to light the complexities of consent, in particular identifying coerced consent. Problematic assumptions around femininity, masculinity and gender roles were reinforced:

> the distinction between permissible and impermissible sexual activities is complicated by the existence of problematic sociosexual scripts of seduction which view men, predominantly, as the sexual initiator and place women in a passive or submissive role.[43]

Discussed further in Chapter 6, conflicting messages around gender roles and issues of consent became apparent and the need for comprehensive education programmes challenging dangerous narratives associated with what is 'harmful' sexual behaviour was advocated for.

Having briefly considered some key theoretical conceptual frameworks which have influenced and dominate social and political thinking on sexuality, particularly within Northern Ireland, the next section will explore more fully how theories on sexuality are shaping modern discourses on adolescent sex and sexuality.

IV. Harmful Sexual Behaviour

A range of literature documents the existence of reports and incidents of child sexual abuse. Yet, the 'institutionalisation of caution' associated with child sexual abuse only started to really consume socio-cultural and political policies and agendas in the latter part of the twentieth century.[44] The emergence of child abuse as a social problem began when Kempe and his fellow colleagues coined the term 'the battered child syndrome'[45] in the 1960s as an 'unrecognised trauma' which stirred significant social and political debate.[46] Discussed further below, within social and political agendas there was a concentration on addressing the *physical* abuse of children. Despite a growing awareness of sexual abuse, the nature and extent of certain forms of harmful sexual behaviour were still not fully recognised, in particular peer-based forms of abuse. The range of sexual abuse and exploitation perpetrated against children and young people (as well as *by* young people) will also be explored below in an attempt to understand more fully how harmful sexual behaviours have come to be conceptualised within modern discourses and to contextualise peer-based 'sexting' debates. This section will therefore explore three key areas of concern: (i) familial abuse; (ii) the image and threat of the

---

[43] E Dowds and E Agnew, 'Rape Law and Policy: Persistent Challenges and Future Directions' in M Horvath and J Brown (eds), *Rape: Challenging Contemporary Thinking – 10 Years On* (Routledge, 2022).

[44] F Furedi, *Culture of Fear Revisited: Risk-Taking and the Morality of Low Expectation* (London, Continuum, 2006) 121.

[45] Kempe describes 'the battered child syndrome' as a clinical condition in children who have suffered serious physical abuse.

[46] CH Kempe et al, 'The Battered-Child Syndrome' (1985) 9 *Child Abuse and Neglect* 143.

'stranger'; and (iii) the narrative associated with the online predator. In doing so, clarity will be acquired regarding the conceptualisation (often narrow in focus), and regulatory responses (often reactive in nature) to certain peer-based behaviours, including bullying and sexting behaviours.

First, *familial abuse*. Initially, focus on intra-familial abuse was primarily concerned with the neglect and physical abuse of children. Recent data illustrates that on average one child a week is killed in the UK, with parents and stepparents often being linked to the death.[47] While the reporting of child deaths involving parents has been noted as early as the 1970s,[48] a number of high-profile deaths involving parents have been recorded over the past decade. To illustrate: the death of 17-month-old 'Baby P', who suffered more than 50 injuries perpetrated by his mother and her partner in 2007;[49] the death of four-year-old Hamzah Khan, who was starved to death by his mother in 2009;[50] the death of four-year-old Daniel Pelka in 2012, who was starved and neglected by his mother and her boyfriend;[51] the death of three year old Riley Siswick who sustained fatal physical injuries at the hands of his mother's partner in 2016;[52] and the death of two-year-old Keigan O'Brien, who died of a head injury inflicted by his mother's partner in 2020.[53] Such accounts of child familial abuse have harrowed an entire nation and have become landmark cases in social care, child protection and child welfare for this generation. Familial abuse has thus been placed on the political radar as more accounts of child physical abuse and neglect begin to dominate media discourses.

As noted above, the accounts illustrated above have concentrated on the *physical* violence and neglect of children. Yet, sexual abuse does happen. As one professional explains:

> We've had a number of young people referred to the service where there's been incest, you know within the family and within the sort of sibling base, older siblings behaving in a sexually harmful way to younger siblings and ranging from touching right through to rape.[54]

Sexual abuse within the family, including sibling abuse, often results in families wanting to 'sort it' themselves and 'keep it quiet'.[55] These narratives highlight how challenging it can be for children to disclose sexual abuse of any kind, but in particular abuse perpetrated by a family member. Despite growing evidence demonstrating that children and young people *can* and *do* display harmful sexual

---

[47] NSPCC, *Statistics Briefing: Child Deaths Due to Abuse or Neglect* (NSPCC, 2021).
[48] See M Hill, 'The Manifest and Latent Lessons of Child Abuse Inquiries' (1990) 20(3) *The British Journal of Social Work* 197.
[49] BBC News, 'Timeline of Baby P Case' (BBC, 8 October 2013).
[50] BBC News 'Amanda Hutton Guilty of Starving Hamzah Khan to Death' (BBC, 3 October 2013).
[51] BBC News 'Starved Boy Daniel Pelka "Invisible" to Professionals' (BBC, 17 September 2013).
[52] BBC News, 'Riley Siswick Murder: Pair Jailed over Boy's Death' (BBC, 13 June 2019).
[53] BBC News 'Keigan O'Brien: Doncaster Couple Jailed over Boy's Death' (BBC, 11 November 2020).
[54] Professional Interview 4 (PDF): Children's Charity.
[55] E Thelen, '"Keep It Quiet": The Family That Covered Up Sex Abuse' (BBC, 10 April 2012).

behaviours within a range of settings including family environments and institutional settings,[56] the reality of such abuse has consistently been ignored. While studies are beginning to scrutinise the extent and nature of harmful sexual behaviour among children, much still remains unknown about the extent of the abuse and the degree of involvement of children as 'perpetrators.'

Second, and discussed in Chapter 2, a focus on the threat of the '*stranger*' has become a key staple within media discourses associated with child sexual abuse and exploitation, for example, the highly publicised murders of eight-year-old Sarah Payne[57] and ten-year-old girls Holly Wells and Jessica Chapman[58] in the very early part of the twenty-first century. These cases shaped public understanding of *who* was a primary threat to their children. While both cases fitted the stranger narrative, this is not the norm when it comes to child sexual abuse and exploitation. Consequently, the prevalence of the 'stranger danger' rhetoric within sex offending discourses presents problems for effective policy reform as it denies the reality of sexual abuse and promotes indifference regarding the multi-faceted nature of sexual crime.[59] The dangers associated with such a narrow interpretation of sexual harm were noted by professionals. For example, one professional interviewee discusses this issue within the context of rape and issues of consent:

> Young people are still in this kind of well, total non-consent really would be the stranger rape, you couldn't see it coming, couldn't protect yourself from it.[60]

Such a restricted construction of harm not only normalises certain forms of coercive and manipulative behaviours, but it can also impact on reporting. Indeed, according to the World Health Organisation (WHO), data to date illustrates that less than 25 per cent of young people exposed to some type of violence seek help, with less than 1 in 11 young people receiving any form of formal support.[61] The image of the 'stranger' within media discourses is presenting 'a selective portrayal of specific facts',[62] a set of facts that do not reflect the lived experiences of harm and abuse for many victims. This socio-political ignorance is mirrored in much of the contemporary debate linked to peer-based sexting behaviours, discussed further in Chapters 6, 7 and 8.

What has resulted from the panic surrounding the stranger is the perception of 'risk' and the image of the 'stranger' in the public imagination feeding into

---

[56] A-M McAlinden, *Grooming' and the Sexual Abuse of Children* (Clarendon Studies in Criminology, 2012).

[57] M Oliver, 'Whiting Found Guilty of Sarah Payne Murder' (*The Guardian*, 12 December 2001).

[58] N Gerrard, 'Holly and Jessica – We'll Never Know' (*The Guardian*, 21 December 2003).

[59] McAlinden (n 56); see also A-M McAlinden, *Children as 'Risk': Sexual Exploitation and Abuse by Children and Young People* (Cambridge, Cambridge University Press, 2018).

[60] Professional Interview 4 (PDF): Children's Charity.

[61] WHO Team, *Violence against Children Online: What Health Systems and Health Care Providers Can Do* (World Health Organisation, 2022) 3.

[62] K Soothill and S Walby, *Sex Crime in the News* (London, Routledge, 1991) 34.

what has been termed the 'precautionary principle'[63] – that is, the uncertainty of 'risky' human conduct giving rise to cautionary behaviour by members of the public influenced by the belief that 'society gains by playing it safe'.[64] Indeed, children are conditioned into a false sense of belief that *all* strangers are dangerous and pose a 'risk' to their safety and wellbeing. Yet, despite official and public discourses promoting a cautionary approach to protect children from certain types of harm, this safety agenda can be extremely counterproductive: a narrow focus of 'harm' and 'risk' leaves children and young people unable to identify certain types of exploitative behaviours within their family networks, school environments and other daily social settings.[65] This is especially pertinent when it comes to young people being able to effectively identify harmful bullying and sexting behaviours.

Finally, given the nature of the behaviours under review, the *online predator* is pertinent to this debate. While discussed in more detail in subsequent chapters, in a similar vein to previous discussions, a common focus is on the adult male predator and the weak vulnerable child. The popular construction of the online predator is inaccurate, and the media rhetoric is synonymous in the description of strangers and online sex offenders as the ubiquitous 'evil' predator.[66] However, literature suggests that online sexual solicitations against children by adult predators are less prevalent than social and political discourses portray. A growing evidence base is noting other forms of online harmful sexual behaviour as being more common, including peer-on-peer abuse.[67] For example, the Secretaries of State for Education and Digital, Culture, Media and Sport commissioned a report investigating online peer-on-peer abuse. The Children's Commissioner for England and Wales, Dame Rachel de Souza, and her office led the inquiry. In 2021 preliminary findings were reported and a number of concerns were expressed regarding young people and participation in a range of online harmful behaviours, including harassment and other forms of abuse.[68] It was also noted that exposure to inappropriate and sexual content online was contributing to young people's engagement in online harmful behaviours.[69] Therefore, failing to acknowledge the variety of harms young people are exposed to online will inevitably hinder effective and informed policy reform in this area. Additionally, safeguarding measures will be limited in the protection they can offer children who suffer harm outside the narrow construction of the online adult male predator.

---

[63] Furedi (n 44) 113.

[64] ibid.

[65] See also McAlinden (n 59).

[66] J Wolak et al, 'Online "Predators" and Their Victims: Myths, Realities, and Implications for Prevention and Treatment' (2008) 63(2) *American Psychologist* 111.

[67] See J Ringrose et al, *A Qualitative Study of Children, Young People and 'Sexting': A Report Prepared for the NSPCC* (London, NSPCC, 2012); E Agnew, 'Sexting among Young People: Towards a Gender Sensitive Approach' (2021) 29(1) *International Journal of Children's Rights* 3.

[68] Children's Commissioner, *Interim Findings on Government's Commission on Online Peer-on-Peer Abuse* (Children's Commissioner for England, 2021).

[69] ibid.

A. The Young Person and Harmful Behaviour

As noted above, literature documenting the potential for children and young people to participate in certain forms of harmful behaviour, especially harmful sexual behaviour, has been noted across a variety of highly publicised cases and reports.[70] Behaviours include physical abuse, sexual abuse, bullying (on- and offline) and emotional abuse.[71] The frequency of young people engaging in wider forms of online harmful behaviours, including online harmful sexual behaviours, is causing concern among professionals and practitioners in the area. As a forensic psychologist explains:

> [T]here's always a problem if somebody becomes a victim because of it and they suffer distress on any level. So wherever that happens it's a problem. But not just for the victim because I believe it's also a problem for the person displaying this type of behaviour because it's really telling us that something is going really wrong for them. That they want or have the capacity and the premeditation to hurt somebody in those ways.[72]

Significantly, this interviewee brings to light the need to not only have effective supports in place for those who are victimised, but also for the young people displaying the harmful behaviour. One of the greatest challenges within contemporary discourses on sex offending and other harmful behaviours has been the introduction of the 'sexually aggressive child' and the young person who displays harmful sexual behaviour.[73] What emerges is an inflation of social anxiety and panic. Young people who are not progressing through the different stages of adolescence as expected are identified as 'at risk' and 'a threat' to appropriate socially constructed socialisation.[74] As discussed in Chapter 2, adolescence is a time when young people are (or should be) given more freedom and autonomy. While this is important for their development, as Firmin emphasises, there is also a need to recognise that young people are still 'emotionally and socially vulnerable' as they try to navigate complex social and peer settings.[75] A careful regulatory balance is therefore required; this is particularly true within the context of sexual exploration.

---

[70] See Chapter 2; Commission to Inquire into Child Abuse, *Report of the Commission to Inquire into Child Abuse (The Ryan Report)* (Dublin, Government Publications, 2009); D Schubotz and P Devine, *Not So Different: Teenage Attitudes across a Decade of Change in Northern Ireland* (Russell House Publishing, 2014); see also McAlinden (n 59).

[71] See eg H Beckett et al, '"It's Wrong … But You Get Used To It" A Qualitative Study of Gang-Associated Sexual Violence Towards, and Exploitation of, Young People in England', A Report Commissioned by the Office of the Children's Commissioner's Inquiry into Child Sexual Exploitation in Gangs and Groups (University of Bedfordshire and Children's Commissioner, 2013).

[72] Professional Interview 3 (PhD): Forensic Psychologist.

[73] E Vizard, 'Adolescent Sexual Offenders' (2007) 6(10) *Psychiatry* 433.

[74] J Wyn and R White, *Rethinking Youth* (London, SAGE, 1997) 22.

[75] C Firmin, 'Contextual Safeguarding: Theorising the Contexts of Child Protection and Peer Abuse' in J Pearce (ed), *Child Sexual Exploitation: Why Theory Matters* (Policy Press, 2019) 65.

In relation to sexting specifically, while there is evidence to suggest that some manifestations of peer-based sexting behaviours are becoming problematic within certain contexts, there is also literature drawing on the sexually curious and naïve young person.[76] The diversity in sexting practices therefore leaves public and official bodies confused and perplexed at how to effectively manage the behaviour. This to date has resulted in either extremely onerous measures to try and regulate behaviours (often *reactively*) being implemented or failing to respond at all. The social anxiety and uncertainty surrounding young people who engage in certain sexual behaviours, including sexting behaviours, and the dangers of current responses, was noted by one of the professional interviewees:

> I feel like there's been a problem over the years where there's been a certain amount of dipping our toe into this conversation with young people and then taking it out again and panicking and then dipping it in another wee bit and then panicking and withdrawing and I think that has really, really been unhelpful for young people as well because they're left sort of floundering and going well, what is it I'm doing or not or what am I meant to be learning about here.[77]

Empirical research is alluding to the tensions and challenges presented for legal and other professionals in providing adequate support and guidance for young people on what are healthy expressions of sexuality. Supports are particularly evasive when it comes to law and policy in the area of sexting behaviours among young people, explored further in Chapters 6 and 8. What *is* known is that, while more reports document the growing trend of harmful behaviours among young people, including online harmful sexual behaviours, the online 'threat' or 'risk' to young people is no longer constructed within the narrow terrain of the adult-child dichotomy.

V. Commercialisation and Sexualisation of Children and Young People

In addition to the features noted above, an interrelated theme for consideration is the premature sexualisation of children. Concerns have been consistently raised that children are living in what has been termed a 'hypersexualised culture'.[78] This includes exposure to sexualised material across a range of platforms, including advertising, magazines and the entertainment industry (film and music). Exposure to such content has been said to perpetuate dangerous and harmful

---

[76] See Wolak et al (n 67); see also A Lenhart, *Teens and Sexting: How and Why Minor Teens are Sending Sexually Suggestive Nude or Nearly Nude Images via Text Messaging* (Pew Research Center Report, 2009).
[77] Professional Interview 4 (PDF): Children's Charity.
[78] RD Egan and G Hawkes, 'Sexuality, Youth and the Perils of Endangered Innocence: How History Can Help Us Get Past the Panic' (2012) 24(3) *Gender and Education* 278.

gender norms. For example, persons within the entertainment industry have come out and voiced concerns. Singers Annie Lennox, Charlotte Church and Sinead O'Connor have all condemned the use of overly sexualised content for selling purposes. Lennox released a statement expressing her dismay by overly sexualised pop stars Rihanna and Miley Cyrus, describing their on-stage performances as 'highly styled pornography'.[79] Charlotte Church said in an interview that young women are encouraged to conform to a certain image, one that is 'hypersexualised' and 'unrealistic',[80] while Natalie Portman recently spoke out about the impact sexualised roles had on her as a young woman.[81] The young people interviewed commented on the prevailing sexualised narrative and were very much aware of marketing agendas, noting: 'if you want to sell this product sexualise it'.[82]

The association between exposure to sexualised material and the internet has also been documented. Children's use of technology is often presented within media discourses as a threat to their healthy development and 'normal' sexual maturity.[83] There is no 'watershed' when it comes to online content, resulting in some young people having continuous and easy access to pornography, sexualised images and violent material.[84] As a result, there is a growing concern that teenagers are becoming desensitised to certain sexual material.[85] The continuous and incessant exposure is pressuring young people to engage in behaviours they do not necessarily want to engage in. Indeed, concerns have been raised that the constant bombardment with overly sexualised content and witnessing 'unhealthy' sexual behaviours, for example, through viewing pornography, can have a detrimental impact on young people's sexual development.[86] As a number of professional interviewees explain:

---

[79] R Williams, 'Annie Lennox "Disturbed and Dismayed" by "Overtly Sexualised" Pop Performances' (*The Telegraph*, 6 October 2013).

[80] K Dutta, 'Charlotte Church Slams "Hyper-Sexualised" Music Industry and "Unattainable Sexbots" Rihanna and Miley Cyrus' (*The Independent*, 14 October 2013).

[81] P Grisafi, 'Natalie Portman Says That Sexualised Roles as a Teen Harmed Her. When Will Hollywood Listen?' *Think Opinion, Analysis, Essays* (13 December 2020).

[82] Young Person Focus Group (PhD): Male.

[83] M Coy, 'Milkshakes, Lady Lumps and Growing up to Want Boobies: How the Sexualisation of Popular Culture Limits Girls' Horizons' (2009) 18(6) *Child Abuse Review* 372.

[84] ibid; ML Ybarra and KJ Mitchell, 'How Risky Are Social Networking Sites? A Comparison of Places Online Where Youth Sexual Solicitation and Harassment Occurs' (2008) 121(2) *Pediatrics* 350; L Lóóf, "Sexual Behaviour, Adolescents and Problematic Content" in E Quayle and K Ribisl (eds), *Understanding and Preventing Online Sexual Exploitation of Children* (London, Routledge, 2012); see also Papadopoulos (n 25).

[85] A Cloete, 'Youth Culture, Media and Sexuality: What Could Faith Communities Contribute?' (2012) 68(2) *HTS Teologiese Studies/ Theological Studies* 1; E Martellozzo et al, '… I Wasn't Sure It Was OK to Watch It …' A Quantitative and Qualitative Examination of the Impact of Online Pornography on the Values, Attitudes, Beliefs and Behaviours of Children and Young People* (NSPPC and Children's Commissioner for England, 2016).

[86] M Flood, 'The Harms of Pornography Exposure among Children and Young People' (2009) 18(6) *Child Abuse Review* 384.

[T]heir viewing of sexualised imagery of children in mainstream media as well, how that's being perceived. And absolutely, young boys, their sexual knowledge, their sexual understanding has been incredibly influenced by the porn that they're watching.[87]

Their sexuality has been distorted perhaps by the availability of images or extreme pornography.[88]

So all those images that they're getting in their head, and all that they're seeing … the attitudes, the beliefs, the values that are held about women within pornography will seep into young people's heads, particularly males.[89]

A lot of the information I think young people get about sex and relationships and … how young men will understand relationships with young women in particular. Unfortunately, a lot of that can be very very coloured by the online world and what they see online and what they observe online.[90]

Concerns were raised specifically in relation to young people viewing pornography and then imitating similar acts/behaviours:

[E]ven from GPs, we're seeing an increase in child[ren] and young people being referred in for, young girls being referred in for [pro]lapse, and anal injuries as a consequence of that, and just the sexual practice is that young people have an expectation … You can see that having a direct influence in the porn that they're watching.[91]

Significantly, and discussed further in Chapter 5, the gendered dimension attached to accessing online pornography was also evident, as the young female participants did not mention pornography in their conversations. While this does not suggest that the young female participants have not watched porn, it does highlight a few interesting interpretations. It could suggest that the female participants interviewed have in fact *not* viewed pornography. Alternatively, the lack of conversation could be directly related to the childhood and sexuality debates discussed previously. That is, as Coppock and colleagues note, when a woman shows any positive sign of sexuality she is somehow viewed as sexually corrupt.[92] The female participants could therefore be very much aware that to watch or view pornographic material of any kind, went against socially constructed gender stereotypes and therefore did not raise this as an issue.

Attempts to address the culture of sex, including the Bailey Review commissioned by the UK Government in 2011, which focused on reviewing the commercialisation and sexualisation of childhood,[93] have made *some* effective changes to policy in the area. For example, retailers should ensure that magazines and other publications which contain sexual imagery/content should be covered

---

[87] Professional Interview 1 (PDF): Independent Social Work Consultant.
[88] Professional Interview 10 (PhD): Statutory Sector.
[89] Professional Interview 3 (PhD): Forensic Psychologist; see also Agnew (n 67).
[90] Professional Interview 18 (PhD): Children's Voluntary Organisation.
[91] Professional Interview 1 (PDF): Independent Social Work Consultant.
[92] Coppock et al (n 18).
[93] R Bailey, *Letting Children Be Children: Report of an Independent Review of the Commercialisation and Sexualisation of Childhood* (Department for Education, 2011).

and not in plain sight of children. Another recommendation related to age-restricted material, age verification processes and parental blocks/controls. Yet, as noted by interviewees, very often it is the young people setting up the parental restrictions, as guardians are not as tech-savvy as their children:

> A lot of work needs to be done with … parents. [They] simply don't understand.[94]

> They're still learning how to use the internet and very often they are asking their young people to set up the parental controls.[95]

In spite of attempts to better protect children and young people online, literature and empirical data suggest that their understanding and knowledge on sex and sexuality is *still* very much motivated and influenced by popular culture, including access to pornography. Further, sexual cultures are constantly being negotiated which can leave children exposed and vulnerable to contradictory messaging around what is healthy and unhealthy sexual behaviour for their age and stage of development.

VI. Conclusion

There is a clear 'emotional investment in children' within social and political discourses, particularly in the area of sexual abuse and exploitation.[96] This chapter and Chapter 2 illustrate how young people can and do engage in harmful and exploitative behaviours which challenge much of the early literature on sex, sexuality and childhood. The panic that often follows is impacting popular constructions of 'the sex offender' within public and official discourses as well as *who* is a threat to children both within on- and offline contexts.[97] The challenges young people who participate in sexting and other harmful and exploitative behaviour present for social and political discourses are multi-faceted. The child who participates in sexual behaviours contradicts well established moulds of the victim and offender within criminal justice and policy debates while also calling into question the fixed notions of children's 'natural' innocence, childhood experience and sexual agency.[98]

These factors further challenge the 'sexualisation of risk'[99] and will inevitably present problems for successful policy reform in relation to sexting and other

---

[94] Professional Interview 1 (PhD): Education Sector.

[95] Professional Interview 11 (PhD): Victim Support Organisation.

[96] F Furedi, *Moral Crusades in an Age of Mistrust: The Jimmy Savile Scandal* (Palgrave Macmillan, 2013) 43.

[97] See A-M McAlinden, 'Deconstructing Victim and Offender Identities in Discourses on Child Sexual Abuse: Hierarchies, Blame and the Good/Evil Dialectic' (2014) 54(2) *British Journal of Criminology* 180.

[98] See A Taylor, 'Reconceptualising the "Nature" of Childhood' (2011) 18(4) *Childhood* 420.

[99] S Scott et al, 'Swings and Roundabouts: Risk Anxiety and the Everyday Worlds of Children' (1998) 32(4) *Sociology* 689.

harmful behaviours displayed by young people. Further, the social construction of the sexual predator as the adult male stranger and the narrow focus within social and political discourses on sex offending and other harmful behaviours is extremely problematic. Children are suffering certain forms of harmful behaviours, including exploitative sexting practices, in silence as they do not see themselves as 'victims' or do not understand the behaviour to be 'harmful'. A challenge becomes clear: the multi-faceted nature of sexual exploitation – including sexting and other harmful behaviour by young people – will only be fully recognised once the constraints of age, gender and youth criminality are dissolved.

To conclude, applying a more nuanced understanding of peer-on-peer abuse and other harmful behaviour will promote a wider public understanding of the *different* types of harmful behaviours young people are engaging in. The real nature and extent of peer-on-peer abuse including exploitative sexting practices and other harmful behaviour can be more fully explored. As a result, the narrow construction of 'risk' and 'harm' presented within contemporary sex offending discourses both on- and offline will be challenged. Deconstructing and renegotiating these categories will present a valuable opportunity to develop innovative policy reforms in tackling sexting and other harmful behaviour perpetrated by young people.

Having scrutinised the inter-disciplinary literature and set the research in a theoretical context, the next three chapters will provide a more thorough overview of the key findings from the author's empirical research projects. Exploring the 'why', which – as Jewkes[100] notes – is so often ignored within research, will assist in providing a more nuanced understanding of the emergence, impact and regulation of 'cyberbullying' and 'sexting' among young people.

---

[100] Y Jewkes, *Media and Crime*, 3rd edn (SAGE, 2015).

4

Narratives on 'Cyberbullying' Among Young People

Bullying behaviours among young people have been conveyed as a customary part of childhood. The normative (and often subtle) dimensions to the behaviour can create a 'culture of secrecy'[1] and cause significant problems when it comes to understanding the prevalence of the behaviour, the extent of harms caused, as well as the effective implementation of law and policy in the area. While existing literature on cyberbullying methods categorise 'sexting' as a form of online bullying behaviour, it will not be a focus within this chapter. Given the unique challenges which sexting among young people can present for legal and other professionals, Chapter 5 will focus on defining and exploring the parameters of this sexual behaviour young people are engaging in. The primary focus of this chapter will therefore be on *other* forms of online bullying behaviours displayed by children and young people.

The chapter is divided into five main sections which outline and explore the dominant themes emerging from the literature and primary research. Initially, in section I, the breadth of definitional and terminological issues which were raised in relation to 'cyberbullying' will be examined. Second, some of the key differences between on- and offline bullying behaviours will be considered. Third, the gendered dimensions to bullying behaviours and other related forms of online harmful behaviour, as part of a continuum of harmful behaviour that young people are engaging in, will also be probed. Fourth, the significant role of the 'bystander' will be explored, with the impact and extent of harm caused by bullying behaviours concluding analysis in section V.

I. Conceptualising (Cyber)Bullying: Definitional Issues

Bullying behaviours among young people are not new; these are not unfamiliar behaviours to adults who work with children and young people, in any setting.[2]

---

[1] R Thornberg, '"She's Weird!" – The Social Construction of Bullying in School: A Review of Qualitative Research' (2011) 25(4) *Children and Society* 258.

[2] See D Olweus, 'Bully/Victim Problems among School Children: Basic Facts and Effects of a School-Based Intervention Program' in D Pepler and K Rubin (eds), *The Development and Treatment*

The behaviour has existed for centuries and has been shaped by the cultural landscape of the period. What *has* happened, since the introduction of the internet, is a shift in how bullying behaviours are displayed and the methods used to perpetrate harm. Consequently, a range of research has been carried out in an attempt to understand more fully the prevalence of the behaviour both on- and offline.[3] Following extensive research, psychologists, policymakers, non-profit organisations, educators and academics have made various attempts to define and conceptualise *exactly* what constitutes bullying behaviour and subsequently cyberbullying. Despite this developing body of research, there is still controversy related to appropriate terminology and a conclusive definition.

While there is no universally agreed definition of bullying, it is generally agreed that bullying (on or offline) includes four key elements: (i) harmful behaviour; (ii) which is repeated; (iii) the person intentionally perpetrates the harmful behaviour; and (iv) there is an imbalance of power (whether that be physical or psychologically, or both).[4] Cyberbullying includes the same key elements with the addition that the harmful behaviour is displayed online using technology, such as smartphones, laptops and gaming devices. To fully understand some of the more problematic aspects of the definition, the key elements will be explored in turn.

We consider *intention* to *harm* first. Intention was an important issue of consideration within interviews with professional interviewees. Some referred to the perpetrators 'original intention'[5] and whether it was their intention to cause harm: 'intention to use aggression to cause harm or distress'[6] and 'the intention is to cause you harm'.[7] Others were more nuanced and included malice, for example, 'really malicious intent'[8] – suggesting it went beyond a simple intention to cause harm. But what do we mean by intention? Within criminal law, the courts have been somewhat unwilling to provide a clear definition of what intention means, simply noting that intention should be given its 'ordinary meaning' and courts should avoid any further elaboration – known as the 'the golden rule'.[9] Other case law has tried to provide some clarity, including *R v Mohan*. In this case intention was described as 'a decision to bring about, in so far as it lies within the accused's power, the commission of the offence which it is alleged the accused attempted to commit'.[10] *Cunliffe v Goodman* also note that 'intention connotes a state of

of Childhood Aggression (Lawrence Erlbaum Associates Inc, 1991); RM Kowalski et al, *Cyberbullying: Bullying in the Digital Age*, 2nd edn (Oxford, Wiley-Blackwell, 2012).

[3] See RA Sabella et al, 'Cyberbullying Myths and Realities' (2013) 29(6) *Computers in Human Behavior* 2703; S Shariff, *Sexting and Cyberbullying: Defining the Line for Digitally Empowered Kids* (Cambridge University Press, 2014).

[4] See Kowalski et al (n 2); see also Chapter 8 and the Addressing Bullying in Schools Act 2016.

[5] Professional Interview 16 (PhD): Independent Researcher on Harmful Sexual Behaviours.

[6] Professional Interview 3 (PhD): Forensic Psychologist.

[7] Professional Interview 19 (PhD): Criminal Justice Sector.

[8] Professional Interview 15 (PhD): Statutory Sector.

[9] *R v Moloney* [1985] AC 905.

[10] *R v Mohan* [1976] QB 1 [11].

affairs which the party ... does more than merely contemplate'.[11] So intention is the person's 'purpose' and 'aim' to perpetrate the harmful behaviour.[12] Yet, interpreting a young person's behaviour online as an 'intention to cause harm' can be complex and not easy to discern.

Even though 'intention' was explored as a fundamental element of a bullying definition by professional interviewees, ambivalence was noted among the young participants:

> When someone says things to you that are harmful without realising the effects that it can have because it's on a computer screen.[13]

> The whole texting stuff. You don't know what they're actually meaning ... people say stuff, but they actually don't mean it ... so [it's] like analysing the actual texting.[14]

Clearly, 'intention' is not easily identified, especially when displayed online. Interview excerpts also highlight that intention can be misinterpreted online. For example, written messages could be construed in different ways by different people and reactions would therefore be incomparable. Important to consider also are the internal factors, such as the period of adolescence, which presents many cognitive, biological and psychological challenges, as well as external factors such as a child's environment. Indeed, Geldard et al explain how 'early childhood experiences, external or environmental stresses and current social conditions' all influence how a young person responds to individual situations.[15] Therefore, even if the sender's intention was not malicious or to cause harm, the receiver (influenced by their own individual stage of development and social experiences) could interpret the message as malevolent and suffer emotional trauma. The subjective nature of harm and singular reactions are discussed further below when examining the impact of bullying behaviours on young people. In addition, and as discussed previously, bullying behaviours are often viewed as part and parcel of childhood and growing up, therefore young people may not recognise certain behaviours as 'harmful' and/or may feel that the harm caused to them is inconsequential. Accordingly, while intention is an important facet of bullying behaviour, measuring intention and the consequential impact of harm, especially within an online bullying situation, can be highly problematic and present many challenges.

Next, the 'imbalance of power'. This was another aspect of bullying behaviour recognised as important. The literature suggests that the 'imbalance of power' between the victim and the young person displaying the harmful behaviour is crucial as it 'distinguishes bullying from other acts of violence or aggression'.[16]

---

[11] *Cunliffe v Goodman* [1950] 2 KB 237 [253].

[12] J Herring, *Criminal Law Text, Cases, and Materials*, 10th edn (Oxford University Press, 2022) 128.

[13] Young Person Focus Group (PhD): Female.

[14] Young Person Interview (PhD): Male.

[15] K Geldard et al, *Counselling Adolescents: The Proactive Approach for Young People*, 4th edn (SAGE, 2016) 19.

[16] MC Aalsma and JR Brown, 'What is Bullying' (2008) 43 *Journal of Adolescent Health* 101.

The professionals interviewed also commented on a power imbalance as an important feature of the behaviour: 'it's to do with that imbalance of power and control'.[17] In particular, the intricacies of how a power imbalance can play out in practice was considered, ie it goes beyond a simplistic understanding of pure physicality (which power imbalances can so often be diminished to):

> We understand that physical side, but we also need to understand the social power that young people have. The manipulation, the, I want you to do this, you can only be my friend if … and so understanding that social power that goes along with that as well.[18]

Acknowledging the social power that can lie at the heart of bullying behaviours was significant. In other words, a young person's lower social status and ranking among peers can also leave them vulnerable to bullying behaviours. Equally, a young person can use their high social status/ranking to bully another young person. This facet of the bullying behaviour speaks directly to some of the more nuanced issues associated with recognising more subtle forms of harm and coercion.[19]

A final aspect of bullying behaviour noted by professionals was that the behaviour was 'repeated'. Considerable research on bullying on- and offline supports the proposition that a distinctive feature of bullying behaviour is the repeated and ongoing nature of the harm inflicted.[20] A professional interviewed explained, 'I talk about it in terms of an onion … you're getting through the layers and layers of behaviour of hurt that have built up over a period of time'.[21] Yet, the speed and wide-ranging audience which technology provides has added a complication to the 'repeated' feature of bullying behaviour online. As some interviewees explain:

> You could see one incident which may have happened in a moment of time but because it's shared repeatedly online by other people then it takes on … a life of its own.[22]

> You're just putting up a photo … or video and then the other people are bullying because they comment.[23]

Although only one picture or video may have been uploaded online, the victim can experience repeated harm and a build-up of hurt by people sharing and commenting on the *same* post. Therefore, confusion was clearly expressed around the repetitive nature of online bullying behaviour and how it should be defined to more accurately reflect the extent of harm that *one* online post can cause and the layers of hurt that can manifest as a result.

---

[17] Professional Interview 19 (PhD): Criminal Justice Sector.
[18] Professional Interview 8 (PhD): Anti-Bullying Organisation.
[19] This is discussed in more detail in Chapter 6 when exploring issues of consent.
[20] Kowalski et al (n 2) 18.
[21] Professional Interview 8 (PhD): Anti-Bullying Organisation.
[22] Professional Interview 6 (PhD): Children's Voluntary Organisation.
[23] Young Person Focus Group (PhD): Female.

Despite some agreement regarding the key elements, a degree of confusion still exists when it comes to defining the parameters of each element and how it applies in practice, particularly online:

> I think that is the problem that we probably have in Northern Ireland. That there doesn't seem to be, that I know of anyway, a very clear definition of what cyberbullying actually is.[24]

Similar concerns have been raised by scholars who explain that defining the boundaries of cyberbullying behaviours 'has proven somewhat difficult'.[25] Further, definitional complications include the fact that bullying on- and offline have similar yet also distinct features, which makes disentangling the facets of the behaviour a complex task. To provide some clarity, this next section attempts to unpack some of these complexities, influenced and formulated by interview participants.

A. Key Terminology Concerns

A common concern expressed was the use of the word 'cyber' and how it has somewhat overshadowed the reality of young people's experiences of bullying behaviour, as very often the two behaviours (on- and offline bullying) cannot be easily detached. As noted earlier, even though we have this new medium (the internet) to display and perpetrate harm, offline bullying *still* continues to be a serious problem among children and young people. In fact, cyberbullying behaviours are often not isolated but are an extension of offline bullying behaviour.[26] Sticca and Perren also argue that there is 'a high degree of overlap' between on- and offline bullying.[27] This analysis is also supported by some of the young people and professionals interviewed:

> A person may become bolder, they may feel empowered by the fact that they can do this to you on a computer so they want to continue on. They may want to see how you would actually react if they did it to you face to face.[28]

> [Their behaviour] went from cyberbullying, internet abuse, Facebook abuse and comments, to in school you know face to face, bullying, ostracised from other friends.[29]

Literature and primary data analysis illustrates that bullying online does not appear in isolation and what begins as online bullying can very quickly infiltrate

---

[24] Professional Interview 18 (PhD): Children's Voluntary Organisation.

[25] Kowalski et al (n 2) 57.

[26] ibid; G Chi En Kwan and MM Skoric, 'Facebook Bullying: An Extension of Battles in School' (2012) 29 *Computers in Human Behavior* 16.

[27] F Sticca and S Perren, 'Is Cyberbullying Worse Than Traditional Bullying? Examining the Differential Roles of Medium, Publicity, and Anonymity for the Perceived Severity of Bullying' (2013) 42 *Journal of Youth and Adolescence* 740.

[28] Young Person Focus Group (PhD): Female.

[29] Professional Interview 14 (PhD): Children's Voluntary Organisation.

the physical world, for example, the school environment. It is becoming clear that bullying behaviours are part of a *continuum* of harmful behaviour among young people. Continuums are discussed further in Chapter 7 (specifically within the context of a 'continuum' of gendered violence).[30] Yet, there is a gap within current literature on the complexity of this relationship and the more nuanced aspects of how young people engage on- and offline. In particular, significant concerns exist regarding the school environment and regulation of harmful behaviours online. For example, and as examined further in Chapter 8, a tension exists regarding legislative provisions, including the Addressing Bullying in Schools Act (Northern Ireland) 2016. The Act was intended to provide a level of certainty among educators and set clear professional expectations when it came to responding to bullying behaviour. Yet, the legislation failed to incorporate the more complex aspects of the behaviour, including the overlap of on- and offline bullying behaviours, and is thus limited in what it can achieve.

Although there is an increasing recognition of the dangers and harms of cyberbullying, the majority of professional participants challenged a specific or tailored cyberbullying definition. For example, one professional explains that it is 'not a new bullying, it's not a different bullying, it is just something that has extended on from other forms of bullying'.[31] It was argued that to make distinctions between bullying cases on- and offline would undermine the complexity of bullying behaviours among young people. Recognising the continuum of bullying behaviours (from on to offline contexts) was also alluded to:

> People think cyberbullying is this brand-new phenomenon. Yes, it is because we have ICT,[32] we have really effective technology these days ... but essentially, it's still bullying.[33]
>
> I think the differentiation between on- and offline with regards to how people behave can sometimes be unhelpful ... Separating behaviour in the real world from behaviour in the online world by the labels we apply ... reinforce[s] the fact, well it's actually different online because it's not real. So, bullying is bullying.[34]

Throughout interviews with professionals (and indeed some of the interviews and focus groups with the young people), participants often referred to online bullying as simply 'bullying'. The use of terminology suggests a reluctance to separate the harms, and this is also reflected in some of the literature. For example, Turbert describes online bullying as 'an old practice with a new twist'.[35] However, while professionals were reluctant to separate bullying behaviours on- and offline, they did recognise some of the unique features of online bullying, including the

---

[30] N Henry and A Powell, 'Sexual Violence in the Digital Age: The Scope and Limits of Criminal Law' (2016) 25(4) *Social and Legal Studies* 398.
[31] Professional Interview 8 (PhD): Anti-Bullying Organisation.
[32] Information and Communications Technology.
[33] Professional Interview 12 (PhD): Education Sector.
[34] Professional Interview 21 (PhD): Safeguarding Sector.
[35] K Turbert, 'Faceless Bullies: Legislative and Judicial Responses to Cyberbullying' (2009) 33(2) *Seton Hall Legislative Journal* 652.

speed at which harmful material can be disseminated, the online disinhibition effect and anonymity.

II. On- and Offline Bullying: A Comparison

The emergence and advancement of technology has provided new opportunities for young people to participate in online harmful behaviours and can challenge the stereotypical and gendered persona of a 'bully', ie a young person (often a boy) who is 'aggressive' and is physically strong.[36] When it comes to online bullying, it can be a 'more convenient' way for young people to perpetrate harm and can therefore be engaged in by young people who would not necessarily exhibit similar behaviours within an offline setting.[37] As a result, in the absence of physical contact, online bullying usually becomes a matter of 'psychological warfare'.[38]

In support of this argument, many professional participants believe the internet has created a platform for those children and young people who may be less 'powerful', whether that be physically or mentally, to bully others due to the absence of physical confrontation. Very often young people who bully online concentrate on 'manipulating'[39] their victim. In other words, as explained by one interviewee, 'those people who would have made really bad face to face bullies are actually psychologically brilliant on the internet'.[40] Further, and interconnected, is the 'online disinhibition effect' which suggests that 'anonymity' and 'invisibility' allow people to explore behaviours online which they would never associate with or express offline.[41]

A. Absence of Physical Confrontation

The physical aspect of bullying behaviour was an important theme and many of the young people commented on the difference between on- and offline bullying through this lens:

> In real life you'll know someone is malicious because they will laugh even if they see that you're hurt. But behind a computer screen they won't see your facial expression when you're looking at all the things they are doing.[42]

---

[36] D Olweus, 'Bully/Victim Problems among School Children: Basic Facts and Effects of a School-Based Intervention Program' in D Pepler and K Rubin (eds), *The Development and Treatment of Childhood Aggression* (Lawrence Erlbaum Associates Inc, 1991) 425.

[37] N Antoniadou and C Kokkinos, 'Cyber and School Bullying: Same or Different Phenomena?' (2015) 25 *Aggression and Violent Behaviour* 364.

[38] S SooHoo, 'Examining the Invisibility of Girl-to-Girl Bullying in the Schools: A Call to Action' (2009) 13(6) *International Electronic Journal for Leadership in Learning* 1–6.

[39] Professional Interview 20 (PhD): Education Sector.

[40] Professional Interview 3 (PhD): Forensic Psychologist.

[41] J Suler, 'The Online Disinhibition Effect' (2004) 7(3) *CyberPsychology and Behaviour* 321.

[42] Young Person Focus Group (PhD): Female.

The physicality of it all. You can't get punched in the face on the internet ... It's not a whole crowd of people shouting in your face.[43]

It was clear that the physical element, or lack thereof, was considered an important distinction between on- and offline bullying. Some young people also acknowledge that physical contact could follow online bullying: as one young person explains, 'and the ones that are bullying you can actually hurt you in real life instead of on the internet. Physically I mean.'[44] As alluded to above, interviewees are again tapping into the concept of a 'continuum' of harmful behaviour. If proactive and successful regulatory frameworks are to be put in place which target peer-based behaviours, such as bullying, recognising that the behaviours cannot always be easily categorised into distinct 'on' or 'offline' contexts is important.

B. All Pervasive Nature: 24-Hour Access

The all-pervasive nature of cyberbullying and the breadth of access online was also highlighted by professional participants. Some professionals focused in on the pervasiveness of online bullying, noting that 'it never goes away' compared to offline bullying which can be 'snappy', 'short' and 'kind of explosive' in that moment.[45] Another professional commented on access and how with offline bullying it is 'periodic',[46] for example if the person who is perpetrating the harm is someone you see in the park on a Friday walking home from school, then access is limited to that period of time. In comparison, when it comes to online bullying, the perpetrator can access you at any time of the day. Another issue raised was the removal of a young person's home as their 'safe place' and how someone can be bullied in their bedroom, leaving a young person feeling very isolated and lonely.[47]

The young people also had similar concerns associated with the pervasiveness of cyberbullying. As one interviewee explains, 'in real life you can walk away but sometimes on the internet you can't'.[48] The same young person also commented on the sophisticated methods young people can use to gain access: 'you have to block them but sometimes they could use other accounts',[49] noting the inescapable feature of bullying online. The constant nature of the harm was also commented on: 'online it's in your house, it's in your phone, and it's constant'.[50] It was clear that some professional and youth participants viewed online bullying as a more pervasive and harmful form of bullying behaviour due to the inescapable and universal nature of the online world.

---

[43] Young Person Focus Group (PhD): Male.
[44] Young Person Interview (PhD): Female.
[45] Professional Interview 3 (PhD): Forensic Psychologist.
[46] Professional Interview 16 (PhD): Independent Researcher on Harmful Sexual Behaviours.
[47] Professional Interview 20 (PhD): Education Sector.
[48] Young Person Interview (PhD): Female.
[49] Young Person Interview (PhD): Female.
[50] Young Person Interview (PhD): Female.

Interestingly, while a number of participants mentioned the all-pervasive nature of cyberbullying behaviours, a number of other professionals challenged some of the proposed 'unique' aspects of online bullying, including the potentially 24/7 aspect that can be attached to cyberbullying. One professional referred to children in care specifically and how offline bullying, for those children, can be ubiquitous:

> With children in the care centre who may be experiencing … bullying from a peer who they go to the same school as, they live in the same children's home as, they're with 24/7, and that's in the physical world.[51]

While online bullying by its very nature gives a perpetrator unlimited access to victims, there are offline cases which can mirror these online features. Children in care homes is one example of this. Recognising the unique contexts in which bullying (on- and offline) can take place, and how certain environments can perhaps magnify the harm caused, is imperative for effective policy reform. For context, by the end of March 2022, it was estimated that approximately 3,624 children were in care in Northern Ireland[52] – in the region of 7 per cent of these children are placed in residential care.[53] While there is very little research to date which explores the impact of bullying behaviours within residential care facilities, the research that does exist notes the relationship between bullying and children in care as an issue of concern.[54] Exposure to bullying has been recorded to be higher in care settings; for example, it has been reported that children in care disclose higher levels of victimisation.[55] Greater clarity is needed regarding the extent and prevalence of bullying behaviours within this particular setting and how effective targeted supports and interventions for this vulnerable group of children could be implemented.

C. Anonymity

Anonymity as a fundamental characteristic of the internet is contested. Christopherson, Suzuki and Calzo propose that anonymity online can provide benefits for young people, for example, privacy and a platform for young people to ask and learn about relationships, health and sexuality free from judgement

---

[51] Professional Interview 8 (PhD): Anti-Bullying Organisation.

[52] In England, it was estimated that approximately 80,000 children were in care in 2021. https://committees.parliament.uk/publications/23006/documents/168514/default/, last accessed 17 July 2023.

[53] Department of Health, *Publication of 'Children's Social Care Statistics for Northern Ireland 2021/22'* (3 November 2022).

[54] See eg Department for Children, Schools and Families, *Safe from Bullying in Children's Homes* (DCSF Publications, 2009).

[55] Anti-Bullying Alliance, *Bullying and Care-Experienced Young People* https://anti-bullyingalliance.org.uk/tools-information/all-about-bullying/at-risk-groups/looked-after-children/bullying-and-care, last accessed 17 July 2023.

and ridicule.[56] Yet, anonymity can also be problematic and can magnify the harm caused by online bullying. Turbert, for example, explains that anonymity can make cyberbullying 'more dangerous' than offline bullying.[57] A main concern noted was how the anonymous perpetrator can use their unidentified status to inflict substantial psychological harm. Yet, total anonymity as a concept was disputed by some professionals interviewed. Indeed, some interviewees were quite dismissive of the notion of 'complete' anonymity and noted the various mechanisms through which anonymity can be broken. For example, one interviewee explains that 'there are mechanisms in place and the PSNI … have very sophisticated systems for breaking through anonymity'.[58] Another interviewee notes, 'people think they can be anonymous online … but technology will catch up'.[59] Despite some professional's reassurances that anonymity was in fact not a safeguard for persons perpetrating harm, the young people interviewed expressed considerable concerns. Some of the comments include:

> It can make them feel like it can be anybody … one of their closest friends to like somebody that lives 10 feet or 10 thousand miles away.[60]

> If you read something from someone anonymous you don't hear it in their voice. You hear it in your own and that is 10 times worse.[61]

> If they don't know who they are being bullied by then … [It can] stress you out wondering who it is.[62]

Two main anxieties in relation to anonymity are noted. First, anonymity leaves a young person questioning their peer and familial relationships. As illustrated by some of the young people above, anonymity could therefore fracture healthy relationships as the young person distances themselves from family and friends due to fear, uncertainty and doubt. Second, anonymity also impacts disclosure as *everyone* becomes a possible or potential suspect. Interestingly, one young person recognised that although anonymity was not absolute, it would have to be a very serious case before the police would activate such measures: 'unless it goes to really higher levels'.[63] Overall, a great level of concern was expressed by the young people regarding anonymity and online harmful behaviours and what help they could actually receive when the person perpetrating the harm is not easily identifiable, ie anonymous.

---

[56] LK Suzuki and JP Calzo, 'The Search for Peer Advice in Cyberspace: An Examination of Online Teen Bulletin Boards about Health and Sexuality' (2004) 25(6) *Journal of Applied Developmental Psychology* 685; KM Christopherson, 'The Positive and Negative Implications of Anonymity in Internet Social Interactions: "On the Internet, Nobody Knows you're a Dog"' (2007) 23(6) *Computers in Human Behaviour* 3038.

[57] Turbert (n 35) 653.

[58] Professional Interview 8 (PhD): Anti-Bullying Organisation.

[59] Professional Interview 19 (PhD): Criminal Justice Sector.

[60] Young Person Focus Group (PhD): Female.

[61] Young Person Focus Group (PhD): Female.

[62] Young Person Focus Group (PhD): Male.

[63] Young Person Focus Group (PhD): Male.

Anonymity in relation to harm caused has therefore not been fully explored in the current literature and is an important theme. Significantly, it was also evident among youth interviewees that they were unclear as to what precisely can be done if someone is anonymously posting harmful content online. Ambiguity around anonymity and response structures could therefore lead to young people not reporting bullying online due to a belief that nothing can be done, thus adding to the extent of harm caused.

III. Online Harms: Beyond Bullying

While bullying online was discussed in its widest sense, some specific forms of bullying behaviours were noted among the young people. By way of an example, 'catfishing' emerged as a problematic practice. 'Catfishing' is defined as being a form of cyberbullying behaviour and describes when someone pretends to be someone else by setting up a fake account and developing relationships online (often romantic) via this fake persona.[64] The below excerpt is taken from the female focus group when discussing some of the negative aspects of the internet:

> Participant C: Catfishing.
>
> Participant D: Oh God.
>
> Interviewer: What is catfishing?
>
> Participant C: It's where you create a fake account using someone else's photos and talk to people on the internet and then get them to like, you can either build a relationship under a fake name or you can get them to like to send you money and send you things.
>
> Interviewer: do you think that happens a lot?
>
> Participant B: All the time.
>
> Participant C: … it's so messed up.[65]

Some of the professional participants also commented on this harmful practice when talking about harmful behaviours more generally but seemed unaware that the behaviour was labelled 'catfishing'. Professionals commented on persons using 'false names, false age'[66] and 'false accounts'[67] to target victims. Despite the young people noting that 'catfishing' happens 'all the time,'[68] and some literature noting the practice as a shared fear among young people,[69] very little scholarly work

---

[64] RA Javier et al, 'Bullying and its Consequences: In Search of Solutions – Part II' (2013) 22(2) *Journal of Social Distress and the Homeless* 59.

[65] Young Person Focus Group (PhD): Female.

[66] Professional Interview 20 (PhD): Education Sector.

[67] Professional Interview 7 (PhD): Children's Voluntary Organisation.

[68] Young Person Focus Group (PhD): Female.

[69] See J Lykens et al, 'Google for Sexual Relationships: Mixed-Methods Study on Digital Flirting and Online Dating among Adolescent Youth and Young Adults' (2019) 5(2) *JMIR Public Health and Surveillance* 1.

exists on exploring the nature, extent and impact of this behaviour on children and young people. Further, the limited discussion afforded to the practice among professionals interviewed speaks to a broader concern regarding the proper identification of 'risks' online.

Another emerging and interrelated strand of bullying behaviours online was a fear among young people that they would fall victim to 'hacking'. A recent European Youth Survey found that 1 in 10 young people (aged 16–19 years) had engaged in hacking.[70] The NSPCC also reported a link between online challenges and hacking. In their 2022 briefing it was noted that young people were fearful of hacking if they did not participate in dangerous online challenges.[71] Hacking is a diverse practice and can also include accessing someone's social media profile without their permission to write insulting messages,[72] or misrepresenting another person's sexual identity.[73]

Similar fears were expressed among the young people who spoke about the risk of hacking and how it was 'the easiest thing to do' and how they had heard 'a lot of horror stories'.[74] There was one specific risk that the young people were particularly attuned to:

> I have a password on my webcam because I'm paranoid because like if I have my phone, because it has … a camera on both sides I'll close it … and then I'll have it sitting away from me just in case.[75]

Despite a range of 'hacking' methods, anxiety was mainly noted among the female participants in relation to personal webcams. The male participants did not mention hacking (or indeed 'catfishing') as a concern at all. The gendered dimension connected to certain risks and harms is interesting and speaks to broader issues associated with contextualising risks within the wider remit of online harms and gender, discussed in more detail in the next section.

IV. Gendered Dimensions to Online Harmful Behaviours

Within the literature, gender has been identified as a significant factor in understanding certain types of harmful behaviour. For example, Newburn and Stanko

---

[70] J Davidson et al, *European Youth Cybercrime, Online Harm and Online Risk Taking: 2022 Research Report* (London, United Kingdom Institute for Connected Communities, University of East London, 2022).

[71] *Children's Experiences of Legal but Harmful Content Online*, Helplines Insight Briefings (NSPCC, 2022).

[72] H Vandebosch and K Van Cleemput, 'Defining Cyberbullying: A Qualitative Research into the Perceptions of Youngsters' (2008) 11(4) *CyberPsychology and Behaviour* 499.

[73] R Kota et al, 'Characterizing Cyberbullying among College Students: Hacking, Dirty Laundry, and Mocking' (2014) 4(4) *Societies* 549.

[74] Young Person Focus Group (PhD): Female.

[75] Young Person Focus Group (PhD): Female.

note 'the most significant fact about crime is that it is almost always committed by men'.[76] Significantly, primary research also demonstrates that gender emerges as a key variable in terms of understanding how and why young people engage or participate in certain forms of online harmful behaviours. Some scholars have explored how gender plays a significant role in understanding bullying at school, specifically within an offline context. For example, Olweus notes that boys often bully 'with physical means' whereas girls are more inclined to use 'subtle and indirect ways' which can include starting and spreading rumours among friendship groups.[77] In addition, Besag describes how friendships among girls 'appear to be more fractious and disputatious than those of boys'.[78]

What is striking is how this gendered dimension of harmful behaviours has transferred online, as illustrated by this excerpt from a focus group below:

> Participant E: Girls are more sneaky about things.
>
> Participant C: I feel girls would be more vicious.
>
> Participant B: Girls are monstrous.
>
> Participant A: They've got like tongues of fire. They like know what to say and how it would hurt you …
>
> Participant C: Boys would just be like 'ha ha you look stupid' but like a girl would like take the photo and put it in a group chat and say look how dopey this girl looks and get like all these other girls like laughing about her and having like this whole discussion and then go back to being her friend in real life.[79]

The girls appear very disparaging of their own gender and their understanding of female interaction within a bullying context reflects wider gender stereotypes regarding how females engage in harmful behaviours, especially in relation to displaying aggression. This analysis was supported by a forensic psychologist who emphasised that verbal attacks were more common among girls than physical manifestations of harm:

> I think we're getting more females because it's more, it gives them more power … a female might be small and petite, over the internet nobody knows that she is.[80]

The online world therefore allows females to display aggression without any physical confrontation.

Despite the literature and interview analysis strongly illustrating gender dimensions attached to expressions of aggression, one male youth participant

---

[76] T Newburn and E Stanko, 'When Men Are Victims: The Failure of Victimology' in T Newburn and E Stanko (eds), *Men, Masculinities and Crime: Just Boys doing Boy's Business?* (London, Routledge, 1994) 1.

[77] D Olweus, 'Annotation: Bullying at School: Basic Facts and Effects of a School Based Intervention Program' (1994) 35(7) *The Journal of Child Psychology and Psychiatry* 1177.

[78] V Besag, *Understanding Girls' Friendships, Fights and Feuds: A Practical Approach to Girls' Bullying* (Open University Press, 2006) 3.

[79] Young Person Focus Group (PhD): Female.

[80] Professional Interview 3 (PhD): Forensic Psychologist.

challenged authoritative theories in relation to female and male sexuality and the notion that gender highly influences displays and acts of aggression. Instead, this young person focused on personality types rather than gender identities:

> Introverts would bully differently to extroverts … like regardless of gender … like some people may choose to be manipulative and some may choose to blackmail people and they may choose to be really sneaky … but other people may choose to be more aggressive and threatening and threaten them with violence in real life … different methods for different personalities but I don't think gender would affect it too much.[81]

Anomalies were also noted by professional interviewees. A minority of the professionals reported acts of physically aggressive behaviours among young females, including organised fights. Such behaviour challenges the presumed manifestations of aggressive behaviour displayed by females. For example, professionals working within the education sector stated there was 'a lot of activity'[82] around organised fights: 'I dealt with a call just last week where a fight between two females was recorded, uploaded and was disseminated.'[83] Awareness of organised fights was also noted by one of the female participants interviewed: 'like there can be ones [videos] that people put [up] about fighting and stuff. It can be like kids in school and no-one's doing anything about it'.[84] While some interviewees challenge the presumption of gender stereotypes in relation to male and female aggression, the predominant narrative suggests that gendered power relations are still very much relevant. Yet, recognising the potential for young people to engage in *any* type of harmful behaviour, regardless of gender, is crucial if effective interventions and supports are to be put in place.

Primary research noted significant gendered dimensions in relation to how young people engage online and consequently the 'risks' they may then be exposed to. By way of an example, a professional working in a safeguarding organisation noted that girls seemed to prefer interacting online through Facebook and Instagram whereas boys were more likely to engage online through gaming sites. The difference in communication was noted as significant as 'there are differences really in terms of risks'.[85] In particular, notable risks associated with gaming sites were put forward:

> We've also heard of you know boys becoming groomed through gaming machines which is … it tends to be young boys' preferred method of online interaction.[86]

Reports of young boys being groomed via gaming sites have also appeared in the media, with devastating outcomes. In 2014, 14-year-old Breck Bednar was killed

---

[81] Young Person Focus Group (PhD): Male.
[82] Professional Interview 1 (PhD): Education Sector.
[83] ibid.
[84] Young Person Interview (PhD): Female.
[85] Professional Interview 6 (PhD): Children's Voluntary Organisation.
[86] Professional Interview 5 (PhD): Safeguarding Organisation.

by 18-year-old Lewis Daynes. Lewis groomed Breck for approximately 13 months via a gaming site before inviting Breck to his flat, where he killed him.[87] To raise awareness of the dangers of online grooming, a short film titled 'Breck's Last Game' was made in partnership with the Breck Foundation and Northamptonshire, Leicester, Surrey and Essex Police departments.[88]

Beyond the harmful connections young people can make on gaming sites, a related concern is the type of content young people are being exposed to. Current research has demonstrated how participation on gaming sites can lead to harmful behaviours being displayed among young people who play certain games. Yang explains:

> Online games generally have violent content, and constantly engaging in violent behavior in virtual situations may lead adolescents, who have yet to attain full maturity, to translate their aggressive acts from the gaming environment into their real-life behaviors.[89]

Concerns were raised by professional interviewees, who were of the opinion that a greater level of caution should be taken when allowing children and young people access to certain material. Schools in particular were 'very concerned' at the material young people were accessing, including 'maybe 18 rated games'.[90] This was leaving young people vulnerable to not only violent but also overly sexualised content. The sexual aspect was mentioned by one of the young people as an issue of concern and related the exposure to participation in sexting: 'most games have some sort of sexual content in it ... would help pressurise them into sexting or something like that'.[91] Significantly, only one young person mentioned gaming as an issue of concern. The lack of discussion among young people could be an indication that they do not perceive gaming sites to be unsafe or pose any real threats. Yet, current literature and interviews with professionals suggests that targeting young people, young males in particular, on gaming sites to exploit them or place pressures on them to engage in harmful behaviour, is a growing concern.

Greater understanding within statutory and voluntary sectors in relation to the full remit of risks gaming sites pose to young people, especially males, is required. That is, greater clarity and understanding in terms of the risks posed and to whom; who are most 'at risk', for example, age demographics and the gendered nature of risk; a fuller understanding of the potential links to online bullying behaviours (in particular engaging in sexting – as noted by the young

---

[87] A Moore, 'I Couldn't Save My Child from Being Killed by an Online Predator' (*The Guardian*, 13 January 2016).
[88] Northamptonshire Police, 'Breck's Last Game' (Northamptonshire Police, 2019).
[89] S Ching Yang, 'Paths to Bullying in Online Gaming: The Effects of Gender, Preference for Playing Violent Games, Hostility, and Aggressive Behaviour on Bullying' (2012) 47(3) *Journal of Educational Computing Research* 236.
[90] Professional Interview 1 (PhD): Education Sector.
[91] Young Person Focus Group (PhD): Male.

interviewee above); the extent and range of harm that can be caused and any other interrelated issues which might emerge. Further discussion on these issues will enhance current analysis and knowledge in this area, especially in relation to safeguarding children and young people from the wider remit of online harmful behaviours.

The range of harms to young people online stems not only from those who actually inflict the harm, but also those who witness the harmful behaviour. Therefore, examining the role of the 'bystander' is also important.

V. The Role of the 'Bystander'

Analysis of the primary data raised questions around those who assume the role of the 'bystander'. Obermann explains: 'bullying is not just an isolated process going on between a bully and a victim but an interaction that takes place in a broader social context'.[92] That includes the young person/people who witness the harmful behaviour being perpetrated and decide whether or not to intervene. Obermaier and colleagues explain that 'bystanders are central in shaping cyberbullying processes, as they can influence the perpetrator's behavior by either supporting the bully or the victim'.[93] Moreover, the role of the bystander can be two-fold as explained by Kowalski and others: 'to the perpetrator, the silence of a passive bystander comes across as support; to the victim, the mere presence of the bystander may amplify an already painful and humiliating situation'.[94]

In tandem with the current literature, a fear was expressed among some of the young people regarding 'bystander' status and the potential negative consequences of intervening (or not). A prominent explanation given for failing to intervene was the concern that they would become a target of online bullying behaviour themselves:

> I know [this] sounds really selfish but I wouldn't want to get involved in case like I started getting bullied ... it's none of my business.[95]

> I would never comment under stuff ... that just causes more shit for you ... It's not my choice ... it's not for me to decide that's wrong, what's right.[96]

> I would try and help them but try not to be in the middle of the fight.[97]

Generally, hesitancy was expressed when it came to standing up for their peers online who were being subjected to bullying. The picture which emerges from

---

[92] M-L Obermann, 'Moral Disengagement among Bystanders to School Bullying' (2011) 10(3) *Journal of School Violence* 239.

[93] M Obermaier et al, 'Bystanding or Standing By? How the Number of Bystanders Affects the Intention to Intervene in Cyberbullying' (2016) 18(8) *New Media & Society* 1492.

[94] Kowalski et al (n 2) 85.

[95] Young Person Interview (PhD): Female.

[96] Young Person Interview (PhD): Male.

[97] Young Person Interview (PhD): Female.

interviews with the young people is a growing tension and uncertainty expressed in relation to how the young people *should* respond in bullying situations and how they actually *do* respond. A delicate balancing exercise emerges; in other words, the young people may want to intervene but are also fearful they too will be subjected to bullying behaviours online or face some sort of retaliation for stepping in.

At times it was clear that the young people interviewed were conflicted regarding intervention. Some young people expressed feelings of shame that they did not intervene when they witnessed bullying online, while others tried to justify their reasoning for not acting. Interview analysis suggests that the young people understand on some level that by not intervening they have added to the harm caused. While other young people seemed sympathetic to bystanders: 'not many people can back you up on online bullying because they don't know who that person is and sometimes your friend can't help you'.[98] It was clear that the 'bystander' role is not one void of emotion. Acknowledging the range of roles that can be present within a bullying case both on- and offline is crucial if effective *preventative* interventions are to be activated, especially in relation to the extent of harm. Indeed, McAlinden, Killean and Dowds discuss a move from recognising 'victim-offender continuums' to more inclusive and comprehensive 'victim-offender-bystander continuums', within certain settings.[99] While discussed within the context of sexual violence, this shift in thinking about the different parties involved when it comes to bullying behaviours would provide a more nuanced analysis of the behaviours under review. This is particularly relevant when considering 'intention' and an 'intention to cause harm'. Overall, examining the potential harm inflicted on the young people who witness the behaviour and who grapple with whether they should intervene or not is an under-researched area and in need of further development, especially within an online context.

VI. The Harmful Impact of Cyberbullying

The literature has documented a variety of harms that can be suffered as a result of being a victim of bullying behaviours on- and offline, especially in relation to adolescent health. Some of the specific concerns noted among academics and practitioners include feelings of depression, anxiety, isolation, anger, helplessness, suicidal thoughts, feeling defenceless, passivity, difficulties socially engaging with others and physical health problems.[100] Similarly, this wide remit of harm was also explored by professional interviewees in the current study. A professional working in safeguarding explained that currently the 'greatest negative impact

---

[98] Young Person Focus Group (PhD): Male.
[99] A-M McAlinden et al, 'Sexual Violence in the Digital Age: Replicating and Augmenting Harm, Victimhood and Blame' (2022) 31(6) *Social and Legal Studies* 871.
[100] K Rigby, 'Consequences of Bullying in Schools' (2003) 48(9) *The Canadian Journal of Psychiatry* 583; R Ortega et al, 'The Emotional Impact of Bullying and Cyberbullying on Victims: A European Cross-National Study' (2012) 38(5) *Aggressive Behaviour* 342.

on children and young people's lives is bullying'.[101] Referring more specifically to online bullying, a number of professionals noted the 'comprehensive impact' bullying can have on a young person and that very often bullying online 'takes control' of that young person's life.[102]

In support of the literature, a professional working in the education sector also explained that young people 'refusing to go to school ... [and their] anxiety levels going through the roof'[103] is a common symptom of bullying online. Moreover, the psychological symptoms of harm were also recorded by some of the young participants:

They don't feel comfortable with themselves. They feel ... scared.[104]

If it gets too far it can lead to like suicide or self-harm or like trying to take a lot of pills or trying to do drugs and stuff like that there.[105]

It's scary but it's also very saddening.[106]

Reading it in your own voice ... in your own head ... you're like dropped down to your emotional boundary.[107]

Empirical findings demonstrate the *wide* range of harm children and young people who are victims of bullying behaviours can experience. It is evident that the impact is extremely variable in nature. Primary analysis suggests that while physical manifestations of harm were something the young people feared, the psychological harm that can result from bullying behaviours among young people seems more varied and wide-ranging. Further, while there is a growing body of research on psychological harm and bullying behaviours, analysis of the interview data demonstrates a lack of understanding regarding the *full* remit of psychological harm. For example, research that explores bullying among young people and the use of drugs as a method of psychological pain relief (as noted by one of the young people) is limited. In addition, the role of the bystander and how 'harm' manifests within that particular context are also under-researched areas within youth culture.

A. Body Image

A growing amount of research has commented on the sociocultural pressures young people are exposed to on- and offline when it comes to self-image and the unrealistic expectations placed on body image.[108] Current research on self-image

---

[101] Professional Interview 21 (PhD): Safeguarding Sector.

[102] Professional Interview 20 (PhD): Education Sector.

[103] Professional Interview 1 (PhD): Education Sector: Participant A; see also V Brown et al, *Estimating the Prevalence of Young People Absent from School Due to Bullying* (Red Balloon Learner Centre Group, 2011).

[104] Young Person Interview (PhD): Female.

[105] Young Person Interview (PhD): Female.

[106] Young Person Focus Group (PhD): Female.

[107] Young Person Focus Group (PhD): Female.

[108] See J Ringrose, 'Are you Sexy, Flirty or a Slut? Exploring Sexualization and How Teen Girls Perform/Negotiate Digital Sexual Identity on Social Networking Sites' in R Gill and C Scharff (eds),

centres mostly on unpacking the relationship between body surveillance and body satisfaction and/or empowerment, especially in relation to females (see Chapter 5). Yet, minimal academic research and analysis explores the relationship between body image, bullying and harm caused.

This issue was raised by interview participants. As an illustration, one young person explained the lengthy process of taking a photo, 'like I might have taken like 20 photos'[109] before uploading the photo she wants her peers to see. Therefore, when a self-image attracts negative commentary online by fellow peers it can have a detrimental impact on that young person, including feelings of self-blame. This was illustrated by a conversation between two young people:

> Participant C: Like a lot of people too put like nice photos of themselves on any media and like want themselves to appear nice to get appreciation and whenever you feel nice and somebody makes fun of you for feeling nice then it can feel like 10 times worse.
>
> Participant B: Because you went from feeling really nice aww that's a lovely photo ... to why did I do this to myself or why did they do this to me?
>
> Participant C: Yeah, it makes it like [it's] your fault.
>
> Participant B: It makes it like you caused it. You're doing it to yourself.[110]

Two issues are significant: first, how young people value a positive online self-image and want to be appreciated and recognised for their physical beauty;[111] second, the confusion around accountability.

Considering a positive online self-image, it is interesting to note that it was the female participants who focused a great deal of discussion on body image. Moreover, while the young people focused primarily on the psychological manifestations of harm, an underlying physical influence was present: puberty and the physical changes that occur during this developmental stage. One young person within a focus group explained: 'It's even worse because we're teenagers and our emotions are all over the place.'[112] This common understanding of puberty and adolescence is also explored by Pesa and colleagues, who note:

> The physical changes that characterize this life stage have been implicated as a trigger for body image problems in both males and females. Boys typically experience positive feelings toward their changing bodies because of the increase in muscle mass ... which may be socially beneficial. Girls generally become more dissatisfied with their bodies following puberty in part because of increased body fat, which conflicts with the cultural ideal of a slender body.[113]

New Femininities: Postfeminism, Neoliberalism and Subjectivity (Palgrave Macmillan, 2011) 106; E Agnew 'Sexting among Young People: Towards a Gender Sensitive Approach' (2021) 29(1) *International Journal of Children's Rights* 3.

[109] Young Person Focus Group (PhD): Female.

[110] Young Person Focus Group (PhD): Female.

[111] The theme of body image emerges throughout interview analysis and is discussed further in Chapter 5 in relation to sexting.

[112] Young Person Focus Group (PhD): Female.

[113] JA Pesa et al, 'Psychosocial Differences Associated with Body Weight among Female Adolescents: the Importance of Body Image' (2000) 26(5) *Journal of Adolescent Health* 335.

While it is suggested that boys 'typically' have a more positive experience in rela-tion to physical changes, interview analysis illustrates the unrealistic pressures faced by girls *and* boys to conform to a particular ideal. However, while research illustrated above suggests that girls are at a higher risk of being subjected to unre-alistic pressures, especially in relation to sexualisation, primary and secondary data analysis also demonstrates the complex and nuanced nature of constructing a 'sexual digital identity', especially among young girls.[114] Indeed, these pressures have a negative impact on young people's understanding and perception of their bodies.

Further, it is evident that the pressures of a positive body image exist on- and offline, yet it could be argued that online technology has created an extra dimen-sion to the pressures placed on young people. For example, the use of filters which allow young people to brush out blemishes or any skin imperfections, enlarge their eyes and reshape their noses. In fact, few young people would upload a self-image online that has not been edited to some degree. For example, it has been docu-mented that as many as 9 out of 10 schoolgirls digitally enhance their photographs before uploading them.[115]

An interrelated issue is the complexity around accountability in relation to body image and bullying online. It was apparent among the young people inter-viewed that when a self-posted image receives negative attention, they feel partly responsible for any antagonistic behaviour directed towards them. An enhanced understanding of the full remit of harm caused by online harmful behaviours, including cyberbullying, will improve child protection and welfare responses, especially within voluntary and statutory organisations.

B. On- and Offline Bullying

Most of the professional participants were hesitant to distinguish between the harm caused by online and offline bullying. For instance, a forensic psychologist considered the range of social and physical factors that contribute to how a young person deals with confrontation and victimisation:

> If somebody's quite resilient and robust to that kind of thing being said to them then they can react very differently to somebody who has had a background that's full of adversity ... so the trigger that the bullying brings can be very different.[116]

The range of harm young people can be exposed to and their coping mechanisms in dealing with harmful experiences are dependent on their own individual life experiences. Factors include the young person's own emotional stability and

---

[114] Ringrose (n 108) 106.
[115] J Bingham, 'Nine out of 10 Teenage Girls Digitally Enhance Their Own Facebook Pictures, Claim' (*The Telegraph*, 19 September 2015).
[116] Professional Interview 3 (PhD): Forensic Psychologist.

wellbeing, any history of exposure to harmful behaviour, the strength (or indeed weaknesses) of their family relationships and their social status within their peer group.

However, other professionals did consider online bullying to be more harmful. A professional within the education sector explained in relation to harm caused, 'I think it's probably more horrific than the offline bullying ... the fact that young people can't escape it'.[117] Some young people in the focus groups also explained that 'it can be like the most emotional form of bullying'[118] and 'it can be very individual and concentrated'.[119] In addition, the long-term impact bullying online can have on young people was noted through various other avenues. For example, a young person's 'digital footprint' was referred to by a professional in the education sector as: 'it's always there'.[120] Current literature comments on the permanent presence of a digital footprint and how it can be one of 'the biggest threats' to a young person.[121] The permanency of an online profile was also noted in relation to both the victim and the young person displaying the harmful behaviour. Considering the former, among professionals the impact of a young person's digital footprint was explained in relation to the harm caused to the victim. A professional working in safeguarding stated, 'that online digital imprint ... aggravates you know the hurt and accelerates their isolation'.[122] Overall, most interviewees concluded that how a young person dealt with being bullied was very individualistic.

VII. Conclusion

Analysis of the literature and empirical data highlights several areas of development in relation to more fully understanding peer-based bullying behaviours. Definitional concerns were noted among most of the professionals interviewed. Lack of an agreed definition restricts progress when it comes to effective response mechanisms being put in place and contributes towards inconsistencies in responses. While there is no conclusive definition of bullying behaviour (on- or offline), most professional conceptualisations of bullying behaviours were almost identical and complemented current definitions within the literature. That is, that bullying online was the intentional perpetration of harmful behaviour using an electronic device; that the harmful behaviour was repeated and involved an imbalance of power between the parties. Yet, explained above, how we understand

---

[117] Professional Interview 12 (PhD): Education Sector.
[118] Young Person Focus Group (PhD): Female.
[119] Young Person Focus Group (PhD): Male.
[120] Professional Interview 20 (PhD): Education Sector.
[121] GS O'Keeffe and K Clarke-Pearson, 'The Impact of Social Media on Children, Adolescents, and Families' (2011) 127(4) *Pediatrics* 802.
[122] Professional Interview 21 (PhD): Safeguarding Sector.

repetition within the context of online bullying requires challenge and this was noted by interviewees.

A significant finding was the reluctance among professionals to catego-rise bullying online as more serious than offline bullying (especially in relation to extent of harm). Moreover, and contrary to popular belief, features such as anonymity and 24/7 access were dismissed by some professionals as unique to online bullying, especially in relation to children in care. However, primary research has also shown that online bullying can and does present distinct challenges for young people. The challenges include a young person's 'digital foot-print', the speed at which information can be disseminated and the global and far-reaching audience. These differences that online bullying presents need to be acknowledged and understood within their unique context without neglect-ing other harmful behaviours displayed by children and young people, including offline bullying. This chapter also established that gender is a contributing factor in terms of understanding young people's interaction online and the various types of online harmful behaviours they can engage in (discussed further in Chapter 5). While gender is not a determinative factor, it is an important indicator and one which cannot be ignored.

One final takeaway from the empirical data was the need to recognise young people's behaviour as part of a continuum. This was discussed in two main ways: (i) the blurring of bullying behaviours within on- and offline contexts; and (ii) the roles of the parties involved, that being the victim-offender-bystander. It is essential that the complexity of behaviours displayed by young people is carefully considered if effective regulatory frameworks (including support mechanisms) are to be put in place.

5

Narratives on 'Sexting' Among Young People

While not an 'old' practice, sexting among young people is a behaviour that young people have been engaging in for some time. In fact, some interview participants noted 2003 as one of the first cases when they were alerted to the behaviour (and it is possible other cases may have arisen before then).[1] Yet, it was not really until circa 2009 that evidence of scholarly debate on this issue became visible.[2] Studies have illustrated a diverse range of motivations among young people including varying levels of pressure – ranging from more subtle forms of peer pressure to more explicitly coercive and exploitative contexts.[3] Non-problematic and harmful motives have also been noted, including engagement in sexting as a form of sexual exploration and sexual expression.[4] Despite the range of motives displayed, participation in the sexual behaviour *at all* has raised significant concerns within law and policy for two main reasons: (i) the behaviour contradicts long-held notions of what it means to be a child and consequently what is a 'normal' childhood experience; and (ii) it is argued that engagement in sexting erodes at the healthy sexual development of the child. As this chapter will illustrate, to categorise *all* sexting behaviours as harmful is failing to consider the complexity of the behaviour. Key is the distinction between *consensual* and *non-consensual* sexting practices. In fact, consent as a legal concept is discussed further in Chapter 6, within the context of sexual behaviours, including peer-based sexting.

It is unclear how many young people participate in the behaviour and given the complex and normative nature of the sexual behaviour, discussed further below, it is unlikely that a *true* figure will ever be known. Despite this, research

---

[1] Professional Interview 1 (PhD): Education Sector.

[2] See A Lenhart, *Teens and Sexting: How and Why Minor Teens Are Sending Sexually Suggestive Nude or Nearly Nude Images via Text Messaging* (Pew Research Center, 2009); R Richards and C Calvert 'When Sex and Cell Phones Collide: Inside the Prosecution of a Teen Sexting Case' (2009) 32(1) *Hastings Communications and Entertainment Law Journal* 1.

[3] See J Ringrose et al, *A Qualitative Study of Children, Young People and 'Sexting': A Report Prepared for the NSPCC* (London, NSPCC, 2012); E Agnew, 'Sexting among Young People: Towards a Gender Sensitive Approach' (2021) 29(1) *International Journal of Children's Rights* 3.

[4] See M Lee and T Crofts, 'Gender, Pressure, Coercion and Pleasure: Untangling Motivations for Sexting between Young People' (2015) 55(3) *British Journal of Criminology* 454.

to date has shed some light on prevalence levels. A recent study carried out by Mori et al illustrates that one in five young people send a 'sext', one in three receive a sext and one in seven would forward a sext on if they received one.[5] The EU Kids Online Survey 2020 also noted that among 12–16-year olds engagement ranged from 8–39 per cent.[6] Earlier studies found that 4 per cent of young people aged 12–17 years (who own a phone) report sending a 'sext'.[7] Figures therefore vary greatly, with more current studies suggesting that the practice is becoming more common.

This chapter will unpack some of the key complexities in conceptualising and managing this evolving form of youth sexual behaviour. Drawing on empirical research, the chapter will argue that a lack of an agreed definition among professionals, practitioners and policymakers is leading to uncertainty of meaning and inconsistencies in responses. Further, advancing on existing narratives in the area, current research demonstrates the *extent* and *range* of conflicting messages surrounding female sexual identity, the highly gendered dimension attached to the practice and the complexity of gender roles. This chapter will therefore provide new insights surrounding the variety of socio-legal tensions which arise from sexting as a sexual behaviour young people are engaging in. Consequently, further clarity and nuance will be provided on a practice knowledge and understanding of which is still being developed within contemporary social, political and legal discourses.

In order to unpack some of these challenges, the chapter is structured as follows. First, key terminology and definitional issues will be considered, and existing tensions probed. Second, the emergence and nature of sexting as a behaviour young people are engaging in will be examined. Third, the chapter will reflect on whether peer-based sexting in certain contexts can be considered 'harmful' sexual behaviour. Fourth, gendered dimensions attached to the behaviour will be analysed. Finally, the chapter will conclude by considering the impact that engaging in sexting behaviours can have on young people.

I. Conceptualising Sexting: Terminology and Definitional Issues

Young people sending naked or semi-naked images is known colloquially as 'sexting'. While 'sexting' was the prevalent term used by past and current researchers, one of the most prominent themes which emerged throughout the primary research was the reluctance to use the word 'sexting' to explain young people's

---

[5] C Mori et al, 'Are Youth Sexting Rates Still on the Rise? A Meta-Analytic Update' (2022) 70 *Journal of Adolescent Health* 531.

[6] D Smahe et al, *EU Kids Online 2020: Survey Results from 19 Countries* (EU Kids Online, 2020).

[7] Lenhart (n 2).

engagement in the practice. This section will identify two collective terminology and definitional issues. Points of concern include: (i) disparity in use of the term sexting between professionals and young people; and (ii) parameters of the sexual behaviour.

A. Sexting: 'A Professional Term'[8]

Hesitancy to use the word 'sexting' was noted by a number of professionals, who believe the word was not effective in communicating with young people who participate in the sexual behaviour 'because an adult created that term'.[9] In a similar vein, others noted the disparity in use of key terminology between adults and young people: 'it's not a word I would hear young people say'.[10] The young interviewees also commented on how their peers do not use the word. When asked if 'sexting' was a term they use within their peer groups to describe the practice, responses include: 'no',[11] 'it's more of a government term',[12] 'no term is really used'[13] and 'young people don't use it because its older people [who] came up with the terminology'.[14] Terminology used to describe the practices young people are engaging in is of vital importance, for three main reasons. One, problems can arise for professionals tasked with identifying the behaviours and activating appropriate supports. Second, issues can arise with the young people who may not readily identify a behaviour as harmful or not due to a divergence in terminology used. Third and finally, use of terminology can perpetuate blame narratives and heighten social anxieties, particularly surrounding a behaviour that has ignited such polarised debates around childhood and youth sexuality. For example, it has been recommended that academics and professionals use the term 'first person produced imagery' over 'self-produced imagery', as the latter possesses victim-blaming connotations.[15]

How are young people describing the practice? The young people were at times more specific in their use of language. For example, when asked how young people refer to the sending of naked and semi-naked images a variety of examples were expressed, from both professionals who work with young people and the young people themselves. Responses include: 'dick pics and tit pics',[16] 'nudes',[17]

---

[8] Young Person Interview (PhD): Male.
[9] Professional Interview 12 (PhD): Education Sector.
[10] Professional Interview 8 (PhD): Anti-Bullying Organisation.
[11] Young Person Interview (PhD): Female.
[12] Young Person Interview (PhD): Male.
[13] PDF Survey: Preferred not to disclose age and gender.
[14] Young Person Focus Group (PhD): Male.
[15] APPG on social media and UK Safer Internet Centre, *Selfie Generation: What's Behind the Rise of Self-Generated Indecent Images of Children Online?* (APPG on social media, 2021) 9.
[16] Professional Interview 1 (PhD): Education Sector.
[17] Young Person Interview (PhD): Male; PDF Survey: Girl, aged 16 years.

'slide into dm's',[18] 'photo',[19] 'pics',[20] 'sending dirts'[21] and 'just messages'.[22] What is interesting is the move from explicit terms such as 'dick pics'[23] to more ambiguous terminology such as simply sending 'messages' or 'pics'. This shift in terminology underlines two issues. First, the normalisation of the process among young people and how within contemporary youth culture the streaming of sexualised content and the sending and receiving of sexualised images is becoming 'increasingly normalised'.[24] As one young person notes: 'sexting has become so common it can nearly be hard to differentiate between that and normal messaging'.[25] Second, using somewhat vague terms such as 'messages' could pose problematic for professionals who may be tasked with distinguishing between written and visual communications. This would be significant when it comes to interventions and potentially the harm caused to the victim.

Using a term such as 'sexting' which has been created by adults also taps into the wider debate regarding the socialisation of young people and the reluctance to include youth voices on issues that directly impact their lives. Indeed, research has shown that when it comes to the socialisation of young people, 'the definitions of appropriate development are not open to negotiation, except between "knowledgeable" adults'.[26] Failing to recognise young people's ability to educate adults on a practice that directly impacts their lives became most apparent within primary research when exploring the conceptual understanding of what exactly sexting was and whether the behaviour was considered to be harmful or not, discussed below. In addition, sexting is now an extremely weighty term that has become automatically associated with 'risk' and 'danger'. As Lee and colleagues put it, sexting is 'a term loaded with moral meaning where sexual expression and childhood literally butt up against one another'.[27] Consequently, empirical findings demonstrate a clear need to move away from the term and move towards a more accurate and neutral term. Yet, we cannot decide on an appropriate term until we more fully understand the practice, including the complex range of motivations and intentions behind the behaviours displayed. This will only be achieved by engaging in further research with young people as active participants and incorporating their voices into the policies tasked with responding to the sexual behaviour.

---

[18] PDF Survey: Boy, aged 17 years.

[19] Young Person Focus Group (PhD): Female.

[20] PDF Survey: Boy, aged 17 years.

[21] PDF Survey: Girl, aged 16 years.

[22] Young Person Focus Group (PhD): Female.

[23] Professional Interview 1 (PhD): Education Sector.

[24] A Powell and N Henry, 'Blurred Lines? Responding to "Sexting" and Gender-Based Violence among Young People' (2014) 39(2) *Children Australia* 122.

[25] PDF Survey: Preferred not to disclose gender and age.

[26] P Scraton (ed), *'Childhood' in 'Crisis'* (UCL Press, 1997) 164.

[27] M Lee et al, '"Let's Get Sexting": Risk, Power, Sex and Criminalisation in the Moral Domain' (2013) 2(1) *International Journal for Crime and Justice* 44.

B. Sexting: Defining the Parameters

Defining the parameters of the sexual behaviour has consistently proved problematic for academics and law and policy makers. Definitions have either been interpretated too widely or are limited in capturing the true nature and extent of the behaviours. Sexting is a blanket term used to describe what is, in reality, quite a diverse practice. Professionals note that sexting can include 'the exchange of sexual messages or images',[28] and the 'video recording of sexual activity' and 'sexual acts'.[29] Some professionals distinguished between the different methods in terms of prevalence, noting that 'it's more images rather than videos',[30] while others commented on the use of sexualised language: 'certainly when we are given access or shown things on phones, as you say, the language is highly sexualised'.[31]

Similarly, the young people also provided a diverse range of answers: 'sexual messages or photos',[32] 'sending sexually explicit pictures or dialogue online',[33] 'sending private images of yourself or another person',[34] 'texting sexually'[35] and 'sending explicit images and videos'.[36] Both professionals and youth participants noted the inclusion of videos and text messages within a definition of 'sexting'. Despite a heightened focus within scholarly debate on the sharing of naked or semi-naked images among young people, there is limited knowledge and understanding in relation to the sharing of text messages and, in particular, videos. Inclusion of these other contexts as a manifestation of sexual behaviours young people are engaging in is indicative of an evolving practice and presents further challenges for professionals in terms of understanding the breadth of the behaviours displayed.

Interrelatedly, the use of one term to describe all methods of sexual communication can cause ambiguity in terms of identifying the extent and level of exposure to potentially harmful sexual content. Uncertainty of meaning in relation to a precise definition was noted by one of the professional interviewees:

> People aren't exactly sure what it means. So, does it mean typing out words you know that might have a sexual connotation … or does it mean sending graphic pictures … and I think there are various other meanings as well but I think whatever it is it's certainly that sexual element and that becomes very dangerous.[37]

---

[28] Professional Interview 5 (PhD): Safeguarding Organisation.
[29] Professional Interview 1 (PhD): Education Sector.
[30] Professional Interview 4 (PhD): Criminal Justice Sector.
[31] Professional Focus Group (PDF): Education.
[32] PDF Survey: Girl, aged 18 years.
[33] PDF Survey: Girl, aged 15 years.
[34] PDF Survey: Boy, aged 16 years.
[35] PDF Survey: Girl, aged 18 years.
[36] PDF Survey: Boy, aged 17 years.
[37] Professional Interview 2 (PhD): Children's Voluntary Organisation.

Professionals were aware that sexting is a term that has 'evolved'[38] as more research is being carried out and understanding of the practice develops. We must also be mindful that some literary commentary refers to 'sexting' as simply the sending of naked or semi-naked images while other research outputs include sexual text messages and/or videos within their data collection. Clarity on what exactly constitutes sexting within individual studies is therefore of critical importance if the nature, extent and impact of the behaviours under review is to be fully understood.

II. Sexting: Emergence and Nature of the Behaviour

While some professionals refer to sexting among young people as a 'new phenomenon',[39] other professionals were reluctant to categorise the behaviour as 'new' but rather a new manifestation of behaviours young people were already engaging in, ie technology simply 'exacerbates'[40] the presence of already existing sexual behaviours. In fact, there is a growing evidence base acknowledging that young people engaging in sexual practices and perpetrating sexual violence constitute 'a significant proportion of all sexual abuse'.[41] For example, the NSPCC estimate that around one third of all sexual abuse is committed by children,[42] with some research reporting higher figures.[43]

Although there was a reluctance among a significant number of professionals to describe sexting as a completely novel behaviour, there were some online facets which were noted as significantly distinctive. For example, the concept of 'distance' was noted as a distinguishing feature when it comes to displaying harmful sexual behaviours online, including sexting:

> It's a barrier between them and [the] actual act. It lessens the consequences … it minimises culpability, responsibility and in many ways, they can justify what they're doing because there isn't somebody sitting in front of them … if you were to ask a young person who carried out those type of offences … would they have carried out a contact sexual behaviour similar to what they were presenting online. Many of them will say no.[44]

In a similar vein, within an institutional context McAlinden refers to specific 'features' within institutions such as 'anonymity, secrecy and power' which can

---

[38] Professional Interview 8 (PhD): Anti-Bullying Organisation.

[39] Professional Interview 6 (PhD): Children's Voluntary Organisation.

[40] Professional Interview 10 (PhD): Statutory Sector.

[41] S Hackett et al, *Services for Young People Who Sexually Abuse: A Report on Mapping and Exploring Services for Young People Who Have Sexually Abused Others* (NSPCC, Youth Justice Board for England and Wales, 2005) 4.

[42] NSPCC, *Statistics Briefing: Child Sexual Abuse* (NSPCC, 2021).

[43] See S Hackett, *Children and Young People with Harmful Sexual Behaviours* (Research in Practice, 2014).

[44] Professional Interview 10 (PhD): Statutory Sector.

'facilitate abuse'.[45] It appears that the online characteristics of anonymity, power and distance can therefore help facilitate online harmful behaviours – including online harmful sexual behaviours – among young people.

The connection between the internet and emerging harmful sexual behaviours among young people can therefore be presented in two ways. First, as noted above, the internet has provided a new platform to display already *existing* harmful sexual behaviours among children and young people. In this context the internet is simply a new platform on which emerging harmful sexual behaviours can be displayed. Second, the internet has created *new* opportunities for young people who may not have displayed harmful sexual behaviours offline to do so online due to the 'distance' element. The latter could be a key variable when examining the prevalence of sexting among young people, especially as it has been described as an impulsive and risk-taking behaviour.[46] Moreover, while both behaviours outlined above *can* be harmful (if coercive or exploitative methods are used), it is important to differentiate the two behaviours as each can present very different challenges, especially regarding appropriate interventions. For example, one is a continuation of harmful sexual behaviour (from offline to online) whereas the other is possibly an impulsive form of harmful sexual behaviour among young people (only displayed online due to the 'distance' facet).

Age composition was also an important factor that needed to be considered. A significant number of professional interviews suggested that the age range for participation in sexting behaviours is getting younger. One professional noted that it would be 'more towards the top end of primary school and then on into the high school'.[47] In agreement, other professionals noted, 'I've dealt with cases at 10 were people have posted pictures of themselves'[48] and 'every year it's getting younger'.[49] While Phippen's research, reported in 2012, noted that there was 'little evidence' to suggest that children aged 10 or 11 years old were 'exposed to sexualised content or asked to self-generate',[50] in the years that have passed, evidence to date within Northern Ireland from professional interviews suggests that the age is now lowering and is an issue of concern for those professionals working within education and child safety and welfare. This development could be for a number of reasons. First, more young people have access to smartphones than ever before, with data suggesting that 10 per cent of six-year-olds have phones and 49 per cent are allowed to use a family phone.[51] This figure continues to rise as the children

---

[45] A-M McAlinden, "'Setting 'Em Up": Personal, Familial and Institutional Grooming in the Sexual Abuse of Children' (2006) 15(3) *Social and Legal Studies* 353.

[46] See JR Temple et al, 'Brief Report: Teen Sexting and Psychological Health' (2014) 37(1) *Journal of Adolescence* 33.

[47] Professional Interview 16 (PhD): Independent Researcher on Harmful Sexual Behaviours.

[48] Professional Interview 3 (PhD): Forensic Psychologist.

[49] Professional Interview 4 (PhD): Criminal Justice Sector.

[50] A Phippen, *Sexting: An Exploration of Practices, Attitudes and Influences* (London, UK Safer Internet Centre and NSPCC, 2012) 3.

[51] C Ibbetson, *How Many Children Have Their Own Tech?* (YouGov UK, 2020).

get older, with an estimated 88 per cent of 12-year-olds owning a smartphone.[52] Second, there is a clear level of uncertainty and doubt among parents and guardians in how they should regulate young people's engagement with technology. A number of professionals commented on parental awareness of how much time their child was spending online but they were often struggling to enforce boundaries: 'it's a battle to get them off their phone'.[53] As children begin to access phones and other technology at a much younger age, these issues will naturally become more heightened. Third, while there is still a lot of work to be done in ensuring we have effective response frameworks in place, professionals are more aware of the issues impacting young people and this could result in an increase in identifying behaviours, reporting and/or seeking help.

III. Sexting: 'Harmful' Sexual Behaviour?

While sexting has mostly been categorised as a form of 'harmful' sexual behaviour within popular socio-legal narratives, an important part of the research was understanding how the professionals and young people respectively conceptualise sexting. In an attempt to understand the more nuanced facets of sexting among young people, and drawing on relevant literature and empirical data, this section explores the typology of sexting. Three main questions are asked. First, a contextual question, how do young people define and conceptualise 'harmful sexual behaviour'? Second, what types of sexting practices are young people engaging in? Third, can sexting be a form of cyberbullying behaviour? In answering these questions, the complexity of sexting practices among young people will be considered.

A. Harmful Sexual Behaviour: Key Features

Young people's engagement in a wide range of harmful sexual behaviours was noted by the professionals, for example: 'it can be a catch all, and it could be very, very wide … sexualised language between one child and another right through to contact sexual abuse, which is violence'.[54] While previously 'harmful sexual behaviour' was often directly associated with child sexual exploitation, as contemporary research to date illustrates, the complexity and varied behaviours young people are engaging in have diversified the term.[55] But how do young people define and understand 'harmful sexual behaviour'?

---

[52] ibid.
[53] Professional Focus Group (PDF): Education.
[54] Professional Interview 1 (PDF): Independent Social Work Consultant.
[55] E Agnew and A-M McAlinden, 'Harmful Sexual Behaviour among Children and Young People Online: Cultural and Regulatory Challenges' in R Killean et al (eds), *Sexual Violence on Trial: Local and Comparative Perspectives* (Routledge, 2021).

A small number of young people provided quite narrow definitions, alluding to specific offences such as 'rape'[56] and 'harassment'.[57] Most young people referred to harmful sexual behaviour in broader terms: 'sexual behaviour that causes harm or distress to others',[58] 'sexual behaviour which negatively effects someone physically or emotionally'[59] and 'sexual behaviour which is dangerous'.[60] The use of terms such as 'harm', 'distress', 'negatively effects' and 'dangerous' suggests the young people understood and accepted on some level that negative consequences and outcomes are strong indicators that the behaviour is 'harmful'.

Consent was also included in some of the definitions. There was an awareness among the young people that a lack of consent was a key element in determining whether a sexual behaviour was harmful or not: 'sexual behaviour without consent',[61] 'non-consensual behaviour'[62] and 'doing something sexual non-consensually'.[63] Such definitions illustrate that the young people appreciate consent as an important factor when it comes to engaging in healthy sexual behaviours. Indeed, some young people displayed quite a nuanced understanding of what a lack of consent looks like. The use of pressure, force or coercion was noted. For example, 'non-consensual or pressured advances',[64] 'someone forcing you to have sex',[65] 'taking advantage of the other person'[66] and 'exploitation of someone for sexual gratification'.[67] Yet, only a small number of participants provided this nuance and thus raised an important question: would the young people be able to differentiate between consent and non-consent in practice?[68]

Interestingly, one young person referred to sexting specifically as being a form of harmful sexual behaviour: 'behaving in a way that is not acceptable like sending naked pics or exposing yourself'.[69] This quote is significant for three main reasons. First, the young person is equating behaviour that is 'not acceptable' with behaviour that is 'harmful'. This feeds into socio-legal debates on childhood and youth sexuality, as discussed early in the book. The prevailing presence of a socio-legal discomfort with youth sexuality and youth expressions of sexuality is influencing how young people view what is 'acceptable' sexual behaviour. Second, and related to the previous point, given the heightened socio-legal anxiety associated with sexting, it is possible that the young person views sexting as unacceptable

---

[56] PDF Survey: Girl, aged 17 years.
[57] PDF Survey: Boy, aged 17 years.
[58] PDF Survey: Girl, aged 15 years.
[59] PDF Survey: Boy, aged 17 years.
[60] PDF Survey: Girl, aged 16 years.
[61] PDF Survey: Girl, aged 17 years.
[62] PDF Survey: Boy, aged 17 years.
[63] PDF Survey: Girl, aged 14 years.
[64] PDF Survey: Neither, aged 15 years.
[65] PDF Survey: Girl, aged 16 years.
[66] PDF Survey: Girl, aged 16 years.
[67] PDF Survey: Boy, aged 16 years.
[68] Issues of consent are discussed further in Chapter 6.
[69] PDF Survey: Girl, aged 16 years.

due to the prevalent 'risk' narratives young people are often exposed to within schools and other settings. As noted in Chapter 1, Northern Ireland as a research site has an extremely moral conservative strain running through most institutions, in particular the education system.[70] Third, and discussed in Chapters 2 and 3, what is 'acceptable' behaviour is often determined by adults and their expectations of how a child and young person should behave.

B. Sexting: Diversification of the Behaviour

Due to a prevailing and heightened 'discomfort with adolescent sexuality'[71] by adults, in particular in relation to sexting among young people, it is not surprising that the behaviour has been predominantly categorised within a 'risk' and 'harmful' frame.[72] Yet, if we look at some of the reasons young people are engaging in the practice, while the behaviour may still be viewed as 'risky', is it always 'harmful' or 'exploitative'? Further, Ashurst and McAlinden explain that what is considered to be 'normal' youth sexual behaviour is 'evolving rapidly' and consequently there is a need to distinguish between what 'is normative or banal and what is potentially harmful or pornographic'.[73]

Some professionals interviewed mirrored Phippen's analysis that it was perceived as a 'flirting' tool to begin a relationship.[74] A professional working in the education sector noted:

> It's seen almost … amongst some groups of young people as part of the beginning of [a] relationship. Let's say … I'll send out my picture of my penis and see do I get a response … it's almost seen amongst some young people as this is how you start a relationship.[75]

While there were some similarities between professional and youth voices (that being that sexting mostly happens within intimate relationships), there were some significant differences. The young people referred to 'trust'[76] and engagement in the sexual behaviour as an indication of being in a 'serious relationship'.[77] Other young people alluded to an element of pressure and not feeling 'comfortable in

---

[70] B Rolston et al, 'Sex Education in Northern Ireland Schools: A Critical Evaluation' (2005) 5(3) *Sex Education* 217.

[71] H Beckett, 'Sexual Exploitation and Sexual Violence in Adolescence' in D Schubotz and P Devine (eds) *Not So Different: Teenage Attitudes across a Decade of Change in Northern Ireland* (Russell House Publishing, 2014) 106.

[72] JR Lippman and SW Campbell, 'Damned If You Do, Damned If You Don't … If You're a Girl: Relational and Normative Contexts of Adolescent Sexting in the United States' (2014) 8(4) *Journal of Children and Media* 373.

[73] L Ashurst and A-M McAlinden 'Young People, Peer to Peer Grooming and Sexual Offending' (2015) 62(4) *Probation Journal* 376.

[74] Phippen (n 50).

[75] Professional Interview 1 (PhD): Education Sector.

[76] Young Person Focus Group (PhD): Female.

[77] Young Person Focus Group (PhD): Male.

their relationship'[78] – suggesting they engage in the practice to establish security within their relationship. This is an important consideration, especially in relation to issues of consent and how certain sexual behaviours, including 'sexting' among young people, have become normalised and viewed as an *essential* part of relationships if you want to 'stay close to someone'.[79] A prominent issue surrounding consent and the normative nature of sexting behaviour, therefore, is understanding the 'cultural paradigm' within which young people must negotiate a sexual identity, while also recognising how these paradigms can shift over time.[80]

Some of the young people also explained that participation in sexting can be to maintain a sexual rapport with their partner or for sexual pleasure: 'for sexual gratification between two or more parties'[81] and 'sending pictures to someone in order to help with sexual pleasure'.[82] What is interesting is that although the quotes refer to sexual pleasure, there is still a level of ambiguity in terms of the young person's exact meaning and intention behind the sending of the images. Depending on the context, the exchange *could* be explorative (small age gap, no evidence of coercion and consent was given by all parties involved). On the other hand, it could be harmful (if the pictures had been sent to someone who did not want to receive them or there is a big age gap, for example). A contextual consideration of the sexual behaviour displayed and the intention behind the behaviour is therefore key (as discussed above).

Of importance is also a recognition of the fragility of youth relationships and how intentions can change. In other words, what was once consensual between two parties may soon become exploitative and manipulative, as interactions between the parties progress and develop, and intentions and motives shift. This was supported by a professional within the criminal justice sector who said:

> In my role what I've come across it's more sort of that boyfriend/girlfriend, they've done it mutually and then it's gone wrong because there's maybe a falling out and a picture is sent somewhere else or to somebody else out of spite.[83]

Primary data illustrates further the complexity of the behaviours displayed among young people and how certain behaviours can overlap. Further, a clear distinction is needed between those cases involving coercion which could signify that a young person may engage in further harmful sexual behaviour on- and/ or offline and those young people who participate in sexting as a flirting tool and may not realise the dangers and potential harms involved.[84] The intentions

---

[78] Young Person Focus Group (PhD): Female; see also Agnew (n 3).
[79] L Lóóf, 'Sexual Behaviour, Adolescents and Problematic Content' in E Quayle and K Ribisl (eds), *Understanding and Preventing Online Sexual Exploitation of Children* (London, Routledge, 2012) 138.
[80] B Simpson, 'Challenging Childhood: Challenging Children: Children's Rights and Sexting' (2013) 16(5/6) *Sexualities* 692.
[81] PDF Survey: Boy, aged 17 years.
[82] PDF Survey: Girl, aged 17 years.
[83] Professional Interview 4 (PhD): Criminal Justice Sector.
[84] Phippen (n 50).

behind the two types of exchanges are distinct and in need of different responses and interventions.

The use of grooming techniques among young people was also explored. While grooming is primarily noted as a concern within a child/adult context,[85] some research to date demonstrates how sexting among young people *can* include grooming components, even if the word 'grooming' is not expressly used. For example, Choi and colleagues explain how sexual coercion within an offline context was 'significantly associated' with requests for naked images among female adolescents.[86] Within primary research the potential among young people to coerce and manipulate peers to receive the images was also noted among professional participants, who noted that in the 'majority of cases it would be different levels of coercion'.[87] In fact one professional explicitly referred to grooming:

> It's the grooming behaviour that takes place to get those images ... at the outset that's really important.[88]

McAlinden offers vital insights in relation to grooming behaviour by noting five significant components. These include: (i) a vulnerable subject; (ii) who is exposed to the use of manipulative and controlling methods; (iii) the grooming behaviour can take place in a variety of interpersonal and social settings; (iv) to establish trust or normalise the harmful behaviour; (v) which in turn facilitates the abuse or prevents exposure.[89] Using McAlinden's grooming definition as a template, primary research is demonstrating that young people can and do use coercive and manipulative techniques: to control a peer who is vulnerable; within a range of settings on- and offline; in order to facilitate the exchange of naked and/or semi-naked images.

Further, as McAlinden notes, due to the 'the difficulties of drawing clear boundaries between innocuous and more harmful intentions', law and policy in the area are struggling to effectively capture the full remit of grooming behaviours.[90] Although McAlinden demonstrates the complexity of grooming behaviours displayed by *adults* and the limits of criminal law regarding proper identification of the harmful behaviour, analysis makes clear that the legal challenges in regulating sexting behaviours which contain grooming elements among young people would present the same if not greater challenges for criminal law, considering the convoluted nature of the practice (see Chapter 8) – for example, the normative nature of the practice among young people and the blurred boundaries in relation to key concepts including consent (see Chapter 6).

---

[85] A-M McAlinden, *'Grooming' and the Sexual Abuse of Children* (Clarendon Studies in Criminology, 2012).
[86] H Choi et al, 'Association between Sexting and Sexual Coercion among Female Adolescents' (2016) 53 *Journal of Adolescence* 164.
[87] Professional Interview 17 (PhD): Children's Voluntary Organisation.
[88] Professional Interview 3 (PhD): Forensic Psychologist.
[89] McAlinden (n 85) 11.
[90] ibid 281.

C. Sexting: Bullying Dimensions

Discussed in the previous chapter, controversy surrounding the lack of a concrete definition for bullying (either on- or offline) has created problems within contemporary discourses when it comes to properly identifying harmful behaviours among young people. A central contention is that 'bullying' and 'cyberbullying' are umbrella terms which can cover a wide range of harmful behaviours. This can create difficulties in understanding the complexity of specific practices, in particular sexual bullying. 'Sexual bullying' has been defined as:

> … behaviour, physical or non-physical, where sexuality or gender is used as a weapon against another … Sexual bullying is also pressure to act promiscuously and to act in a way that makes others uncomfortable.[91]

While there is evidence to suggest a strong relationship between sexting, gender and pressure among young people (discussed further below) – is all sexting a form of bullying? This question was put to the professional interviewees and the importance of distinguishing between sexting which could be considered a form of online sexual bullying and other sexting practices was noted:

> I think there are elements of bullying in sexting … but you've got to break it into different areas.[92]

> If they're doing it to threaten them or intimidate them or make them feel stupid or make them feel scared then it's bullying … whereas if a boy who just fancies a girl and he wants to try and attract her, that's not bullying. That's inappropriate sexual behaviour … It can be as titillating or romantic and flirty to extreme harassment. It becomes criminal.[93]

Interestingly, the repetitive nature of the exchange or interaction was not considered, a key facet of bullying behaviours (as noted in Chapter 4). In addition, while most young people stated that sexting could be 'a gateway'[94] to cyberbullying, they did not believe the act of sending or receiving naked or semi-naked images should automatically be considered cyberbullying behaviour. Therefore, there was a clear call to separate the different types of behaviours being displayed and 'intention' was noted as a significant determining factor.

IV.   Gendered Dimensions to Sexting

Primary research strongly demonstrates the interplay between a wide range of pressures, often subtle and gendered in nature, influencing young people's

---

[91] Family Lives, *Sexual Bullying* https://www.familylives.org.uk/advice/bullying/general-advice/what-is-sexual-bullying, last accessed 17 July 2023.
[92] Professional Interview 21 (PhD): Safeguarding Sector.
[93] Professional Interview 19 (PhD): Criminal Justice Sector.
[94] Young Person Focus Group (PhD): Female.

engagement in sexual behaviours. An expectation of engaging in sexting practices was noted among the young people. Some of the male participants referred to the sharing of images being similar to a transaction: 'I send you this, you send me that'.[95] A noteworthy number of the female youth participants referred to different levels of pressure feeling like 'they have to'[96] engage in the behaviour rather than an actual desire to. Two important points can be made here. First, analysis speaks to gender stereotypes and the prioritisation of one partner's sexual needs and desires over another, very often displayed within a heteronormative setting.[97] Second, the quote noted above, 'I send you this, you send me that', suggests an expectation among some young people that they will receive an image and the subtle undertones of pressure within this setting. Empirical data suggests that this expectation is often gendered, with males often sending images first and/or requesting the images. As one professional explains:

> I've had a number of girls over the years where just the pressure, it starts with one boy in school requesting an image and then suddenly five boys are and then suddenly 40 boys in one school and one girl and then you're thinking, how many other girls in your school are being pressured by similar groups of boys.[98]

The pressure on girls to send images is clear, but what is also poignant is the potential pressure on boys to *receive* such images. While this was not noted within this research study, it has been noted elsewhere. Indeed, Harvey and Ringrose comment on images of girls' bodies as a form of 'value' within peer settings and a 'recognition of hegemonic masculinity'.[99] Yet, as noted by Setty, a presumption that boys receive 'value' from receiving such images is misplaced.[100] For example, it was noted that receiving images would often result in a boy being labelled 'more positively' like a 'player'[101] or 'stud'.[102] But what does this mean for boys who do not receive sexual images? Potential exposure to homophobic bullying, exclusion and isolation have been noted.[103] Such outcomes can therefore impact how boys interact and engage with female peers. A significant scholarly gap is also presented; further research on LGBTQ+ young people's motivations and intentions when it comes to engaging in peer-on-peer sexting behaviours is much needed.

Interrelated to the narrative on gender roles and pressure, female participants spoke about wanting to please their partner by sending images – to 'make him

---

[95] Young Person Interview (PhD): Male.

[96] Young Person Focus Group (PhD): Female.

[97] M Burkett and K Hamilton, 'Postfeminist Sexual Agency: Young Women's Negotiations of Sexual Consent' (2012) 15(7) *Sexualities* 815–833; see also Chapter 3.

[98] Professional Interview 4 (PDF): Children's Charity.

[99] L Harvey and J Ringrose, 'Sexting, Ratings and (Mis)Recognition: Teen Boys Performing Classed and Racialized Masculinities in Digitally Networked Publics' in E Renold et al (eds) *Children, Sexuality and Sexualisation* (Palgrave Macmillan, 2015) 361.

[100] E Setty, '"Confident" and "Hot" or "Desperate" and "Cowardly"? Meanings of Young Men's Sexting Practices in Youth Sexting Culture' (2020) 23(5) *Journal of Youth Studies* 561.

[101] Young People Focus Group (PhD): Male.

[102] Young People Focus Group (PhD): Male.

[103] Setty (n 100). See also Ringrose et al (n 3).

want me more'.[104] This finding relates not only to women's negotiations of sexual identity but also broader discourses on female objectification and body surveillance, practices that are extremely prevalent within western societies. In fact, some of the young female participants noted how uploading an image can be instantly sexualised:

> if a girl puts up a full body photo there will maybe be a 100 people going you look really nice … but the things that will be called on the most will be her figure and her assets. And like girls will compliment her on her figure and boys will compliment her on like if she has boobs or a bum or if she's skinny … they'll sexualise a photo that could be like literally, 'I got an expensive dress. Look at it, it's so pretty'.[105]

The above excerpt speaks to the female body being seen as 'a collection of body parts'.[106] In addition, the quotation also reinforces how young people are receiving conflicting messages around sexual agency and autonomy. As one young person explains: 'it's like all shame but at the same time it's all sexualised'.[107] The cultural context in which young people are receiving these messages is therefore significant and is influencing young people's understanding of their bodies and gender roles, often resulting in 'habitual body monitoring'.[108] One professional interviewee commented on female role models within youth and pop culture such as The Kardashians and how they can be 'highly sexual' in the content that they share.[109] This often leaves young females thinking, 'why can't I look that' and 'why can't I have that beautiful photo on Instagram'.[110] While most discussed within a female context, exposure to a range of socio-cultural pressures was not unique to females. Some of the male participants explained: 'everything is based on looks'.[111]

The young people also commented on puberty and the physical changes that a young person goes through during this concentrated developmental stage, often leaving them feeling 'self-conscious', noting also that this would be a 'key factor' explaining why young people engage in sexting practices.[112] Clearly, there is a heightened pressure to conform to a particular body image within youth culture and this is having a negative influence on how young people, male and female, not only place value on their *own* bodies (self-objectification), but also the value placed on *other* bodies (sexual objectification), including their peers. This analysis is significant for two main reasons: (i) it furthers understanding regarding the normalisation of the practice and the broader gender and pressure debate in

---

[104] Young Person Focus Group (PhD): Female.
[105] Young Person Focus Group (PhD): Female.
[106] RM Calogero, 'Objectification Theory, Self-Objectification, and Body Image' in T Cash (ed), *Encyclopedia of Body Image and Human Appearance* (Academic Press, 2012) 574.
[107] Young Person Focus Group: Female.
[108] BL Fredrickson and T Roberts, 'Objectification Theory: Toward Understanding Women's Lived Experiences and Mental Health Risks' (1997) 21(2) *Psychology of Women Quarterly* 173.
[109] Professional Interview 4 (PDF): Children's Charity.
[110] ibid.
[111] Young Person Focus Group (PhD): Male.
[112] Young Person Focus Group (PhD): Male.

relation to sexting among young people; and (ii) related to the first point, analysis questions the extent of the gender disparity when it comes to body surveillance among young people.[113] While it cannot be disputed that females are exposed to greater levels of sexual objectification and surveillance,[114] examining existing cultural contexts in which young people are negotiating their sexual identities, pressures placed on young boys to conform to a particular (and often unrealistic) body ideal are increasing.

V. The Harmful Impact of Sexting

The far-reaching harmful impact sexting can have on young people has been examined in its broadest sense. Emotional and psychological implications have been raised which can vary from embarrassment, feeling extremely upset and afraid,[115] to self-harming and suicidal thoughts/ideation.[116] Socially, a young person can also experience exclusion from peer groups and a sense of isolation.[117] In addition, Gillespie and others comment on the potential legal ramifications that can befall a young person who engages in the sexual behaviour (see Chapters 6 and 8 for more on legal frameworks).[118] This section will unpack some of the emotional, psychological and physical harms in more detail by exploring issues associated with: (i) a young person's environment; (ii) the intention behind the original exchange of sexual content; (iii) victim and blame narratives; and (iv) gender dynamics.

A. Environment

Professionals often focused on the psychological manifestations of harm and explained that how a young person responded was highly dependent on individual circumstances, personal history and exposure to any childhood adversity. As one professional explains:

> Their capacity to manage their attitudes or self-manage or emotionally regulate, is all a consequence of their background, their circumstances, their early years trauma, whatever it might be, has all contributed to who they are at that particular moment and time.[119]

---

[113] See Ringrose et al (n 3).

[114] ibid. See also Agnew (n 3).

[115] KJ Mitchell et al, 'Prevalence and Characteristics of Youth Sexting: A National Study' (2012) 129(1) *Pediatrics* 13.

[116] AC Milton et al, 'Sexting, Web-Based Risks, and Safety in Two Representative National Samples of Young Australians: Prevalence, Perspectives, and Predictors' (2019) 6(6) *JMIR Mental Health* 1.

[117] GS O'Keeffe and K Clarke-Pearson 'The Impact of Social Media on Children, Adolescents, and Families' (2011) 127(4) *Pediatrics* 800.

[118] AA Gillespie, 'Adolescents, Sexting and Human Rights' (2013) 13(4) Human *Rights Law Review* 623.

[119] Professional Interview 10 (PhD): Statutory Sector.

Another professional explained that when it comes to young people's engagement in sexual practices, including harmful sexual practices, it is 'very diverse' and you have to focus on 'each individual child and their experiences, their background'.[120] Only by doing this can you get 'a real sense of why they've done what they've done'.[121] Analysis corresponds with existing literature in the area, such as Faure-Walker and Hunt, who note that young people who display harmful sexual behaviours have often experienced some sort of adversity in their life, such as trauma.[122] Within the context of peer-based sexting behaviours, where there is evidence of coercion or manipulation, considering the child's background will be of crucial importance if appropriate and effective interventions are to be activated.

B. Intention

A significant proportion of professionals commented on the 'variable' impact of sexting behaviours among young people and how 'the purpose of the original exchange' is a fundamental factor to be considered when assessing impact and the extent of harm caused.[123] For example, as noted above, sexting among young people can start off as consensual and explorative and then become exploitative as interactions change, often when a relationship breaks down. When intentions shift, the young person often feels an element of blame. Therefore, the true extent of harm may not be visible from the outset. Indeed, a professional working in the education sector described how some children initially feel 'embarrassed' when their photos have been shared amongst peers.[124] However, as time moves on and the photo continues to be forwarded and more and more peers know about it, the harm becomes magnified. This can result in the young person wanting to leave school, for example. As one professional explains, 'it very quickly became something else. Not a joke anymore.'[125] Further, due to the normalised culture associated with sexting practices, young people may not easily identify the behaviour as harmful. One professional explained how a young person who had received up to 15 unwanted sexual images in one day 'was quite blasé' about being bombarded with unrequested sexual content.[126] Yet, often if the exchange is unwanted or involves grooming behaviours, for example, the impact on the young person who is being manipulated can be significantly heightened.[127]

---

[120] Professional Interview 1 (PDF): Independent Social Work Consultant.
[121] ibid.
[122] D Faure-Walker and N Hunt, 'The Prevalence of Adverse Childhood Experiences Among Children and Adolescents Who Display Harmful Sexual Behaviour: A Review of the Existing Research' (2022) 15 *Journal of Child and Adolescent Trauma* 1051.
[123] Professional Interview 16 (PhD): Independent Researcher on Harmful Sexual Behaviours.
[124] Professional Interview 20 (PhD): Education Sector.
[125] ibid.
[126] Professional Interview 4 (PDF): Children's Charity.
[127] See Ringrose et al (n 3).

C. Blame

It was also noted by a few participants that young people often do not report cases of sexting because they feel partly to blame and responsible for the harm caused and often do not see themselves as a 'victim'. Indeed, a number of professionals commented on the internal turmoil young people often feel after engaging in sexual practices. This can include feeling that they have somehow been 'complicit in what's happening' because they have produced and distributed the image to someone.[128] Young people can also think, 'I must have done something that led to this, you know, it must have been my own behaviour'.[129] As discussed in Chapter 2, blame can be heightened when the victims have been made to perform 'their own abuse',[130] whether that be taking and sending an image or recording themselves engaging in sexual activity. In those situations, often the young person cannot recognise the coercion and manipulation and therefore does not identify as a victim.

While a young person *might* more readily identify coercion within an adult-child paradigm, when it comes to peer-on-peer abuse, an extra level of difficulty is that often young people do not associate their peers with being 'perpetrators' of sexual abuse (see Chapters 2 and 3). Allocation of blame and victim identity also feeds into the academic literature on socially constructed victim and offender moulds[131] – in particular, victim and offender stereotypes in relation to sexual offences, especially child sexual offences, which portray children as a 'passive victim'.[132] Finally, blame narratives can add to feelings of apprehension in relation to reporting the abuse alongside fears of criminal sanctions being imposed if they were to report – all of these issues become intensified within coercive or manipulative peer-based sexting contexts (see Chapter 8).

D. Gender

Finally, explored above, gender was an important factor when it came to the circumstances surrounding the sending of a 'sext' and the impact of harm. Professional participants said that girls seem to be more distressed by sexting behaviour than boys, noting, 'in terms of the area of sexting my experience is that we're getting more calls in terms of girls concerned about doing that'.[133] Despite

---

[128] Professional Interview 17 (PhD): Children's Voluntary Organisation.
[129] Professional Interview 4 (PDF): Children's Charity.
[130] ibid.
[131] A-M McAlinden, 'Deconstructing Victim and Offender Identities in discourses on Child Sexual Abuse: Hierarchies, Blame and the Good/Evil Dialectic' (2014) 54(2) *British Journal of Criminology* 180. See also Chapter 2.
[132] J Kitzinger, 'Who are you Kidding? Children, Power and the Struggle against Sexual Abuse' in A James and A Prout (eds), *Constructing and Reconstructing Childhood* (Falmer Press, 1997) 169.
[133] Professional Interview 1 (PhD): Education Sector.

the gendered nature of online harmful behaviours being noted by professionals, concerns were also raised that boys may not be reporting incidents due to 'a strong culture that keeps them quiet'.[134] Literature also suggests that a focus on female victimisation has contributed to a 'mistaken public impression' that boys either do not get abused at all or are infrequently victims of such abuse.[135] In addition, male victimisation contradicts long-held and problematic presumptions on victimhood and challenges traditional perceptions of male sexuality.[136]

While a significant amount of research to date illustrates that girls and women are exposed to greater levels of sexual victimisation,[137] and males are 'overwhelmingly' the perpetrators of unlawful activity,[138] under-reporting among male victims, particularly within a sexually abusive context, is a significant child protection and welfare concern.[139] Further, there are concerns that boys are not as well educated or informed when it comes to issues of sexual abuse and therefore may not identify the abuse as readily as their female counterparts.[140] More research is needed to explore the prevalence of boys as 'victims' of online harmful behaviours and specifically online harmful sexual behaviours. Culturally entrenched gender stereotypes need to be challenged within schools and within homes to encourage boys to talk about being victims of online harmful behaviour. Male-focused research would provide further scrutiny of a practice that is becoming increasingly prevalent among young people.

In sum, understanding that online harmful behaviours impact children and young people differently, and examining not only the varying contextual factors of each situation but also the internal and external factors which are influencing how a young person reacts to a particular situation, are crucial.

VI. Conclusion

This chapter has explored emerging issues relating to peer-based sexting among young people. Complexities associated with terminology, the wide-ranging pressures young people are exposed to, gender dynamics and the varying levels of

---

[134] ibid.

[135] D Finkelhor et al, *A Sourcebook on Child Sexual Abuse* (SAGE, 1986) 63.

[136] See R Graham, 'Male Rape and the Careful Construction of the Male Victm' (2006) 15(2) *Social and Legal Studies* 187.

[137] Rape Crisis estimate that 1 in 4 women compared to 1 in 18 men have been raped or sexually assaulted: see Rape Crisis England and Wales, *Rape and Sexual Assault Statistics* https://rapecrisis.org.uk/get-informed/statistics-sexual-violence/, last accessed 17 July 2023.

[138] EA Stanko and K Hobdell, 'Assault on Men: Masculinity and Male Victimisation' (1993) 33(3) *British Journal of Criminology* 413.

[139] ML Paine and DJ Hansen, 'Factors Influencing Children to Self-Disclose Sexual Abuse' (2002) 22 *Clinical Psychology Review* 271.

[140] J Brown and A Saied-Tesser, *Preventing Child Sexual Abuse: Towards a National Strategy for England* (NSPCC, 2015).

harm sexting can cause, have been considered. In brief, using correct terminology is imperative not only for response frameworks but also because terms play 'a vital expressive role'.[141] There is a clear need to move beyond adult-generated dialect and incorporate language more relevant to the young people directly affected by the practice. Furthermore, a clear definition and accurate use of terminology is critical if practitioners are to properly identify harmful behaviours.

Inextricably linked to the sexting debate are varying levels of pressure alongside gender and power relations. While primary research does suggest that some young people are engaging in 'sexting' voluntarily and within peer relationships, a noteworthy amount of data puts forward the idea that many young people are feeling pressured into participation (some young people experiencing more subtle forms of pressure, with others experiencing more overt pressures). Intention and consent are therefore fundamental factors in need of consideration. Yet, it is not always easy to identify consent or a lack of consent in practice, particularly due to a range of conflicting messages associated with gender roles, sexual identify and performance. It is this tension and understanding between what constitutes consent and coercion in practice which requires a more nuanced debate (discussed further in the next chapter). Finally, and interrelated, while it is important to acknowledge the potentially coercive elements of sexting, within social and legal policy, youth sexual expression is being solely understood in terms of 'risk' and 'harm'.[142] Yet, as one young person notes: 'sexting is perhaps this generation's smoking or this generation's drinking at a young age'.[143] Noting the normative dimension attached to the behaviour and 'risk-taking' behaviours among young people, there is an urgent need to move beyond the narrow interpretation of childhood, youth sexual agency and identity.

[141] C McGlynn and E Rackley, 'Image-Based Sexual Violence' (2017) 37(3) *Oxford Journal of Legal Studies* 535.

[142] See eg, K Albury et al, 'Young People and Sexting in Australia: Ethics, Representation and the Law' (ARC Centre for Creative Industries and Innovation/Journalism and Media Research Centre University of New South Wales, 2013).

[143] Young Person Focus Group (PhD): Male.

6

Peer-Based Sexting, Law and Issues of Consent

It becomes incredibly problematic when it becomes online, or through some sort of medium, or it's not person to person, and what does consent really look like. Is it encouragement? Is it asking, persisting and asking to the point of coercion? Is it chancing your arm in the young person's landscape? All of those things. Great challenges for that young person to navigate and understand if what they're doing is harmful, coercive, or inappropriate, or just part of what it means to engage in some sort of sexual behaviour. It's not easy.[1]

Critical engagement with empirical findings reinforces the significant role of consent in determining whether peer-based sexting is harmful or not. If consent is to be considered a key element when differentiating between explorative and exploitative and/or more coercive sexting behaviours, understanding its current limitations as a legal concept is important. It is therefore necessary to consider young people and the role of consent alongside consent law and sexual behaviours in a broader context. With this in mind, the first section of the chapter will critically engage with the current literature and policies governing young people and the role of consent. Wider consent laws, alongside significant legislative frameworks governing sexual offences in Northern Ireland, will then be probed. In doing so, some of the more problematic areas of consent law will be considered. In addition, the chapter will scrutinise national legislative frameworks, citing the problematic and confusing social and legal messages surrounding sexual offences and issues of 'consent'. In light of such analysis, the need for regulatory reform will be advocated for.[2]

While a portion of this chapter will be focused on scholarly debate that relates to offline sexual offences (specifically rape) and issues of consent, the range of concerns expressed within the literature resonate, as the empirical data will demonstrate, with many of the themes emerging from interviews with professionals and young people within the context of coercive or manipulative peer-based sexting behaviours. In addition, considering the complexity of sexting behaviours young people are engaging in, ranging from consensual to exploitative, the chapter will

---

[1] Professional Interview 1 (PDF): Independent Social Work Consultant.
[2] Discussed further in Chapters 7 and 8.

conclude by introducing a key argument to be discussed in later chapters (albeit a contentious issue) – the need to frame certain non-coercive peer-based sexual behaviours within a consensual, 'youth sexual agency' and 'children's rights' framework. This would ensure young people are not being criminalised unnecessarily and that proper educative rather than retributive responses are being activated.

I. Sexual Behaviours and the Role of Consent: A History in Northern Ireland

The concept of 'consent' features as a key element for most sexual crimes both nationally and internationally. For example, in Northern Ireland (and indeed in England and Wales), under Part 2 of the The Sexual Offences (Northern Ireland) Order 2008, to be acquitted of a sexual offence, it must be proven that the complainant *consented* to the behaviour and that the defendant *reasonably believed that the complainant was consenting* to the behaviour.[3] In determining what a 'reasonable belief' in consent is, the court must consider 'all the circumstances' and any steps the defendant took to ascertain whether the complainant was in fact consenting.[4] For context, historically in practice, whether a sexual offence was committed focused on the presence of force or resistance.[5] Recently, there has been a shift towards examining the presence (or lack thereof) of consent within a particular sexual encounter. Yet, discussed further below, placing greater emphasis on the presence of 'consent' raises a number of important contextual questions around what sexual activities or encounters are outside the boundaries of consensual sexual conduct.[6] What becomes apparent is that, while consent is a key factor in determining whether a sexual encounter (including within the context of peer-based sexting) was exploitative or not, it is also important to recognise that the law is 'both a site of authority and of contestation'.[7]

First, how has consent been defined in law? Consent is defined in Article 3 of The Sexual Offences (Northern Ireland) Order 2008 as follows: '[a] person consents if he agrees by choice and has the freedom and capacity to make that choice'.[8] It was said that this legislative definition was placing sexual autonomy and freedom of choice as two key tenets when it came to understanding consent

---

[3] See Arts 5–7 of the Sexual Offences (Northern Ireland) Order 2008, which deals with the offences of rape, assault by penetration and sexual assault. Sections 1–3 of the Sexual Offences Act 2003 (for England and Wales) deal with the same offences.

[4] Sexual Offences (Northern Ireland) Order 2008; Sexual Offences Act 2003.

[5] R West, 'Consent, Legitimation, and Dysphoria' (2020) 83(1) *The Modern Law Review* 1.

[6] See E Dowds, 'Consent, Autonomy and Coercion: A Response to Robin West' (2020) *The Modern Law Review* 1.

[7] ibid 2.

[8] Consent is defined in the Sexual Offences Act 2003, s 74 for England and Wales.

and sexual offences.[9] Yet, as Dowds and other scholars illustrate, interrogating key concepts such as 'freedom' and 'capacity' presents significant challenges, particularly within the context of coerced consent.[10] In addition, enshrined in law are 'evidential' and 'conclusive' presumptions about consent which provide *some* clarity on what circumstances would be considered outside the scope of 'free' and 'voluntary' consent.[11] Evidential presumptions deal with a range of circumstances in which: (i) if proven to exist; and (ii) the defendant was aware that those circumstances did in fact exist, it will be said that the complainant did not consent unless 'sufficient evidence' is adduced to rebut the presumption.[12] There are six circumstances noted, which can include, for example, that the complainant was asleep at the time of the relevant act, and/or at the time of the relevant act the complainant was subjected to violence. Conclusive presumptions on the other hand cannot be rebutted and if proven to exist it will be determined that the complainant did not consent, and the defendant did not reasonably believe that the complainant consented. Given its conclusive nature, there are only two circumstances that fall into this category: (i) deception; and/or (ii) impersonation.[13] While these presumptions have helped provide some counsel and direction for legal professionals, there are concerns that the presumptions do not consider the wide remit of coercive circumstances that currently exist.[14] Consequently, despite developments in law regarding consent, the concept within the context of criminal law and serious sexual offences has been described as 'complex',[15] a 'vague concept',[16] a 'difficult legal area'[17] and 'subject to manipulation'.[18]

Common law has also tried to create some clarity regarding a more nuanced understanding of consent and what constitutes an 'absence of consent'. For example, in the case of *R v Olugboja*, the Court of Appeal noted that consent 'covered a wide range of states of mind ... ranging from actual desire on the one hand to reluctant acquiescence on the other'.[19] This quote from the Court of Appeal,

---

[9] Sir John Gillen, 'Report into the Law and Procedures in Serious Sexual Offences in Northern Ireland' (Gillen Review) (Department of Justice, 2019) 20.

[10] E Dowds and E Agnew, 'Rape Law and Policy: Persistent Challenges and Future Directions' in M Horvath and J Brown (eds), *Rape: Challenging Contemporary Thinking – 10 Years On* (Routledge, 2022); S Cowan 'Freedom and Capacity to Make a Choice: A Feminist Analysis of Consent in the Criminal Law of Rape' in V E Munro and C F Stychin (eds), *Sexuality and the Law: Feminist Engagements* (Taylor and Francis, 2007); V Munro, 'Constructing Consent: Legislating Freedom and Legitimising Constraint in the Expression of Sexual Autonomy' (2008) 41 *Akron Law Review* 923.

[11] Evidential and conclusive presumptions about consent are defined in Arts 9 and 10 of the 2008 Order for Northern Ireland and ss 75 and 76 of the 2003 Act for England and Wales.

[12] Art 9(2) of the 2008 Order.

[13] Art 10(2) of the 2008 Order.

[14] Dowds and Agnew (n 10).

[15] C Sjolin, 'Ten Years On: Consent under the Sexual Offences Act 2003' (2015) 79(1) *The Journal of Criminal Law* 20.

[16] E Dowds, 'Sexual Consent in Northern Ireland: The Social and Legal Dimensions' (2020) *Queens Policy Engagement* 1, 3.

[17] Gillen Review (n 9) 19.

[18] V Tadros, 'Rape without Consent' (2006) 26(3) *Oxford Journal of Legal Studies* 517.

[19] *R v Olugboja* [1982] QB 320 [331].

in particular the reference to reluctant acquiescence, powerfully illustrates what Catherine Mackinnon notes, 'the presence of consent does not make an interaction equal'.[20] Further, *R v Malone (Thomas Patrick)*[21] also expanded on the concept of consent by noting that the complainant does not have to say 'no' and/or physically resist to show a lack of consent – recognising the wide range of settings and contexts in which sexual abuse and exploitation can take place.[22] In addition, *R v Bree*[23] is a significant case that considers consent within the context of voluntary intoxication. In this case, problematic societal attitudes towards complainants who were voluntarily intoxicated and then subsequently subjected to sexual violence became apparent.[24] This is significant when exploring young people and party culture (see below). Further, and importantly, when considering consent with the wider context of what are potentially coercive and exploitative settings (including among young people), MacKinnon notes:

> Psychological, economic, and other hierarchical forms of force – including age, mental and physical disability, and other inequalities, including sex, gender, race, class, and caste when deployed as forms of force or coercion in the sexual setting, that is, when used to compel sex in a specific interaction – would have to be expressly recognized as coercive.[25]

While laws within Northern Ireland and England and Wales have been moving away from models primarily based on force and resistance in an attempt to recognise the more nuanced and complex dimensions associated with human interactions, themes associated with force and resistance still very much infiltrate the criminal justice system when determining whether a person consented or not to a particular sexual act.[26] This is powerfully illustrated in the below case.

A. Consent Law and the 'Rugby Rape Trial' in Northern Ireland

Despite increased interest regarding the law and procedures surrounding sexual offences alongside notable concerns associated with the proliferation of a range of gendered myths and stereotypes, it was not until 2018 that concrete action was taken in Northern Ireland. The Gillen Review was commissioned by the

[20] C MacKinnon, 'Rape Redefined' (2016) 10 *Harvard Law and Policy Review* 440.

[21] *R v Malone (Thomas Patrick)* [1998] 2 Cr App R 447 [458].

[22] In New Zealand, the Crimes Act 1961, s 128A(1) explicitly notes: 'A person does not consent to sexual activity just because he or she does not protest or offer physical resistance to the activity'.

[23] *R v Bree* [2008] QB 131.

[24] See P Rumney and R Fenton, 'Intoxicated Consent in Rape: Bree and Juror Decision-Making' (2008) 71(2) *Modern Law Review* 279.

[25] MacKinnon (n 20) 474.

[26] See E Dowds, 'Rethinking Affirmative Approaches to Consent: A Step in the Right Direction' in R Killean et al (eds), *Sexual Violence on Trial* (Routledge, 2020); R Burgin, 'Persistent Narratives of Force and Resistance: Affirmative Consent as Law Reform' (2019) 59 *British Journal of Criminology* 296.

Criminal Justice Board and was initiated in the wake of a high-profile case known colloquially as 'The Rugby Rape Trial'.[27] In this case, a number of rugby players were charged with a range of sexual offences including rape and sexual assault. While a verdict of 'not guilty' was returned after a lengthy nine-week trial, the case persuasively highlighted a range of problematic procedures when it came to investigating and prosecuting serious sexual offences in Northern Ireland.[28] While all parties involved in the case were over 18 years old, the reporting and commentary that stemmed from the case directly links to wider discourses on young people, consent and sexual behaviours.

One key area of concern highlighted during and in the wake of the 'Rugby Rape Trial' related to myths and stereotypes associated with sexual behaviours and issues of consent. For example, great concerns were expressed regarding the line of questioning the complainant was subjected to and the perpetuation of a range of harmful and highly gendered myths and stereotypes.[29] By way of an example, the line of questioning from the defence included 'if you didn't like him, why were you kissing him in his bedroom?'[30] In fact, a focus on the complainant 'following' Jackson to his bedroom was put forward by the Defence as a sign of consent.[31] This narrative directly links to issues around 'ongoing consent' and the right for young people to withdraw consent at any time.[32] This was highlighted by professionals in the context of peer-based sexting, as two professionals explain:

> The young person essentially goes and finds themselves suddenly in a scenario where sex or a sex act is expected, and they feel like well I've implied consent by coming here. Because I've already implied consent I have to follow through with it.[33]

> Well, if you've been sending me that imagery, and we've been communicating like this, well why wouldn't I feel it's okay to now touch you when we've been doing this. So, there is an underlying bit of, there's been an implying consent by the imagery and sexual communication they've been having.[34]

What has become evident is that the misunderstanding and blurred boundaries surrounding the parameters of consent apply both to on- and offline contexts for young people. For example, the first quote clearly illustrates the confusion surrounding consent and a lack of understanding that consent can be withdrawn at any time. The second quote brings two issues to the fore: (i) misunderstandings

---

[27] See S McKay, 'How the "Rugby Rape Trial" Divided Ireland' (*The Guardian*, 4 December 2018).

[28] See Killean et al (n 26).

[29] ibid; see also E Dowds, 'I Presume She Wanted It to Happen': Rape and Reasonable Belief in Consent, and Law Reform in Northern Ireland' (2022) 73(1) *Northern Ireland Legal Quarterly* 74.

[30] E Crossey Malone, "The Ulster Rugby Rape Trial: No to Victim-Blaming & Rape Culture' (*Socialist Party*, 7 March 2018).

[31] Dowds (n 29) 94.

[32] E Agnew, 'Sexting, Consent and Young People: Regulatory Challenges' (2021) 9 *Queen's Policy Engagement* 3.

[33] Professional Interview 4 (PDF): Children's Charity.

[34] Professional Interview 3 (PDF): Independent Social Work Consultant.

associated with 'ongoing consent' – this could include a young person who sends a sexual image to another young person, and they feel that because they participated in one type of sexual behaviour then other sexual behaviours are 'expected'; and (ii) the transition from non-contact to contact peer-based sexual behaviours. That being, the movement from online to offline settings and the role consent plays within those different (and at times blurred) contexts for young people. These quotes also speak to a 'continuum of gendered violence' that young people can and do engage in.[35]

Interrelated to this point are problematic assumptions associated with victim blaming which were also perpetuated during the trial. For example, it was put to the complainant, 'It was witnessed by others that you were staring at Paddy Jackson?'[36] The complainant's behaviour was a key feature throughout cross-examination and used to reinforce victim blaming narratives. As Hadley Freeman notes, '[d]id you smile at him? You asked for it. Did you not smile at him? You hurt his feelings. Were your clothes sexy? You're a slut. Were they frumpy? You're a frigid bitch.'[37] As discussed in detail in Chapter 5, this narrative directly links back to young people, gendered pressures, sexting and issues of consent. As a professional interviewee explains, young people can feel pressured to engage in certain sexual behaviours and failing to do so can result in them being labelled and/or isolated from peer groups: 'am I a bit of a prude? Maybe I am no fun.'[38] Victim and blame narratives can also lead to young people, mostly girls and women, trying to negotiate conflicting messages around female sexuality and identity: the dual representation of women as having to be both 'sexy' and 'innocent'.[39] In particular, the young people referred to the presence of shaming discourses within youth culture and wider society.[40] The young people powerfully highlight how gender stereotypes, victim blaming/shaming and gendered power dynamics are greatly influencing young people's perceptions of intimacy and specifically their participation in sexting behaviours and understanding of consent.[41] Further, empirical analysis speaks to the 'damned if you

---

[35] Discussed further in Chapter 7. See also N Henry and A Powell, 'Sexual Violence in the Digital Age: The Scope and Limits of Criminal Law' (2016) 25(4) *Social and Legal Studies* 397; R Killean et al, 'Sexual Violence in the Digital Age: Replicating and Augmenting Harm, Victimhood and Blame' (2022) 31(6) *Social & Legal Studies* 871.

[36] Cited in Dowds (n 29) 93.

[37] H Freeman, 'What Does the Belfast Rape Trial Tell Women? Make a Complaint and You'll Be Vilified' (*The Guardian*, 4 April 2018).

[38] Professional Interview 4 (PDF): Children's Charity.

[39] J Ringrose, 'Are you Sexy, Flirty or a Slut? Exploring Sexualization and How Teen Girls Perform/Negotiate Digital Sexual Identity on Social Networking Sites' in R Gill and C Scharff (eds), *New Femininities: Postfeminism, Neoliberalism and Subjectivity* (Palgrave Macmillan, 2011); see also E Agnew, 'Sexting among Young People: Towards a Gender Sensitive Approach' (2021) 29(1) *International Journal of Children's Rights* 3.

[40] Young Person Focus Group (PhD): Female; Chapter 5.

[41] Agnew (n 39).

do, damned if you don't' argument'[42] as young people struggle to negotiate 'the body, its "normality" and its potential'.[43] Indeed, the hyper-sexualised culture in which young people currently live is placing heightened pressures and unrealistic demands in relation to their bodies and sexual identity, both on and offline.

Commentary on 'The Rugby Rape Trial' was documented daily during the nine-week trial and summaries of the case were posted widely on social media platforms, news sites, radio shows and newspapers. The message coming from this case was received by people of all ages, including young people: the victim was held 'responsible' for her actions (or inactions) and the expectation that young people (in particular girls) must act, dress and speak in a way that minimises 'risk'.[44]

II. Consent Law and Broader Rape Mythology

Empirical findings further mirror popular narratives on rape myths and broader discourses on sexual violence, which are predominantly framed within a heter-onormative context.[45] Indeed, Bohner et al situate rape mythology within four general types of myths including *blame, disbelief, exoneration* and *typology*.[46] Significantly, the four myths were expressly noted by both professionals and young people within the context of peer-based sexting behaviours, some with gendered undertones. This reproduction of concerns surrounding sexual violence and harmful sexual behaviours powerfully illustrates the extent to which rape mythology resonates with and influences understanding and conceptualisation of a diverse range of sexual behaviours, including peer-based sexting and issues of consent.

First, *blame*. This theme was highly gendered in nature when discussed within the context of peer-based sexting behaviours. That being, girls can 'provoke' certain types of harmful behaviours. One professional interviewee explains how young people question whether their actions led or contributed to the harm caused:

> If I hadn't done this. If I hadn't taken those drugs. If I hadn't been hanging around with those people then it wouldn't have happened … maybe I led that person on, maybe I behaved in some way that he thought that that was okay.[47]

---

[42] J Lipmann and S Campbell, 'Damned If You Do, Damned If You Don't … If You're a Girl: Relational and Normative Contexts of Adolescent Sexting in the United States' (2014) 8(4) *Journal of Children and Media* 371.

[43] K Corteen and P Scraton, 'Prolonging 'Childhood', Manufacturing 'Innocence' and Regulating Sexuality' in P Scraton (ed), *'Childhood' in 'Crisis?'* (UCL Press, 1997) 76.

[44] See Dowds (n 29).

[45] Dowds and Agnew (n 10).

[46] G Bohner et al, 'Rape Myth Acceptance: Cognitive, Affective, and Behavioral Effects of Beliefs that Blame the Victim and Exonerate the Perpetrator' in Horvath and Brown (n 10) 19. See also R Cowan 'Asking for It' in Killean et al (n 26) Chapter 7.

[47] Professional Interview 4 (PDF): Children's Charity.

This quote speaks to the 'ideal' victim and how certain behaviours can challenge those 'deserving' or 'worthy' of victim status.[48] This also directly links to 'responsibilation'[49] – the idea that a person should conduct themselves in a way which is risk-averse and failing to do so places an element of blame and responsibility on the victim for the harms suffered.[50] This is evident when the professional reiterates what young people say to them: 'If I hadn't done this'. This narrative is consistent with broader rape mythology and blame discourses. Significantly, during the Rugby Rape Trial one of the defendants said, 'she didn't have to stay. She could have left'.[51] Again, this places focus on what the victim did or did not do, rather than on what the defendant did or did not do to establish consent. In a similar vein, the young person asks 'maybe I led that person on' – questioning whether *their* behaviour implied consent. Finally, the above interviewee excerpt also speaks to young people who engage in 'risky' behaviour – 'If I hadn't taken those drugs. If I hadn't been hanging around with those people'. A 'good' or 'credible' victim is someone who 'exercises appropriate caution' and does not engage in a 'high risk lifestyle'.[52] Consequently, engaging in behaviour which is deemed to be outside the normal boundaries of what is 'acceptable' places a level of responsibility and blame on the young person.

Second, *disbelief*. Within the context of peer-based sexting, disbelief was discussed in two main ways. The first relates to the previous point: young people are concerned they will not be believed if they come forward, as they are somehow to 'blame' for the harm caused to them. For example, one young person who recalled being cat-called in the street, notes 'you just think you never want to dress like that again'.[53] Although the young person was simply walking down the street minding her own business when she was sexually harassed, the young person placed a level of blame on herself because she was wearing a particular outfit. In this view, the young person begins to think, by wearing this outfit did I lead the person on? Second, young people not identifying as a 'victim' due to the perceived 'normative' nature of the sexual behaviour (including other harmful behaviours such as sexual harassment). The same young person explained how the sexual harassment she was subjected to was minimised by her parent – 'she said this is normal basically'.[54] In fact, blame and disbelief are powerfully interlinked,

---

[48] N Christie, 'The Ideal Victim' in EA Fattah (ed), *From Crime Policy to Victim Policy* (Palgrave Macmillan, 1986); A-M McAlinden, 'Deconstructing Victim and Offender Identities in Discourses on Child Sexual Abuse: Hierarchies, Blame and the Good/Evil Dialectic' (2014) 54(2) *British Journal of Criminology* 180.

[49] Responsibilation is discussed further in Chapter 7 when examining sexual behaviours as a continuum of behaviour.

[50] See Chapter 7 and also Dowds (n 29).

[51] Dowds (n 29) 85.

[52] L Gotell, 'Rethinking Affirmative Consent in Canadian Sexual Assault Law: Neoliberal Sexual Subjects and Risky Women' (2008) 41 *Akron Law Review* 866, 867.

[53] Young Person Focus Group (PhD): Female. See also Agnew (n 39).

[54] Young Person Focus Group (PhD): Female.

as one professional explains: 'the young person will still be judged even though they are a victim'.[55] Disbelief can therefore result in young people dismissing their experience(s) as irrelevant and minimising the true harm caused to them.

Third, *exoneration*. This again was a highly gendered dimension attached to peer-based sexting. The misplaced presumption that boys cannot control their 'sex-drive', coupled with the prevailing pressure on boys – both within media forums and within peer settings – to convey a 'dominating sexual persona' became apparent.[56] This discourse problematises understanding of consent among young people as sexual decision-making is contextualised via a range of gendered myths and stereotypes. Indeed, a British survey explored sexual coercion in the context of adolescent relationships and described one participant as saying, 'girls don't seem to be driven by their hormones half as much as guys'.[57] This misplaced understanding of the body, sex and sexuality suggests that boys have no control over their bodies and are therefore in some way less responsible for their actions. As one young person explains, if a boy sends an image 'it's overlooked' whereas the same cannot be said of their female counterparts.[58] Consequently, boys are often excused/exonerated and treated less harshly than their female peers for sending content of a sexual nature or engaging in other types of sexual behaviour due to their 'active masculine sexuality'.[59] This is heavily influenced by a range of persisting gender stereotypes alongside the presence of a prevailing sexual double standard within socio-cultural and legal discourses surrounding sexual behaviours.[60]

Fourth and finally, *typology*. This theme directly links to blame, gender and victimhood and the suggestion that a certain 'type' of young person engages in sexting. The typology argument is problematic in multiple ways. The narrative links back to blame discourses, popular victim/offender moulds and what Ringrose and Renold have termed the 'digital slut'.[61] Indeed, research and scholarly commentary illustrate how girls who participate in sharing images are often labelled with derogatory terms such as 'whore'[62] by challenging 'ideal victim' status[63] and the prevailing presumption that female sexuality is 'passive'.[64] As Penney notes in relation to sexting among young people, 'this shaming has

---

[55] Professional Interview 14 (PhD): Children's Voluntary Organisation.

[56] C Barter, 'Attitudes and Behaviour in Teenage Intimate Relationships' in *Premature Sexualisation: Understanding the Risks: Outcomes of the NSPCC's Expert Seminar Series* (NSPCC, 2011) 8.

[57] MJ Hird and S Jackson, 'Where "Angels" and "Wusses" Fear to Tread: Sexual Coercion in Adolescent Dating Relationships' (2001) 37(1) *Journal of Sociology* 31.

[58] Young Person Interview (PhD): Male.

[59] Gotell (n 52) 877.

[60] Agnew (n 39).

[61] J Ringrose and E Renold, 'Slut-Shaming, Girl Power and "Sexualisation": Thinking through the Politics of the International SlutWalks with Teen Girls' (2012) 24(3) *Gender and Education* 337.

[62] See Agnew (n 39).

[63] Christie (n 48) 17–30. See also Chapters 2, 3 and 5.

[64] Gotell (n 52) 877.

generational and gendered overtones … and moral panics regarding girls' digital sexual expression'.[65]

The above analysis highlights how wider and dominant rape mythology can influence social understandings of youth sexual behaviours, including peer-based sexting behaviours. In doing so, a prevalent gender imbalance when young people engage in peer-based sexting behaviours (as well as other sexual behaviours) and how those behaviours are received and understood within the socio-legal landscape, was noted. Most significantly, this section explores the construction of peer-based sexting behaviours within youth culture and how it reflects broader literature on sexual communication – that boys/men are the 'sexual initiators' and girls/women are the 'sexual gatekeepers'.[66] This narrative speaks to the ongoing challenges young people face when trying to negotiate consent.

III. Sexting, Consent and Young People

What has therefore become apparent, while cases such as *Olugboja*, *Malone*, *Bree* and the 'Rugby Rape Trial' were unpacking consent within the context of other sexual offences (the offence of rape specifically), is that the complexities of consent as a legal concept and what amounts to an 'absence of consent' can be applied to a range of sexual behaviours among young people. Not surprisingly, the ongoing confusion surrounding consent and a lack of education on this important concept was noted by the young people:

> It [consent] was mentioned but we weren't like taught about consent … they kind of just said you need consent before you do this but they kinda didn't explain what *kind* of consent.[67] (Emphasis added)

Young people also expressed a desire to learn more on: 'how to say no'[68] and 'toxic traits in a relationship'.[69] The 'culture of confusion'[70] surrounding sexual behaviours and what amounts to harmful and abusive sexual behaviours was also noted by the professionals:

> [T]here's so many people that come in, and you have to sit and work out whether or not they consented to it, because they don't know themselves, because in their head they're like, well, I didn't say no, or I was drunk. Well, I did like him, but he wouldn't take no for an answer, so I just gave up. We hear that constantly. That's horrendous.[71]

---

[65] R Penney, 'The Rhetoric of the Mistake in Adult Narratives of Youth Sexuality: the Case of Amanda Todd' (2016) 16(4) *Feminist Media Studies* 721.

[66] H Frith, 'Sexual Scripts, Sexual Refusals and Rape' in Horvath and Brown (n 10) 99.

[67] Young Person Focus Group (PhD): Female.

[68] Young Person Survey (PDF): Girl, 16 years.

[69] Young Person Survey (PDF): Girl, 18 years.

[70] A-M McAlinden, *Children as 'Risk': Sexual Exploitation and Abuse by Children and Young People* (Cambridge, Cambridge University Press, 2018) 122.

[71] Professional Interview 2 (PDF): Sexual Health Charity.

Therefore, understanding the complexity of coercive settings and power dynamics that are often at the centre of a wide range of sexual behaviours, including peer-based sexting, is imperative. Further, and significantly, professionals also spoke to the influence of environment and family dynamics. As one professional explains:

> They can come home and see a relationship that is quite toxic, and quite dysfunctional, and that will have a greater message to that young person than the half an hour they've learnt in school on what consent is.[72]

A young person's relationship with parents/guardians/carers, and the experiences they are exposed to in their home can strongly influence how they view 'healthy' and 'unhealthy' relationships. When it comes to responses and education (discussed further in Chapters 8 and 9), including those key care providers is therefore essential if toxic traits are to be effectively challenged and healthy and safe messaging around relationships promoted.

Relevant also to issues of consent and young people's engagement in a range of sexual behaviours, including harmful sexual behaviours, is the emergence and prevalence of 'party culture'.[73] Within a peer context, young people often socialise by attending 'house parties' and while such parties can be a positive outlet for young people to engage and interact with their fellow peers in a social setting (often outside of the school environment), these parties can also act as gateways to coercive environments where young people are pressured to participate in certain sexual behaviours.[74]

Moreover, when differentiating between exploitative and more coercive forms of sexting behaviours, understanding the complex settings of 'gang culture', issues of consent (or lack thereof) and how participation in sexual behaviours can exist and manifest in these circumstances, will also be essential when determining appropriate supports and interventions. Not surprisingly, professionals commented on the coercive settings young people can find themselves in within an offline setting. For example, one professional notes:

> [A] couple of young people I work with who maybe don't have that feeling of they've been the victim of it … they would say 'oh no … like I got what I wanted from him'. It might have been alcohol or drugs and they're of that mindset and that is just how they're justifying it I suppose to themselves. And I've said 'but that situation you were in that you ended up having sex with two older males' and she would say 'I know but I got a bottle of vodka out of it and that's what I wanted so really, I'm the winner'.[75]

This correlates with Pearce's analysis of 'coerced consent' and the social and environmental factors which underpin whether consent was 'freely' and

---

[72] Professional Interview 1 (PDF): Independent Social Work Consultant.

[73] McAlinden (n 70); E Agnew and A-M McAlinden, 'Harmful Sexual Behaviour among Children and Young People Online: Cultural and Regulatory Challenges' in R Killean et al (eds), *Sexual Violence on Trial: Local and Comparative Perspectives* (Routledge, 2021).

[74] M Melrose, 'Twenty-First Century Party People: Young People and Sexual Exploitation in the New Millennium' (2013) 22(3) *Child Abuse Review* 155; McAlinden (n 70).

[75] Professional Interview 4 (PhD): Children's Charity.

'voluntarily' given[76] – ie where a young person finds themselves in an abusive situation but due to the provision of gifts, such as alcohol and/or drugs, the young person believes they have 'freely' consented to participate in certain sexual behaviours. In reality, the young person is being manipulated and is in an exploitative situation. Their ability to 'freely' choose and exercise 'choice' has in fact been taken away from them.[77]

Interlinked into scholarly commentary on coercive consent, one professional commented on 'treat' coercion versus 'threat' coercion:

> [T]reat based that feels flirtatious. It makes me feel good, it makes me feel good about my body, it makes me feel good because somebody wants to see me, I'm excited that they want to see me ... the different one will be the coercive threat based one, which is, if you don't show me more of those I'm going to do, which is then down into much more of the coercive threat based, blackmail base.[78]

The same professional also commented on the move from 'treat' to 'threat' coercion:

> [W]hat might have been initially excitement ... moves to anxiety ... Then you're into what originally might have been 'treat based', becomes then ... well now that I've got it, so then it could become[s] 'threat' and 'coercive'.[79]

This shift in behaviour can be extremely problematic. First, the young person *may* recognise the change in behaviour but due to engaging in certain sexual behaviours previously, feel they are somehow to blame for their current situation and/or fear the consequences if they ask for help and support through a misplaced belief that they gave an impression of consent. This links back to previous analysis on rape myths, blame discourses and their association with peer-based sexual behaviours, including sexting.[80] Second, the young person *may not* recognise the shift in behaviour (from 'treat' to 'threat') and therefore does not come forward as they do not recognise the behaviour as coercive and abusive.

A final issue noted was that involving access to pornography and issues of consent. Empirical data demonstrated that sexting behaviour can be part of a wider display of harmful sexual behaviour, for example problematic viewing of pornography.[81] These more concerning facets of sexting behaviour were noted by some professionals who commented on how pornography can '*distort*'[82] perceptions of sexuality, thus feeding into prevailing gender stereotypes on femininity and masculinity. Misconceptions include the idea that men are aggressive and

[76] J Pearce, 'A Social Model of "Abused Consent"' in M Melrose and J Pearce (eds), *Critical Perspectives on Child Sexual Exploitation and Related Trafficking* (Palgrave Macmillan, 2013) 59.
[77] ibid 59.
[78] Professional Interview 3 (PDF): Independent Social Work Consultant.
[79] ibid.
[80] Pearce (n 76) 59; Bohner et al (n 46) 19.
[81] See also L Ashurst and A-M McAlinden, 'Young People, Peer to Peer Grooming and Sexual Offending' (2015) 62(4) *Probation Journal* 374.
[82] Professional Interview 10 (PhD): Statutory Sector.

powerful and women are weak and submissive,[83] which can impact on how a young person views consent and whether consent has been given and received.[84] While young people's access to pornographic material has been a concern for governments and policy-makers for quite some time and should not be dismissed,[85] it is also clear that there are a range of issues, some more prevalent in nature, that are impacting young people's engagement online, including bullying and other forms of harassment, for example.[86]

It is evident that indicators associated with consent and non-consent have historically been and *continue* to be a 'central concern' within *all* discourses associated with sexual behaviours.[87] Within the context of peer-based sexting behaviours specifically, empirical research illustrates the need to be aware of existing tensions between what constitutes consent and coercion in practice.

IV. Sexting, Consent and Current Legislative Provisions

Having carefully considered the history of consent law in Northern Ireland and current legal parameters, the next section will examine the current legislative provisions governing peer-based sexting in Northern Ireland, with a focus on image-based sexting behaviours and issues of consent. In doing so, a number of notable concerns and challenges will be probed. While the law associated (inadvertently) with peer-based sexting has already been briefly outlined in the introduction to the book, this section aims to provide a more thorough and nuanced analysis of the legislation. In particular, why consent, to date, has not featured in any of the applicable legislative provisions will be considered.

When it comes to the sending of naked or semi-naked images, depending on the age of the parties, different legislative provisions can be activated. If the parties are 18 years or over, the relevant offence is 'disclosing private sexual photographs and films with intent to cause distress'.[88] This is often referred to colloquially as 'revenge porn'. Several scholars have contested the use of this phrase, arguing that 'revenge porn' fails to fully capture the complex motivations involved (moving beyond 'revenge') and can lead to harmful and negative connotations, including

---

[83] A Oakley, *Sex, Gender and Society* (Maurice Temple Smith Ltd, 1972).

[84] Agnew (n 39).

[85] See M Horvath et al, *'Basically … Porn is Everywhere' A Rapid Evidence Assessment on the Effects That Access and Exposure to Pornography Has on Children and Young People* (London, Office for the Children's Commissioner, 2013).

[86] A Phippen, *Children's Online Behaviour: Policy and Rights Challenges* (Palgrave Macmillan, 2017) Chapter 3.

[87] L Pineau, 'Date Rape: A Feminist Analysis' (1989) 8(2) *Law and Philosophy* 218.

[88] Criminal Justice and Courts Act 2015, s 33.

victim-blaming.[89] 'Image-based sexual abuse' has been adopted to more accurately denote the range of behaviours displayed and recognise the full scope of harm caused.[90]

If the parties are under 18 years of age (the primary focus of this book), the offence falls under indecent image legislation. The legislative framework is Article 3 of the Protection of Children (Northern Ireland) Order 1978 (1978 Order),[91] as amended by Article 42 of the Sexual Offences (Northern Ireland) Order 2008 (which raised the age of a 'child' as defined under law from 16 to 18 years).[92] There are some significant points to note about this particular piece of legislation. First, the original intention behind the framing of the 1978 Order was to protect young people (ie those under 18 years) from adults who wished to sexually exploit children and young people. In fact, the English and Welsh equivalent of the legislative provision (The Protection of Children Act 1978) explicitly notes that the Act was designed to 'prevent the exploitation of children.'[93] When it came to drafting the legislative provision, consent was therefore not deemed to be a key priority or an essential element of the offence – as it would be held that a child cannot consent to an adult taking indecent photographs of them. It was not anticipated that young people *themselves* would begin to engage in, what has become colloquially known as, 'sexting'. Professionals also commented on the primary regulatory aim of the legislation:

> We're criminalising children unnecessarily by virtue of a legislation that was designed 30 years ago for a particular purpose.[94] It is currently not fit for purpose.[95]

Second, while consent or reasonable belief in consent does not feature in the framing of the offence under Article 3 of the 1978 Order, there are a number of defences available. The defences are complex and include: (i) exception for criminal proceedings/investigations;[96] (ii) legitimate reason; (iii) lack of knowledge;[97] and marriage/other relationships.[98] The first exception applies to defendants who are being charged under Article 3(1)(a) but who work in the criminal

---

[89] C McGlynn et al, *Shattering Lives and Myths: A Report on Image-Based Sexual Abuse* Project Report (Durham University; University of Kent, 2019).

[90] ibid.

[91] This legislation (and the English and Welsh equivalent) should not be confused with s 62 of the Coroners and Justice Act 2009 which applies to England, Wales and Northern Ireland. Section 62 outlines the offence of 'possession of prohibited images of children'. This offence captures non-photographic images, for example, computer-generated images. Such images are not the focus of this book.

[92] In England and Wales, the legislative framework is s 1 of the Protection of Children Act 1978 (1978 Act) as amended by s 45 of the Sexual Offences Act 2003.

[93] Protection of Children Act 1978, s 37.

[94] 'Particular purpose' being to protect young people from adult perpetrators of child sexual exploitation.

[95] Professional Interview 1 (PDF): Independent Social Work Consultant.

[96] Protection of Children (Northern Ireland) Order 1978, Art 3A; Protection of Children Act 1978, s 1B.

[97] Protection of Children (Northern Ireland) Order 1978, Art 3(3)(a)–(b); Protection of Children Act 1978, s 1(4)(a)–(b).

[98] Protection of Children (Northern Ireland) Order 1978, Art 3B; Protection of Children Act 1978, s 1A.

justice sector. All that must be established is that the defendant's actions were 'necessary' for the prevention, detection or investigation of crime.[99] The defence of legitimate reason focuses primarily on 'legitimate research'. In the conjoined case *Atkins v DPP; Goodland v DPP*,[100] it was noted that it is a question of fact for the court when determining whether research satisfied a 'legitimate reason'. The case also emphasised that the research must be 'honest' and courts were encouraged to 'bring a measure of scepticism' when deliberating and 'should not too readily' come to the conclusion that the defence had been made out.[101] A lack of knowledge considers cases where the defendant argues that they had not seen the photograph in question and/or had 'no cause to suspect' that the image was an 'indecent photograph of a child'.[102] The defence of legitimate reason and lack of awareness can only be raised as a potential defence if the defendant is being charged under Articles 3(1)(b) or (c) of the 1978 Order (distribution or possession).[103]

Finally, to avail of the defence under marriage or other relationships[104] the defendant must prove that the child was 16 years or over at the time the photograph was taken and that they were married/civil partners or lived together as partners in an 'enduring family relationship'.[105] The courts have been very clear that the defence under Article 3B of the 1978 Order/section 1A(4) of the 1978 Act is to be used in a very limited number of cases. For example, in *R v M*[106] the court refused to incorporate a 'one-night stand' within the scope of the defence. In this case, the defendant was 23 years old, and the complainant was 17 years old. While the key facts of the case go beyond the parameters of the defence,[107] for the purposes of this chapter, focus will be on how the court interpreted section 1A(4) of the 1978 Act. The Court of Appeal were clear that when the legislative provision was drafted, a careful balance was sought between protecting children and ensuring minimum interference with a person's rights under the European Convention on Human Rights (such as Article 8).[108]

It was argued that to include 'brief sexual relationships' within the scope of section 1A(4) of the 1978 Act would 'diminish the protection provided' to

---

[99] Protection of Children (Northern Ireland) Order 1978, Art 3A(1)(a); Protection of Children Act 1978, s 1B(1)(a).

[100] *Atkins v DPP; Goodland v DPP* [2000] 1 WLR 1427.

[101] ibid.

[102] *R v Collier (Edward John)* [2005] 1 WLR 843.

[103] In England and Wales, it is s 1(1)(a) or (b) of the 1978 Act.

[104] This defence is available to a defendant who is being charged under Arts 3(1)(a)–(c) of the 1978 Order; in England and Wales, s 1(1)(a)–(c) of the 1978 Act.

[105] Protection of Children (Northern Ireland) Order 1978, Art 3B(1)(a)–(b); Protection of Children Act 1978, s 1A(1)(a)–(b).

[106] *R v M* [2011] EWCA Crim 2752.

[107] The prosecution argued that the defendant raped the complainant and took pictures of her while she was undressed and asleep. The defence argued that the complainant had consented to the sexual intercourse and the taking of the photograph and was therefore entitled to avail of the defence under s 1A(4) of the 1978 Act by stating that a 'one night stand' fell within the scope of this defence.

[108] Right to respect for private and family life.

children and young people under 18 years.[109] The Court of Appeal therefore held that the decision not to allow the defendant to try and avail of the defence under section 1A(4) of the 1978 Act was compatible with his rights enshrined under the European Convention on Human Rights.[110] The defendant's counsel argued that it was 'irrational' to say a child could consent to sexual activity but not to the taking of a photograph unless they were in a marriage, civil partnership or an enduring family relationship.[111] In response, the Court of Appeal noted that the defendant had 'no right' to make the child in question the 'subject of pornography'[112] and the 'protection of children from sexual exploitation is necessary and a "pressing social need"'.[113]

What the *R v M* case powerfully illustrates is that the purpose of this legislative provision was to protect children from exploitative relationships involving an adult (someone over 18 years) as the perpetrator. Consequently, upon careful reading of this case, it seems clear that 'other relationships' and 'enduring family relationship' will not extend to peer-based sexting relationships. Further, it is questionable whether widening the scope of this defence to include peer-based relationships is even appropriate, given the intention behind the drafting of the legislation and the child protection issues raised by the Court of Appeal. What *is* clear, however, is that the Protection of Children (Northern Ireland) Order 1978 and the Protection of Children Act 1978, as they currently stand, are not designed to cater to the breadth of peer-based sexting behaviours displayed by young people. It is therefore inappropriate to activate this legislative provision within the context of peer-based sexting.

Further, as discussed in Chapter 5, criminalising and holding young people 'responsible' and somehow to 'blame' for engaging in sexting behaviours is dismissing significant motivations and influences behind the behaviour. As Salter and colleagues explain:

> The twin processes of criminalisation and responsibilisation, both of which either censure or shame the individual, overlook sexting as part of a broader pattern of gendered sexual negotiations.[114]

Other regulatory concerns have been raised, associated with the use of indecent image legislation, criminalisation and a child's welfare. This was reinforced by one professional who suggested:

> we need to be better placed in both our understanding of what a good screening looks like for those young people who engaged in some sort of behaviour, through a medium

---

[109] *R v M* (n 106) [37].
[110] This case dealt with the English and Welsh equivalent – s 1A(4) of the 1978 Act.
[111] *R v M* (n 106) [17].
[112] ibid [36].
[113] ibid [13].
[114] M Salter et al, 'Beyond Criminalisation and Responsibilation: Sexting, Gender and Young People' (2013) 24(3) *Current Issues in Criminal Justice* 304.

that has been made available to them, in order to explore their sexuality, that may have blurred boundaries … and doesn't suggest that they're likely to persist in engaging in that behaviour.[115]

In the wake of intense debates on these issues, both nationally and internationally, countries are trying to ascertain the best way to regulate and respond to peer-based sexting.[116]

V. Sexting, Young People and Sexual Development

There are a plethora of writings available on what is considered to be 'normal' and 'healthy' sexual development among children and young people.[117] Empirical findings and scholarly literature suggests that traditional theoretical thinking on the child as *always* 'innocent' and 'asexual' has resulted in western culture taking measures, sometimes extreme in nature, to protect children from premature sexualisation, including engaging in certain forms of sexually explorative behaviours. Seemingly, the fear and anxiety expressed within modern discourses on child sex abuse has become panic and is influencing social and political agendas on risk management.[118] An example would be the *Gillick* case.[119] In this case it was held that a child under the age of 16 years could consent to medical treatment and/or examination if they had 'sufficient maturity and intelligence to understand the nature and implications of the proposed treatment.'[120] This has been referred to as '*Gillick* competence'.[121] Although *Gillick* competence does not set a 'lower age limit' per se, literature suggests that a child under 13 years would usually require parental consent for medical examinations and/or treatments.[122] This aligns with the law on sexual consent and the discretion that police possess when dealing with parties aged 13–15 years.[123]

---

[115] Professional Interview 1 (PDF): Independent Social Work Consultant.

[116] International responses are critiqued in Chapter 8 of this book.

[117] See Chapter 3 of this book and S Hackett, 'Children and Young People with Harmful Sexual Behaviours' in C Barter and B David (eds), *Children Behaving Badly? Peer Violence between Children and Young People* (John Wiley and Sons, 2010) 122.

[118] McAlinden (n 70).

[119] *Gillick Respondent v West Norfolk and Wisbech Area Health Authority First Appellants and Department of Health and Social Security Second Appellants* [1986] AC 112.

[120] ibid [113].

[121] Note that '*Gillick* competence' and 'Fraser guidelines' can often be used interchangeably but Fraser guidelines relate to the giving of advice specifically relating to contraception and sexual health whereas *Gillick* competence is used in a wider range of settings involving young people.

[122] Care Quality Commission, 'GP Mythbuster 8: Gillick Competency and Fraser Guidelines' (23 December 2022) https://www.cqc.org.uk/guidance-providers/gps/gp-mythbusters/gp-mythbuster-8-gillick-competency-fraser-guidelines, last accessed 17 July 2023; Chester West and Chester Council, 'Young People and Consent: Guidance Notes' https://www.cheshirewestandchester.gov.uk/documents/social-care-and-health/children/team-around-the-family/young-people-and-consent-guidance-notes-130219.pdf, last accessed 17 July 2023.

[123] As discussed further in Chapter 8, the police have discretion to divert cases involving sexual activity away from the Public Prosecution Service in Northern Ireland (the Crown Prosecution

The significance of the outcome of the *Gillick*[124] case was brought to the fore when a range of societal fears associated with sex, sexuality and young people was posited.[125] In brief, it was argued that providing young people with 'secret medical advice' would encourage 'promiscuity' among young people and the 'stability of family life threatened'.[126] Commentary on the case mirrored the misplaced belief that young people who are 'sexually mature' for their age are seen to be a threat to traditional perceptions of the 'innocent' child.[127] It is important to protect children and young people from harms that can manifest both on- and offline and ensure children receive proper support and intervention if their behaviour is deemed to be harmful. However, over-regulation of *all* sexual behaviours is counterproductive and can result in young people being labelled 'deviant' and consequently criminalised for behaviour that is in fact a normal part of their sexual development.

Interestingly, EU Directive 2011/92/EU on combating the sexual abuse and sexual exploitation of children and child pornography specifically notes:

> This Directive does not govern Member States' policies with regard to consensual sexual activities in which children may be involved and which can be regarded as the *normal discovery of sexuality in the course of human development*... [including] new forms of establishing and maintaining relations among children and adolescents, including through information and communication technologies. These issues fall outside of the scope of this Directive. (Emphasis added)

Article 8(3) of the Directive deals with consensual sexual activities, noting that it is within the discretion of Member States whether to convict parties under Article 5(2) and 5(6) (acquisition, possession and production of child pornography) if the parties involved have reached the age of sexual consent, there is no evidence of abuse, and the images were for the 'private use' of the parties involved.[128] This provision protects (or directs Member States to provide adequate protection to) young people between the ages of 16–18 years from being unnecessarily criminalised for peer-based consensual image sharing.

Yet, greater attention should be afforded to young people engaging in the sexual behaviour who are below the age of consent. More careful consideration therefore is required of how to respond appropriately to this cohort of young people, in particular those young people who fall within the police's discretionary powers to divert away from the Public Prosecution Service (13–15 years). This idea was supported by a number of professionals: 'sexting can be healthy as well, it's just

---

Service in England and Wales) if the child is aged 13–16 years and there is no evidence of coercion or manipulation.

[124] *Gillick* (n 119) [112].

[125] See Scraton (n 43).

[126] *Gillick* (n 119) [147].

[127] S Jackson and S Scott, 'Risk Anxiety and the Social Construction of Childhood' in D Lupton (ed), *Risk and Sociocultural Theory: New Directions and Perspectives* (Cambridge University Press, 1999) Chapter 4.

[128] Directive 2011/92/EU, Art 8(3).

the different medium for exploration. The same as anything'.[129] But there was also a recognition that with every healthy behaviour, there is room for manipulation and coercion, 'sex can be corrupted by somebody who has a deviant aspect of what they want to do. It's the same on-line'.[130] Appropriate regulatory responses are therefore imperative.

Specifically, children who engage in sexual behaviours that are considered to be 'problematic' and/or 'developmentally unusual' for their age should receive the necessary supports and interventions required to minimise potential nega-tive outcomes.[131] This would be particularly relevant for those children who are engaging in the sexual behaviour at a very young age. For example, a number of professionals noted 'primary school children'[132] and 'the lower years' in secondary education[133] as being the most common age group they have had to deal with for sexting behaviours. On the other hand, young people engaging in certain sexual activities and behaviours which are considered to be 'normal' and 'healthy' for their age and stage of development should not be unnecessarily regulated. In such instances, consent will feature as a key element in determining whether the behav-iour is 'normal' and 'healthy'. In addition, consideration of the wider contextual factors, including consent, will also determine whether education or health-based interventions are more appropriate regulatory responses.

This analysis, however, also highlights that while consent is an important feature within the context of peer-based sexting behaviours, existing legal and societal tensions within consent law must also be recognised. The literature cited above highlights how consent law (and the scope of some key legislative provi-sions as they are currently framed and applied in practice) fail to capture the complexities of human relationships and interactions.[134] Within the context of peer-on-peer sexual interactions, there is a pressing need to acknowledge the presence of a 'culture of confusion'[135] when it comes to young people negotiat-ing consent and sexual agency. How girls in particular 'consent' to certain sexual behaviours and express sexual agency must be considered alongside prevailing gender norms, dominant heteronormative narratives and the nuances of youth culture.[136] This is why legal reforms must be carefully considered and would only form *part* of the regulatory picture. Non-legal responses and interventions, such as gender-sensitive education programmes, must also be engaged and are indeed preferred over criminal sanctions for young people (discussed further in Chapter 8).

---

[129] Professional Interview 2 (PDF): Sexual Health Charity.
[130] ibid.
[131] Hackett (n 117) 122. See also Chapters 3, 5 and 7.
[132] Professional Interview 3 (PDF): Independent Social Work Consultant.
[133] Interview 20 (PhD): Education Sector.
[134] See eg Dowds and Agnew (n 10).
[135] McAlinden (n 70) 122.
[136] See K Schobert et al, '"I Thought We Were Vibin"': A Qualitative Exploration of Sexual Agency and Consent in Young People' (2021) 24(7) *Sexualities* 906.

VI. Conclusion

It is clear that young people are using technology to not only educate themselves on issues relating to sex and sexuality but are also using technology to explore sexual boundaries.[137] Consent therefore becomes a crucial factor to be taken into consideration when determining whether a sexual behaviour is explorative (consensual) or exploitative (non-consensual). In particular, the socio-cultural context and the circumstances surrounding the peer-based interaction become imperative in establishing consent. Yet, despite ongoing reforms and developments in the area of consent law, scholars including Dowds have noted that laws surrounding consent 'continue to perplex academics and practitioners'.[138] In addition, despite context being a key feature within a wealth of academic literature on consent, as Andersson and Bladini note '[t]he lack of context has been criticised in relation to sexual violence … due to the inability to consider power imbalances, vulnerabilities and coercive circumstances that follows from such a perspective'.[139] While discussed within an adult context, as empirical analysis demonstrates, similar complexities arise with peer-based sexting behaviours.

Drawing on the lived experiences of young people and the broader regulatory tensions associated with sexting, noting in particular the diverse range of circumstances sexting can involve, proposals to consider *consensual* peer-based sexting to be outside the scope of current legal frameworks (and indeed inappropriate to utilise in these types of cases) has been strongly promulgated.[140] Reforms in law would strongly align with empirical findings and scholarly commentary on the issue. Reconstructing law and policies in the area to better reflect the lived experiences of young people would therefore challenge dangerous narratives associated with young people, criminalisation and sexual agency. It would also provide a valuable opportunity to present clarity on consent law and acknowledge the need to recognise the complex contextual settings that are often at the centre of these peer-based interactions.[141] Finally, placing consent as a key feature within regulatory frameworks would provide a platform to contest stereotypical understandings of 'sexual risk' and 'harm' while also challenging problematic normative dimensions associated with peer-based sexual behaviours. Yet, discussed further in Chapter 8, careful consideration should also be given as to whether *any* form of peer-based sexting behaviour should fall within the remit of indecent image legislation.

---

[137] See Chapter 3 of this book.

[138] E Dowds, 'Refining Consent: Rape Law Reform, Reasonable Belief, and Communicative Responsibility' (2022) 49(4) *Journal of Law and Society* 845.

[139] W Andersson and M Bladini, 'Autonomy and Beyond – Voluntariness in the Light of Lived Autonomy' (2021) (3 & 4 /170) *Retfærd. Nordic Legal Journal* 35, 39.

[140] Note: whether *any* type of peer-based sexting behaviour should be dealt with via the legal landscape, will be probed further in Chapter 8.

[141] See also Chapter 3.

Alongside changes in law and policy, research also advocates for public awareness campaigns on consent. The blurred boundaries surrounding negotiating 'free and informed' consent was a prevalent theme which emerged in the study. In this vein, such campaigns should focus on issues including 'withdrawing consent' and the different contexts in which these interactions can manifest. Awareness campaigns could be a powerful tool in helping alleviate some of the confusion felt by young people when it comes to what is 'healthy' and 'consensual' sexual behaviour. Indeed, there is research to show that campaigns including 'I Just Froze' have infiltrated mock jury deliberations.[142] Further, awareness campaigns – if activated successfully –can not only challenge myths and stereotypes, inform wider public audiences on healthy sexual interactions but can also 'make visible' victims' experiences of sexual violence.[143]

Reflecting on these debates and the importance of consent within the context of peer-based sexting behaviours, the next chapter will consider the work of Liz Kelly and Simon Hackett to help professionals and practitioners differentiate between *consensual* and *non-consensual* sexual behaviours (focusing on sexting behaviours).

---

[142] See Dowds and Agnew (n 10).
[143] S Doherty, 'Exhibition Review: A Reflection on Ruth Maxwell's Not Consent Exhibition as a Method of Challenging Rape Myths in Ireland' (2020) 14(2) *Law and Humanities* 279.

7

Sexting Among Young People: A Continuum of Sexual Behaviour

The available literature and research on sexting among young people has illustrated significant cultural and legal challenges when it comes to identifying and responding to the sexual behaviour. In broad terms, current regulatory frameworks fail to grapple with the complexity of sexting behaviours young people experience daily. Further, and importantly, despite academic interest in this area, limited understanding exists regarding the variety and severity of harms to which young people can be exposed when subjected to unwanted or coercive sexting practices, including physical, emotional and psychological harm. This gap in knowledge has been facilitated by an increasing awareness of peer-based sexting behaviours and the subsequent framing of the practice purely within a 'risk' and 'harmful' context. This has created a range of tensions, in particular challenging traditional perceptions of children, childhood and youth sexuality (see Chapters 2 and 3). In addition, the narrow framing of the sexual behaviour creates two core problems. First, young people struggle to negotiate a sexual identity with prevailing competing and conflicting messages associated with sexual agency and autonomy. Second, and interrelated to the previous point, young people struggle to identify themselves as either the person being harmed ('victim') or the person instigating the harm ('offender'), or indeed both. As a consequence, very few young people come forward to receive the support and help they may need. Accordingly, attempts to manage and regulate the behaviour become extremely difficult and at times futile.

This chapter argues that before any interventions are activated, proper identification and framing of the sexual behaviour is crucial. In this respect, Chapters 5 and 6 are important contextual chapters. The wide range of sexting behaviours young people engage in (Chapter 5) and how consent can play a role in distinguishing between the different types of behaviours displayed (Chapter 6), highlight that peer-on-peer sexting behaviours cannot easily be categorised into distinct branches of behaviour. In laying out the framework for the continuum, the seminal work of Liz Kelly and Simon Hackett will be considered. Critically engaging with Kelly and Hackett's contributions in this field will not only identify some of the broader issues at play but also explain why sexting between young people is on a continuum with other forms of peer-based sexual behaviours, including other harmful sexual behaviours. Moving toward a continuum of behaviour, a more holistic approach can be taken when responding to sexting among young people – one that moves away from criminalisation and mostly punitive responses, to one which considers alternative responses, such as gender sensitive education programmes.

Finally, before unpacking the key issues in more detail, it is important to clarify the age group to which the below discussion relates. While the primary research suggests that increasingly children of younger ages are participating in sexting, this section will place emphasis on those young people who fall within 'the grey area' of age limits within criminal law – ie young people aged 13–17 years. This age range is significant for a number of reasons. First, it takes account of the disparity in age limits regarding sexual consent at 16 years and the age at which a young person can legally send sexual content of themselves via an image and/or video at 18 years and above. Second, as noted by a number of professionals interviewed, when dealing with sexual offence cases that involve a young person under the age of consent but aged between 13–15 years inclusive, the police possess a level of discretion. This discretionary power can be used depending on a number of contextual factors, for example, if the two parties are of a similar age and there is no evidence of coercion. Third, in contrast to sexual activity involving 13–15 year olds, sexual activity with a child under 13 years is a strict liability offence and the police officers have no discretion but to forward the case to the Public Prosecution Service (the Northern Ireland equivalent to the Crown Prosection Service for England and Wales). Children under the age of 13 therefore require a different type and level of intervention due to their age and stage of development (physical, emotional and psychological). Fourth, the majority of social networking sites where images, videos and messages can be shared among young people have an age restriction of 13 years and over (this includes Facebook, Instagram and TikTok). Within this broader context, recommendations discussed below to view sexting behaviours as part of a continuum of sexual behaviour will be solely focused on the age range 13–17 years.

I. Sexting: Beyond a Purely 'Risk' and 'Harmful' Framework

Sex and sexual practices among young people have always instigated a level of panic and concern, not only within the public arena but also within regulatory bodies. Concerns include poor sexual health outcomes including, sexually transmitted infections (STIs) and unwanted pregnancies.[1] Child protection and welfare concerns have also been noted, primarily around early initiation and/

---

[1] See H Young et al, 'Sexual Intercourse, Age of Initiation and Contraception among Adolescents in Ireland: Findings from the Health Behaviour in School-Aged Children (HBSC) Ireland Study' (2018) 18(362) *BMC Public Health* 1.

or engagement in more harmful sexual practices which are said to be 'outside normative developmental parameters'.[2] In addition, early sexual activity, adverse outcomes and a range of contextual factors, including socio-economic status and the level of education the young person has received, have been identified as key factors.[3] Such debates become heightened when trying to distinguish between what is 'normal' and 'healthy' behaviour and what is 'unhealthy' and potentially 'problematic' sexual behaviour for a child or young person of a certain age and stage of development. Simon Hackett has been a pioneer in the area and has developed a continuum of sexual behaviour for practitioners and professionals to work from (discussed further below). The NSPCC, one of the leading children's charities, has also provided guidance according to age group, for example, young people aged between 13–17 years may start to experiment sexually with peers of the same age.[4] As long as this interaction is consensual, it is not considered to be outside the boundaries of healthy sexual development. Yet, as discussed earlier in the book, there is a continued and prolonged societal discomfort with young people engaging in any kind of sexual activity, particularly below the age of consent (16 years).

Sexting among young people under 18 years has raised similar concerns regarding what is considered to be healthy behaviour for their age. At the heart of this discourse is youth sexual agency and how it has come to be understood within the technological age. As noted in the introductory chapter, technology is an integral part of youth culture and identity, and it is not going away. While the internet and use of ICTs (information and communication technologies) among young people has raised many varied and complex regulatory challenges, one issue that seems to continually perplex academics, educators and legal practitioners alike is that of peer-based sexting. This is mostly due to the narrow framing of childhood, adolescence and youth sexuality. Emphasis on traditional notions of these key concepts and stages of human development continue to be mobilised within popular contemporary narratives on children and young people. As Lesko argues: 'adolescents' identities are simultaneously sites of broader cultural debates about knowledge, identity, representation, and power'.[5] Consequently, when it comes to understanding current framings of youth sexual agency both on- and offline, important issues to consider are the varied socio-cultural factors influencing how young people view their bodies, and power dynamics (often gendered) – all of

[2] C Smith et al, 'Practice and Policy in the UK with Children and Young People Who Display Harmful Sexual Behaviours: An Analysis and Critical Review' (2014) 20(3) *Journal of Sexual Aggression* 267; S Hackett, 'Children and Young People with Harmful Sexual Behaviours' in C Barter and B David (eds), *Children Behaving Badly? Peer Violence between Children and Young People* (John Wiley and Sons, 2010).

[3] MJ Palmer et al, 'Prevalence and Correlates of "Sexual Competence" at First Heterosexual Intercourse among Young People in Britain' (2019) 45 *BMJ Sex Reproductive Health* 127.

[4] NSPCC, *Sexual Development and Behaviour in Children* (NSPCC, 5 August 2022) https://learning.nspcc.org.uk/child-health-development/sexual-behaviour accessed 21 May 2023.

[5] N Lesko, *Act your Age!: A Cultural Construction of Adolescence* (New York, Routledge Farmer, 2001) 50.

which are influencing how young people communicate and negotiate their sexual identity and representation.

Studies suggest that young people are engaging in a wider range of sexual activities and at an earlier age.[6] While not all sexual experiences have elements of coercion or manipulation, concerns have been raised regarding pressurised and unwanted sexual encounters, including coercive sexting behaviours.[7] Sexually exploitative behaviours and the contextual factors at play during the decision-making processes both within on- and offline settings, including in party and gang contexts, have been probed.[8] In addition, a range of socio-cultural factors including a prevailing culture of sex, gendered power relations and easy access to pornography have all helped influence and shape how young people negotiate sexual relations and understand sexual agency.[9] Indeed, Lee and Crofts note three origins of pressure within the context of peer-based sexting: individual (this can include pressure within relationships); peer pressure (this can include group pressure to engage in sexting behaviours or the young person could be isolated); and socio-cultural pressures (this can include a culture of sex within pop culture).[10] It is against this backdrop of complex sexual interactions, social pressures and daily exposure to sexual content that young people are trying to establish, negotiate and express their sexual identity in a positive and healthy way.

As established in previous chapters, it is clear young people engage in a wide range of behaviours, some of which are more harmful and abusive in nature than others. Yet, due to the convoluted nature of some of the interactions, it is not always easy to establish who is being harmed and who is perpetrating the abuse. In addition, due to hierarchies of victimhood and who are perceived to be the most credible victims, alongside the prevailing public narrative that victims must be 'sexually innocent', there is a danger of neglecting victims or misidentifying them as the perpetrator.[11] Discussed previously in Chapter 2, victims of the Rochdale child sex abuse ring were the 'wrong type of victim' and were treated as perpetrators for bringing their friends to the ringleaders.[12] This was despite one

---

[6] R Lewis et al, 'Heterosexual Practices among Young People in Britain: Evidence from Three National Surveys of Sexual Attitudes and Lifestyles' (2017) 61 *Journal of Adolescent Health* 694.

[7] See M Wood et al, *'Standing on My Own Two Feet': Disadvantaged Teenagers, Intimate Partner Violence and Coercive Control* (NSPCC, 2011); J Ringrose et al, *A Qualitative Study of Children, Young People and 'Sexting': A Report Prepared for the NSPCC* (London, NSPCC, 2012).

[8] M Melrose, 'Twenty-First Century Party People: Young People and Sexual Exploitation in the New Millennium' (2013) 22 *Child Abuse Review* 155.

[9] See A-M McAlinden *Children as 'Risk': Sexual Exploitation and Abuse by Children and Young People* (Cambridge, Cambridge University Press, 2018).

[10] M Lee and T Crofts, 'Gender, Pressure, Coercion and Pleasure: Untangling Motivations for Sexting between Young People' (2015) 55(3) *British Journal of Criminology* 454.

[11] ibid; J Woodiwiss, 'Dramatising a Contemporary Childhood Sexual Abuse Narrative: Reinforcing a Hierarchy of Victims' (2022) *Feminist Media Studies* 1; T Horeck and D Negra, 'Reconsidering True Crime and Gendered Authority in Allen v Farrow' (2022) 22(6) *Feminist Media Studies* 1564.

[12] Woodiwiss (n 11) 3.

girl noting that she was forced to have sex with at least 20 men in one night.[13] Similar to other forms of peer exploitation, young people who engage in coercive or other harmful sexting behaviours and the young people who are victimised, are not a homogenous group.[14]

While young people can view sexting behaviours as a form of 'digital flirtation',[15] as noted previously, the predominant discourse among adults is one of discomfort. This is not unexpected given the laws that surround the sharing of sexual images of persons under 18 years of age and the potential long-term consequences for young people if images are shared (see Chapter 8 for a more detailed analysis of the law and suggested reforms). What is a particularly concerning facet of the narrative, however, is how young people are denied sexual agency by arguing that they are still (or should be) dependent on adults as they are going through a significant developmental stage and are therefore in need of protection. Yet, they are potentially criminalised if they do engage in the sexual behaviour as they 'should have known better'.[16] Further, as illustrated in cases such as the Rochdale case, another troubling account emerges where the young person who is sexually aware or active is deemed to be no longer in need of safeguarding – they are 'located outside the protective cloak of childhood innocence'.[17]

The responsibilisation discourse, which places a level of responsibility on young people to manage potential 'risks', is also significant. This discourse is often highly gendered in nature and manifests via a sexual double standard alongside shame and blame dialogues, such as 'slut shaming'.[18] As one professional explains in relation to sexual behaviours among young people in general and gender inequality:

> You're a slut if you do, you're frigid if you don't. These are the terms that people use. There is a no win there. Do you know what I mean? It's a catch twenty-two completely, and always for girls, and never for guys, and that's really, really disheartening.[19]

What is deeply precarious is that within this gendered responsibilisation discourse there is a presumption that young girls can simply say 'no'. This is reflected in a number of campaigns designed to prevent young people from engaging in sexting. For example, in 2016 Staffordshire County Council released

---

[13] J Bindel, 'Rochdale Victim: "I Was Groomed at 14, Then the Courts Came for My Children"' (*The Guardian*, 17 April 2022).

[14] Melrose (n 8).

[15] J Ringrose et al, 'Teen Girls, Sexual Double Standards and "Sexting": Gendered Value in Digital Image Exchange' (2013) 14(3) *Feminist Theory* 312.

[16] K Albury and K Crawford, 'Sexting, Consent and Young People's Ethics: Beyond Megan's Story' (2012) 26(3) *Continuum: Journal of Media & Cultural Studies* 463.

[17] Woodiwiss (n 11) 5.

[18] See L Karaian, 'Policing "Sexting": Responsibilization, Respectability and Sexual Subjectivity in Child Protection/Crime Prevention Responses to Teenagers' Digital Sexual Expression' (2013) 18(3) *Theoretical Criminology* 282.

[19] Professional Interview 2 (PDF): Sexual Health Charity.

a #saynotosexting campaign.[20] It was said the campaign was designed to 'raise awareness of child sexual exploitation and in particular the dangers for young people around sexting'.[21] Reflecting on the prevailing presence of a range of socio-cultural factors influencing how young people negotiate their sexual agency, in particular girls, it is clear that advice to simply say 'no' is to overly simplify key facets of youth sexual culture, including the presence of gendered power dynamics.

Further, the dual representation of women in the media as both sexy and innocent, and the representation of men as dominant and assertive, sends conflicting messages to young people when it comes to negotiating consent and expressing their sexuality and agency.[22] What is becoming reality for many is how the 'sexually powerful' girl/woman that is so frequently publicised, particularly within advertising,[23] must overcome the persistent presence of sexism within youth culture.[24] This was also reflected in the work of Burkett and Hamilton, who explain that 'just saying no' is suggesting that men and women negotiate sexual agency and identity in equal ways:

> the 'just say no' approach to sexual consent is deeply problematic in light of the contradictory ways in which women's empowerment is assumed within postfeminist discourses whilst masking ongoing gender imbalances.[25]

Consequently, reflecting on the diverse range of sexual practices young people can engage in and be exposed to, ranging from consensual to coercive and more harmful and abusive behaviours, to avoid overly simplistic accounts of conceptualising the behaviours, the use of a continuum seems most apt.

II. Existing Continuums: Key Features

Kelly's research pioneered the exploration of women's experiences of sexual violence as part of a 'continuum' of violence.[26] Indeed, a number of scholars have since used continuums to more effectively chart the range and scope of sexual behaviours young people are displaying, including Hackett (in relation to young

---

[20] Staffordshire Commissioner, 'Young People Urged to Say No to Sexting in New Campaign' https://staffordshire-pfcc.gov.uk/young-people-urged-to-say-no-to-sexting-in-new-campaign/ accessed 17 July 2023.

[21] ibid.

[22] See E Agnew, 'Sexting among Young People: Towards a Gender Sensitive Approach' (2021) 29(1) *The International Journal of Children's Rights* 3.

[23] R. Gill, 'Empowerment/Sexism: Figuring Female Sexual Agency in Contemporary Advertising' (2008) 18(1) *Feminism and Psychology* 35.

[24] See Ringrose et al (n 7).

[25] M Burkett and K Hamilton, 'Postfeminist Sexual Agency: Young Women's Negotiations of Sexual Consent' (2012) 15(7) *Sexualities* 815.

[26] L Kelly, *Surviving Sexual Violence* (Cambridge, Polity, 1988).

people and harmful sexual behaviour),[27] McGlynn (regarding image-based abuse between adults)[28] and McAlinden (speaking to a typology of harm along a continuum of peer-based relationships, peer-based recruitment and peer-based risk).[29] This section will focus on the pioneering work of Kelly on continuums and sexual violence and the work of Hackett as one of the leading scholars in the area on young people and sexual behaviours.

Kelly typified the continuum of sexual violence as the range of harmful behaviours women are exposed to, some on a daily basis, and the far-reaching and diverse settings and contexts in which the violence manifests. This has implications for policy and understanding the lived experience of sexual violence including: (i) legal frameworks and other regulatory mechanisms were not properly equipped to capture either the complexity of the behaviours or the sheer level of exposure; (ii) the relationship between dangerous messaging associated with male power and female resistance and sexual violence; and (iii) how the range of behaviours that fall under sexual violence can and do 'shade into one another'.[30] Kelly hoped that the concept of a 'continuum' of sexual violence would help women 'make sense' of the harmful and abusive behaviours they were experiencing, some on a daily basis.[31] Kelly also recognised the peculiar features of coercive control and how certain behaviours over a period of time can amount to sexual violence.[32]

In comparison, Hackett's continuum was proposed to assist professionals and practitioners in identifying the breadth of sexual behaviours *young people* are displaying – ranging from 'normal' to 'violent'.[33] In advocating for the use of a continuum, Hackett challenges the notion of 'a one size fits all' approach, explaining that young people who display harmful sexual behaviours within any setting, 'are a varied and complex group with diverse needs'.[34] The diversified behaviours young people engage in are broken down into five categories within Hackett's model: normal; inappropriate; problematic; abusive; and violent.

Hackett defines 'normal' behaviour as 'socially acceptable' and 'developmentally expected' where young people have engaged in 'mutual' and 'shared decision-making'. 'Inappropriate' behaviour can often be 'socially acceptable behaviour within a peer group' and there is a general sense of consent, but the context in which the behaviour has been displayed makes the behaviour 'inappropriate'.

---

[27] Hackett (n 2).

[28] C McGlynn et al, 'Beyond Revenge Porn: The Continuum of Image-Based Sexual Abuse' (2017) 25 *Feminist Legal Studies* 25.

[29] McAlinden (n 9) Chapter 6.

[30] Kelly (n 26) 75.

[31] ibid.

[32] Kelly (n 26) 77.

[33] Hackett (n 2).

[34] S Hackett et al, 'Harmful Sexual Behaviour Framework: An Evidence-Informed Operational Framework for Children and Young People Displaying Harmful Sexual Behaviours' Project Report (London, NSPCC, 2016) 15.

'Problematic' behaviour is 'developmentally unusal' and 'socally unexpected', and consent issues are more blurred and there may be a power imbalance. Towards the other end of the continuum are 'abusive' and 'violent' sexual behaviours. 'Abusive' behaviours can involve elements of coercion, misuse of power and there may be displays of 'expressive violence'. Finally, 'violent' sexual behaviour is 'higly intrusive' and the behaviour would be 'physically violent'.[35]

In addition, and related to Hackett's continuum, before exploring the peculiar features of peer-based sexting behaviours as part of a continuum of sexual behaviour, it is important to consider what *types* of sexual behaviours are considered to be 'safe' and 'healthy'. Brooks, a sexual health charity, uses a traffic light tool system to distinguish between the different categories of behaviour.[36] The tool was designed to enhance existing safeguarding procedures by providing greater clarity in relation to what is 'healthy' sexual behaviour. The behaviours have been divided into green, amber and red. Green behaviours are said to be developmentally normal and healthy and are 'reflective of natural curiosity, experimentation, consensual activities and positive choices'.[37] Amber behaviours would include more 'risky' and 'uncharacteristic' behaviours but have not reached the more serious threshold of 'coercive' or 'threatening' behaviour. Professionals should therefore be mindful of the 'activity type, frequency, duration or context' of the sexual behaviours when determining an appropriate intervention.[38] Red behaviours would require immediate support and intervention as the behaviour is said to be unquestionably concerning, due to, for example, a notable age gap and an obvious power imbalance between the parties. In addition, Brooks has also noted a range of behaviours according to age group: 0–5 years, 5–9 years, 9–13 years and 13–17 years. For extra clarity, concerning the oldest age group (13–17 years) as the key age range for this piece of research, Brooks has noted some green behaviours to include sexually explicit conversations with peers and having sexual relationships. Amber behaviours include taking and sending naked or sexually provocative images of self or others ('sexting') and accessing exploitative or violent pornography. Red behaviours include sexually aggressive behaviour and non-consensual sexual activity.[39]

III. Sexting: A Continuum of Sexual Behaviour

Boyle refers to 'continuum thinking' as important when exploring gender and violence as it can 'unsettle binaries', recognise 'grey areas' and 'avoid the "othering"'

---

[35] Hackett (n 2).
[36] See S Hackett, *Children and Young People with Harmful Sexual Behaviours* (Research in Practice, 2014) 19.
[37] ibid 19.
[38] ibid.
[39] ibid 21–22.

of certain groups of people.[40] These features are important as peer-on-peer sexting behaviours have tested popular conceptions of childhood and youth sexuality, often leading to the 'othering' of young people who behave outside the boundaries of what is considered to be 'normal' sexual development.[41] Henry et al also argue that continuums are an important part of the analysis process when examining online behaviours as 'it is no longer accurate to treat technologies as representing a separate sphere of behaviours, practices and experiences to those in the material world'.[42] Moreover, using a continuum: (i) means that connections can be made between harmful peer-based sexting behaviours and wider debates on gender-based forms of harm; (ii) highlights the multi-faceted nature of the behaviours being displayed (ranging from consensual to more harmful); (iii) acknowledges how the behaviours can merge from the on- to offline world (or vice versa); and (iv) recognises the varied experiences of those young people being victimised but also those young people displaying the behaviours.

In providing this extra analysis, this section will further clarify why an appropriate graduated response is required when examining sexting behaviours among young people. While some of the previous discussion has already explored the sexting context and how it speaks to some of the broader themes emerging, the purpose of this section is to tease out the particular risk factors associated with peer-based sexting that have come to the fore during the development of the research. In doing so, the author argues that placing the behavours on a continuum will assit in challenging some of the misconcpetions associated with sexting behaviours as well as provide an opportunity for more appropriate, robust and diverse interventions to be engaged.

Five main issues should be carefully examined when examining sexting as part of a continuum of sexual behaviour. First, as noted in Chapters 2 and 3, social perceptions and understandings of the behaviour are viewed primarily through an extremely narrow lens – a risk and harm-based frame. Consequently, attention to popular constructions of childhood and youth sexuality would need to be carefully monitored, to ensure that young people's behaviour is not viewed as 'socially unexpected' simply because there has been 'an explosion of anxiety' associated with peer-based sexting behaviours.[43] Second, contextual factors – including motivation and settings – are hugely important. As one professional explains, a distinction needs to be made between 'two 14-year olds having sexual intercourse in their home, and there's no issues around necessarily consent' and 'the same two 14-year olds engaging in sexual intercourse in a church, and obviously that can

---

[40] K Boyle, 'What's in a Name? Theorising the Inter-Relationships of Gender and Violence' (2019) 20(1) *Feminist Theory* 19.
[41] See Chapter 2.
[42] N Henry et al, 'Technology-Facilitated Domestic and Sexual Violence: A Review' (2020) 26(15–16) *Violence against Women* 1828.
[43] S Angelides, 'Technology, Hormones and Stupidity: The Affective Politics of Teenage Sexting' (2013) 16(5–6) *Sexualities* 665.

bring its own constraints.'[44] In the context of peer-based sexting and settings, is the young person sending an image in the privacy of their own home consensually, or creating and sending the image in the school bathroom, for example. Contextual factors are therefore extremely important in determining whether the behaviour is normal or atypical for a young person of that age. In addition, illustrated within the literature, motivations can 'differ markedly' when it comes to young people engaging in sexual behaviours.[45] In the context of sexting specifically, the scope and range of motivations present emphasise the complexity of the behaviours. Noted previously, studies reveal a diverse range of motivations which can include sexting as a form of sexual exploration or expression.[46] Problematic motivations can include where the exchange or sending of images is seen 'as a joke' and more harmful motivations can include varying levels of pressure or coercion.[47]

Third, consideration needs to be given to the medium through which young people are displaying their sexuality. One professional comments on young people trying to negotiate a sexual identity using a tool that is not only readily available in today's society but is also constantly advancing, so no-one really knows the limits and boundaries of what it can do. This is important when looking at whether there has been an abuse of power but also in ensuring appropriate interventions, eg education:

> It's a tool by which a young person explores their sexuality, and I think then there are occasions where it will border over into harmful, and problematic, and inappropriate usage, but that in itself, as we know, doesn't make a person harmful or abusive. It's how they're navigating their understanding of their sexuality through a tool, that fundamentally, do they really have a full comprehensive understanding of the implications of that tool in their exploration.[48]

Fourth, viewing pornographic material and its relationship with more harmful sexting practices. Depending on the age of the parties and content being viewed, it could be considered highly problematic.[49] The ability to access 'quite explicit pornography' and to do so 'fairly easily' was noted during empirical research.[50] Indeed, the relatonship between exposure to pornography and young people engaging in more problematic or harmful sexual behaviours was rasied as a key factor of consideration among most professional interviewees. For example:

> Particularly early adolescents, 13 onwards, particularly to their porn use, and their viewing of sexualised imagery of children in mainstream media as well, how

---

[44] Professional Interview 1 (PDF): Independent Social Work Consultant.
[45] L Ashurst and A-M McAlinden, 'Young People, Peer to Peer Grooming and Sexual Offending' (2015) 62(4) *Probation Journal* 378.
[46] See Agnew (n 22); Ringrose et al (n 7).
[47] ibid.
[48] Professional Interview 1 (PDF): Independent Social Work Consultant.
[49] See also Brook Traffic Light Tool in Hackett et al (n 34) 25.
[50] Professional Interview 15 (PhD): Criminal Justice Sector.

that's being perceived. And absolutely, young boys, their sexual knowledge, their sexual understanding has been incredibly influenced by the porn that they're watching.[51]

Viewing of pornography is therefore an important contextual factor when looking at the broader sexual pressures young people are being exposed to and determining whether there was a clear intent to cause harm or not.

Fifth and finally, when accessing the young people's behaviours, consideration is also given to any adversity the child may have been exposed to. In the context of young people engaging in harmful sexual behaviours, one professional explains:

> Normally what we're seeing is dysfunctionality attachment, some adversities around that child or young person, or isolation, particularly as they enter into secondary school that may be a consequence of that early dysfunction, and impact on their own relationships with those core protective adults that maybe should have had an influence on guiding them a wee bit better.[52]

Research has shown that familial and other environments which may expose young people to potentially harmful behaviours, can result in young people adopting similar behaviours in other social contexts.[53] In other words, as Firmin notes, 'abuse between young people does not occur in a vacuum but rather within interplays between contexts and individual agency'.[54]

A. Sexting as 'Explorative', 'Problematic' or 'Harmful'

With this in mind, the author will focus on three main areas: (i) sexting as 'normal/ explorative'; (ii) sexting as 'problematic'; and (iii) sexting as 'harmful' sexual behaviour. The categories were chosen taking into consideration some key issues highlighted throughout the primary research and analysis of the secondary literature, in particular Hackett and Kelly's continuums on sexual behaviours. While the author will be discussing peer-based sexting behaviours in three main areas, these are not mutually exclusive groupings and recognition of blurred boundaries and 'grey areas' of young people's experiences of sexting behaviours will be considered throughout.

First, sexting as 'normal/explorative': this recognises the sending of naked or semi-naked images as a form of 'risky' behaviour young people are engaging in but acknowledges that the behaviour can be displayed 'consensually' among young people. Throughout the interview analysis, when it came to distinguishing 'explorative' sexting behaviour from other forms of sexting behaviour, a key issue was whether the parties involved 'consented' to the sending or receiving of

---

[51] Professional Interview 1 (PDF): Independent Social Work Consultant.
[52] Professional Interview 1 (PDF): Independent Social Work Consultant.
[53] C Firmin, *Abuse between Young People: A Contextual Account* (Routledge, 2018).
[54] ibid 162.

the sexual material. For example, as explained by a professional in the criminal justice sector, 'it's to do with that imbalance of power and control and maturity and is there the freedom and capacity to consent'.[55] Therefore, while consent cannot *legally* be given under 18 years of age in relation to sending a naked image, within this context, consent refers to the sending of an image without coercion. Scholars including Albury and Crawford also note consent as an important factor when differentiating between the sexual behaviours: 'in situations where images were made with full consent, there needs to be an acknowledgement of young people's potential for sexual agency, rather than casting them solely as either victims or perpetrators'.[56]

An important feature of 'normal/explorative' sexting is therefore recognising that sending images can happen within young intimate relationships, but it can also happen among peer groups. As noted by some professionals, young people can send images for body reassurance: 'as a comparison thing'.[57] Yet, it is also important to note that if this is done as a form of body surveillance where pressure is involved or one of the parties sends the images on without consent, then the behaviour would move into the problematic or harmful category of sexual behaviour, depending on the context.

Interrelated, and noted above, in determining whether a young person consented, the age of the parties would be considered. While the professionals interviewed were reluctant to expand on what was meant by 'a similar age', it was clear from existing literature and the interview excerpts below that an appropriate age range was between one to two years.[58] As one professional interviewee explains:

> There's a slightly different context than if you're an 11-year-old saying, "but I consent to sex" … It doesn't matter, you're 11. The law recognises the vulnerability [with] that age [regarding] freedom and capacity … Do you have the capacity at 11 to really understand what it is we're doing? No. A 15-year-old? Yeah, maybe … What we don't want to do is unnecessarily put the 16- or 17-year-old boyfriend on a sex offender register for raping his 15-year-old girlfriend. When it wasn't quite like that … So, there's a safeguarding side [for] the victim but there's also the safeguarding side [for] the suspect.[59]

The interviewee raises an important issue about the level of risk an individual actually poses and how this should be reflected in the intervention activated. Overly onerous regulatory responses within low level risk cases are inappropriate and can lead to unnecessarily severe outcomes for one or all parties involved.

Hackett differentiates between 'socially acceptable' behaviour (which can be categorised as 'normal') and 'socially acceptable behaviour within [the]

---

[55] Professional Interview 19 (PhD): Criminal Justice Sector.
[56] Albury and Crawford (n 16) 471.
[57] Professional Interview 1 (PhD): Education Sector.
[58] See also McAlinden (n 9).
[59] Professional Interview 19 (PhD): Criminal Justice Sector.

peer group' (which can be categorised as 'inappropriate').[60] It is clear from the primary research that despite young people viewing sexting as 'normative' within peer networks, professionals and practitioners working within education, child protection and child welfare sectors have raised a number of significant concerns. In particular, concerns regarding a young person's mental health and wellbeing if the sexual behaviour becomes more harmful, eg images are forwarded on after the breakdown of a relationship, and in addition, the legal ramifications that could potentially befall a young person (see Chapter 8).

As noted previously, there is a high level of social anxiety associated with peer-based sexting and it is unlikely that sexting would be considered 'socially acceptable'. Yet, there is a danger in labelling *all* sexting as inappropriate or problematic as it negates young people's sexual autonomy and right to sexual expression. Noting that sexting behaviour can be 'explorative' within the digital era acknowledges that the behaviour is 'risky' (recognising that once the image is sent you no longer have control over what happens to it) but does not stigmatise *all* sexting behaviour as 'problematic' or 'harmful'. If we reflect back to Brooks' traffic light system, green behaviours for the category 13–17 years can include sexual relations. This type of sexual behaviour can also be 'risky' in that it can result in unwanted pregnancies or contracting a range of sexually transmitted infections. If comparisons are made with producing sexual content such as a naked image, while there are notable and legitimate concerns regarding a young person's digital footprint and the worldwide platform in which images can be shared, there is also a need to recognise that the sexual behaviour is being displayed using a tool that has become an integral part of a young person's life. This relates back to previous discussions on technology use among young people and their 'digital native' status, as one professional explains:

> Why are we blaming young people for being on-line and exploring themselves as a digital native? We give them iPads, we give them telephones, we created the internet, we give them passwords on the Wi-Fi. It just seems a bit hypocritical to me.[61]

A careful balancing exercise is therefore required: one which recognises a number of key factors to be taken into account when determining what type of intervention is required: (i) young people, particularly during adolescence, will naturally engage in risk-taking behaviours; (ii) the use of technology to communicate is a common feature within contemporary youth culture and electronics are being used as a tool for sexual exploration and risk-taking behaviour; (iii) the context in which the images were created and shared, eg whether it was 'consensual'; and (iv) whether the young people are aware of the potential consequences if an image is sent on – in particular, thinking about a young person's 'digital footprint'.[62] This

---

[60] Hackett (n 2).

[61] Professional Interview 2 (PDF): Sexual Health Charity.

[62] See GS O'Keeffe and K Clarke-Pearson, 'The Impact of Social Media on Children, Adolescents, and Families' (2011) 127(4) *Pediatrics* 800; L Allen, 'Sexual Assemblages: Mobile Phones/Young People/ School' (2015) 36(1) *Discourse: Studies in the Cultural Politics of Education* 120.

should help identify whether an educative response is appropriate or whether a more in-depth risk assessment should be made.

This leads the discussion on to 'problematic' displays of peer-based sexting behaviour. In contrast to explorative behaviours, more concerning behavioural traits may start to become apparent. This could include, for example, use of bullying techniques. As one professional interviewee explains, 'there's sexting and there's cyberbullying and there's a bit in the middle where they meet'.[63] Both professional and young participants strongly advocated that sexting should not automatically be categorised as 'cyberbullying' unless there are clear bullying elements present. There is also an acknowledgement that exposure to the harmful behaviour can intensify as time moves on and shift the behaviour to a more 'harmful' context. Recognition of this during the information-gathering process is therefore significant when it comes to engaging appropriate interventions.

Further, 'problematic' sexting behaviours could include cases where different levels of pressure are present and/or the blurring of boundaries regarding consent has become more apparent. These traits are not always easily identifiable. Indeed, Kelly speaks to pressurised sex and how simplifying heterosexual relations as either consensual or non-consensual does not account for a significant proportion of women's sexual encounters, noting that sexual interactions can involve 'a range of pressure and coercion'.[64] Similarly within the context of young people's sexual experiences, Powell refers to 'subtle pressures' that can lead to 'unwanted' or 'compliant' sexual encounters: 'subtle pressures relate to the gendered social norms or expectations as to what men and women are "supposed" to do in a relationship'.[65]

Empirical data also highlights a range of pressures young people are exposed to, some gendered in nature. This included 'unwanted' exposure to sexual content and pressures that blur boundaries between consent and a lack of consent, for example, sending an unwanted image to another peer to 'flirt'. Issues with consent immediately arise and the potential harm that receiving an unwanted image could cause to the recipient must be considered. There were concerns voiced by a number of professionals surrounding the contexts in which images were being shared. As two professionals explain:

> P: … young people are being sent images that they never asked for.
>
> F: On a regular basis.
>
> P: And they haven't engaged in any kind of conversation that suggests [they] should now receive a naked image from you or I should receive a dick pic or I should receive a picture of a girl's naked boobs. But that's what's happening. Unsolicited messaging of sexual images.[66]

---

[63] Professional Interview 16 (PhD): Independent Researcher on Harmful Sexual Behaviours.
[64] Kelly (n 26) 82.
[65] A Powell, 'Sexual Pressure and Young People's Negotiation of Consent' ACSSA Newsletter No 14, (Australian Institute of Family Studies, 2007) 11.
[66] Professional Interview 4 (PDF): Children's Charity.

This analysis is supported by an EU Online Kids survey, also confirming a gendered dimension to the behaviour. In this study it was reported that more girls experience unwanted sexual requests online than boys.[67] Added to this are the different levels of coercion a young person can experience, which can determine if a behaviour is problematic or more harmful in nature. One professional explains (and referred to in Chapter 6): 'they're not recognising treat-based coercion',[68] ie the compliments, the treats and gifts to pressure and coerce a young person into engaging in certain activities. Equally, for professionals identifying the behaviour, it is easier to pinpoint certain types of coercive behaviour but the 'subtlety of language' and the 'cajoling' that can occur in youth interactions, for example, can sometimes be more difficult to recognise:

> I think most people would see, if you don't show me your boobs, I'm going to do [X or Y]. So, I think most people would say, oh my God, that's just awful. But aren't your boobs just fabulous, oh my God, show me those fabulous boobs, they're just fabulous. I just think they're lovely, and they're the nicest I've ever seen. I don't [think] most people would see that as equally as coercive by cajoling.[69]

Interrelated to the broader discourse on sexual behaviours, a number of external pressures were also apparent. By way of an example, a professional interviewed spoke of 'a lot of silent pressure' and young people having sex 'to get it out of the way'.[70] Relating specifically to socio-culture pressures to have sexual intercourse, the same professional found that: 'it filters in to how you look, how you act, what you're supposed to do, what you're supposed to be doing at a certain point'.[71] This was primarily discussed within a heteronormative context. A clear gender dynamic was present – it was often boys applying the pressure and girls who were at the receiving end of it. It is important to emphasise that although there was a clear gendered dimension attached to this narrative, pressure to engage in sexual activities was also noted in relation to boys. This was often framed in relation to toxic masculinity and a need to fulfil a dominant masculine persona: 'there's obviously a lot of pressure on young men to be sexual and be interested in sex with girls and to be manly and display their masculinity'.[72]

In addition, cases where there are elements of pressure but they are not overt could also fall under 'problematic' behaviour. Note, however, similar to bullying behaviours, the presence of pressure could be considered more harmful behaviour if, for example, there was a clear intention to coerce and cause harm, or the behaviour is part of a broader picture of engagement in harmful practices. This could include evidence that the young person has been exposed to degrading

---

[67] D Smahel et al, *EU Kids Online 2020: Survey Results from 19 Countries* (EU Kids Online, 2020) 7.
[68] Professional Interview 3 (PDF): Independent Social Work Consultant.
[69] ibid.
[70] Professional Interview 2 (PDF): Sexual Health Charity.
[71] ibid.
[72] Professional Interview 4 (PDF): Children's Charity.

sexual behaviours such as frequently viewing violent pornography. This can lead to significant competency differentials, both in terms of power and knowledge. As one professional interviewee explains:

> Fundamentally, where I consider whether or not a young person needs that full assessment, I'm looking at the behaviour, I'm looking at the context of the behaviour, the age difference, the knowledge differential, the understanding differential between the perpetrator and the other person, before deciding whether or not that young person requires either something much more comprehensive, or some re-direction, and that re-direction may [be] best placed with parents, or carers, as opposed to professionals.[73]

This brings the discussion on to focus on 'harmful' sexting behaviours. Some of the key distinctive differences between problematic and harmful sexual behaviour would be an explicit intent to cause harm or a notable distinction in relation to the methods used to receive an image, such as use of coercion and exploitation. This could include, for example, when young people forward images on as an act of revenge with a clear intention to cause harm to another young person. In fact, some of the young people commented on images being forwarded as a result of a 'break-up', noting it to be 'a very serious issue'.[74] Other research has recognised such behaviour as a sexual offence.[75] Within this case example, a range of contextual factors must also be considered which can determine the level of support and type of intervention required – for example, as noted previously, problematic viewing of violent pornography, which has been shown to 'distort'[76] perceptions of sexuality. Other contextual factors could include evidence of partner violence – physical, sexual or psychological. Indeed, scholars including Drouin, Ross and Tobin have noted a potential link between coercive sexting practices among young university students and partner violence.[77] While this was not specifically mentioned during primary data collection, the relationship between sexting among young people (under 18 years) and other forms of violence within young intimate relationships should be more carefully considered in the context of the broader remit of harmful sexual behaviour being displayed. Exploring connections between different types of harmful behaviours helps distinguish whether the behaviour is a one-off incident or part of a broader picture of violence – eg a display of harmful behaviour against one victim or numerous one-off incidents with multiple victims.

There is also a growing literature base surrounding the increase of other online gendered-based forms of crime, including upskirting, down-blousing,

---

[73] Professional Interview 1 (PDF): Independent Social Work Consultant.
[74] Young Person Interview (PhD): Female.
[75] See McGlynn et al (n 28).
[76] Professional Interview 10 (PhD): Statutory Sector.
[77] M Drouin et al, 'Sexting: A New, Digital Vehicle for Intimate Partner Aggression' (2015) 50 *Computers in Human Behaviour* 197.

sexual harassment and recording of sexual offences, including sexual assaults.[78] Consideration of these behaviours is important as harmful sexting practices can be part of a broader continuum of harmful sexual behaviour.[79] 'Upskirting' describes when someone takes a picture underneath's someone skirt without their consent, often in a public place. 'Down-blousing' is the taking of an image, non-consensually, down someone's top. Both are inherently gendered-based forms of abuse where women and girls are targeted, primarily by men. The Crown Prosecution Service has noted that approximately one third of perpetrators who commit 'upskirting' offences also commit other serious sexual offences, including sexual assault and alternative voyeurism offences.[80] While these offences were not discussed within the context of sexting, they are an important consideration due to the increased number of such offences being committed.

Indeed, identifying the more concerning elements of peer-based sexting behaviour was commented on by the professional interviewees. This is where the behaviour can 'become frightening. It becomes grooming.'[81] As noted previously in this chapter, the 'subtlety of language' that can have grooming or harmful undertones must be carefully considered. In addition, there may be a significant age gap between the parties; more than two years is typically outside what would be considered 'a similar age'. Yet, while two years would be the benchmark, as one professional in the criminal justice sector pointed out, what is understood as 'a similar age' must be a factor that is reviewed alongside a range of other considerations – there is a need to look 'at the context of it all'.[82] Another professional explains:

> That cut out off point of two years, to make it a call as to whether or not it's being abusive or not, isn't sufficient. We need to understand more about the relationship, and the attraction … and what was driving that.[83]

A certain amount of professional discretion is therefore required when dealing with young people and sexual behaviours, and assessing at times the subtler communications. Yet, as noted previously, with any type of discretion there can be an element of 'cloudiness'.[84] Guidance and training on how to identify these subtle interactions is therefore crucial.

---

[78] See McGlynn et al (n 28); R Lewis and S Anitha, 'Upskirting: A Systematic Literature Review' (2023) 24(3) *Trauma, Violence and Abuse* 1.

[79] See McGlynn et al (n 28).

[80] The Crown Prosecution Service, *Upskirting: Public Urged to Report Offenders as Prosecutions Double* (CPS, 3 December 2021) https://www.cps.gov.uk/cps/news/upskirting-public-urged-report-offenders-prosecutions-double, last accessed 17 July 2023.

[81] Professional Interview 19 (PhD): Criminal Justice Sector.

[82] ibid.

[83] Professional Interview 1 (PDF): Independent Social Work Consultant.

[84] Professional Interview 4 (PDF): Children's Charity.

Finally, placing peer-based sexting behaviours on a continuum underscores the need for a multi-disciplinary regulatory framework which considers the importance of responses beyond the legal landscape, including education programmes. This would provide opportunities to consider the range of potential risk factors at play, the varying settings in which abuse can take place and the agency of the young people involved. In doing so, a proper assessment can be made as to whether the young person is in need of low-level intervention or more specialist and targeted supports.[85] But this approach must be applied consistently. As one professional explains:

> A child or a young person engaging in some sort of sexting or sending images of themselves, on some occasions may result in this full assessment being carried out, and in others nothing occurring. So, there's not a uniformity in terms of how the statutory agencies, particularly in children's services, respond to that … probably what I would see is, those cases that do get referred to me further down the track, there are points earlier where interventions could have occurred that might have had an impact that may not have resulted in this young person being referred at a later point in time.[86]

The importance of appropriate and early intervention at suitable junctures was therefore strongly advocated for to prevent future adverse outcomes.

Related to the previous point, while there are a range of assessment tools, guides and a growing literature base in relation to young people and harmful sexual beahviours, deciding what assessments to engage and for how long was noted to be subjective. A professional interviewee explains: 'the problem can sometimes lie in who's making the call, because it's maybe based on their knowledge or understanding of the literature as to whether or not that young person requires something more or less'.[87] This narrative also relates to prevailing myths and stereotypes associated with certain types of sexual behaviours and a growing concern associated with digital sexual behaviours. A professional interviewee questions whether consideration has been given to shifting norms and ideas associated with youth sex and sexuality when identifying whether a behaviour is normal or more problematic:

> The difficulty is when we're talking about stereotypes and myths, it tends to be potentially my generation who's giving those stereotypes and myths, but those are stereotypes and myths based on, well, oh my God, in my day that wouldn't have happened.[88]

Attention should therefore be afforded to such myths and stereotypes when certain boundaries are being reinforced. Are interventions being activated from

---

[85] See J Henniker et al, 'An Inter-Agency Assessment Framework for Young People Who Sexually Abuse: Principles, Processes and Practicalities' (2002) 8(2) *Child Care in Practice* 114.
[86] Professional Interview 1 (PDF): Independent Social Work Consultant.
[87] ibid.
[88] Professional Interview 3 (PDF): Independent Social Work Consultant.

a child protection and welfare perspective, or a desire for a young person to conform to a particular 'ideal'?

In sum, using a continuum to document the behaviours being displayed by young people, as Kelly notes, 'the range of abuse, intimidation, coercion, intrusion, threat and force' can be better captured as well as recognising that there are no 'clearly defined and discrete analytic categories'.[89] In terms of young people and peer-based sexting, recognising the range of behaviours– from explorative to more harmful and abusive – is significant. Identifying the range and complexity of behaviours will not only help with managing and responding to the sexual behaviour but will also provide a more conducive setting for helping young people safely navigate their sexual identity and agency in a constantly increasing and evolving digital landscape. In addition, from a child protection perspective, as child sexual abuse and exploitation is a key issue of concern within law and policy, noting also the steady levels of peer engagement in sexual exploitation and other forms of harmful sexual behaviour,[90] properly identifying behaviours can ensure that appropriate interventions are activated early. This includes with peer-based sexting practices that possess coercive and exploitative dimensions.

IV. Conclusion

Proposing that peer-based sexting be considered as a continuum of sexual behaviour recognises the diversity of the behaviour being displayed and also its evolving nature. It has thus been argued that the complexity of sexting behaviours among young people can only be fully understood and responded to by acknowledging that the behaviour may be explorative, problematic or harmful, and one can easily become the other. A certain amount of professional discretion is therefore required when determining whether the behaviour has moved from explorative to problematic and/or harmful. This distinction in behaviour is essential if effective safeguarding measures are to be put in place for all parties involved.

In addition, the sexual pressures and gendered dynamics at play must be carefully considered when accessing a young person's behaviour. The diversity of pressures a young person can be exposed to can range from individual pressures that they can be subjected to within inter-personal relationships, to wider pressures that they can be exposed to on a daily basis within pop and youth cultures. A distinction therefore needs to be made between sexting behaviours that have become 'normalised' and are part of the digital landscape within which young people are now operating; and 'normalised' sexting behaviours within youth culture which are a direct result of persistent and prevalent problematic and conflicting socio-cultural messages surrounding sexual agency and identity,

[89] Kelly (n 26) 76.
[90] NSPCC, *Statistics Briefing: Harmful Sexual Behaviour* (NSPCC, 2021).

Empirical findings suggest that while peer-based sexting can be explorative and a digital form of sexual expression, it can also sit on the continuum of more problematic and harmful sexual behaviours. Recognising the wide range of experiences – and how easily the behaviour can shift from being explorative to being more harmful – will better reflect the reality for many young people who engage in or are exposed to sexting behaviours. It is also hoped that by placing sexting behaviours on a continuum, the importance of education and specifically gender-sensitive education programmes, will become apparent.[91]

With this in mind, the next chapter will explore the legislative and policy consequences to recognising sexting as part of a continuum of behaviour and outside a purely 'harmful' framework, noting in particular why criminal law is not an effective regulatory framework in this area.

---

[91] Discussed further in Chapter 8.

8

Cyberbullying and Sexting: Law and Policy

This chapter will address some of the core issues surrounding the current regulation of cyberbullying and sexting among young people. Progress in developing appropriate regulatory measures which acknowledge the complexity of online harmful behaviours has been extremely slow within the social and political realm. Contributing factors include, and discussed previously in this book, a reluctance to challenge the dominant schools of thought within the disciplines of childhood, youth sexuality and criminalisation. This chapter critically examines some of the challenges legal professionals and others face in an attempt to regulate the highly complex and evolving practices displayed between young people.

While bullying behaviours online will be discussed, greater attention will be afforded to the tensions surrounding peer-based sexting (with a focus on image-sharing), due to the complex nature of the behaviours displayed and the unique legal challenges the behaviour presents. As discussed in Chapter 7, correctly categorising online harmful behaviours, particularly the practice of sexting among young people, has caused significant academic debate. As Shariff notes, 'the first step to curbing the problem is to acknowledge it for what it is, which is much larger than any individual law or judicial system'.[1] Framing the behaviour solely as an infringement of criminal law does not consider the complexity of the sexual practice and therefore fails many of our young people in the process. One of the principal objectives of this chapter is therefore to test the boundaries and limitations of criminal law as an effective regulatory tool, using previous chapters as a backdrop to the analysis – in particular Chapters 6 and 7. In doing so, some international legal frameworks will also be examined as a comparative tool.

The chapter will end by advocating for a children's rights framework – one that accounts for the evolution of children's rights and the contexts in which such rights exist. Particular attention will be paid to some of the general principles laid down in the UN Convention on the Rights of the Child (UNCRC). As this chapter will illustrate, there is an increasing recognition of children as right holders and a need to ensure that the welfare of children is of paramount consideration and

---

[1] S Shariff, *Sexting and Cyberbullying: Defining the Line for Digitally Empowered Kids* (Cambridge University Press, 2015) 85.

at the heart of laws and policies which directly impact their lives. Yet, attempts to situate some of these rights within certain contexts present significant challenges. A notable socio-legal discomfort and reluctance to fully accept and incorporate the voices and agency of young people is examined. Emerging tensions within this area, particularly surrounding the legal landscape, will also be probed.

I. A Review of the Law: Limitations

Before discussing the regulatory frameworks that govern the behaviours under review, it is necessary to present an overview of the legal age limits. Although these age limits have been briefly alluded to already in the book, this section will provide a broader overview of the main issues and contextualise such debates within the setting of peer-based bullying and sexting behaviours.

A. Age Limits

As explained previously, the minimum age of criminal responsibility (MACR) is 10 years old in England, Wales and Northern Ireland. This is one of the lowest MACR in Europe, with other countries including France (13 years), Italy (14 years), Sweden (15 years) and Lithuania (16 years), all having age limits more in line with the recommendations laid down by the UNCRC. Indeed, the UNCRC has consistently noted that the MACR in England, Wales and Northern Ireland is not in accordance with international standards. In 2007, the UN Committee had previously asked State Parties not to set a MACR too low and encouraged State Parties to have a MACR of 12 years as the 'absolute minimum'.[2] The age was raised to 14 years in 2019[3] and this age was reiterated by the UN Committee in its most recent report, released in June 2023.[4] In fact the UN Committee has said that it is 'deeply concerned' when it comes to the administration of child justice within Great Britain and Northern Ireland, in particular, the 'draconian and punitive nature of its child justice system'.[5]

Engaging the law to criminalise children at 10 years of age for *any* offence has faced considerable opposition across many public and private sectors. By way of

---

[2] General Comment No 10 (2007) *Children's Rights in Juvenile Justice*, 25 April 2007, CRC/C/GC10 [32].

[3] General Comment No 24 (2019) *on Children's Rights in the Child Justice System*, 18 September 2017, CRC/C/GC/24 [22].

[4] Committee on the Rights of the Child, *Concluding Observations on the Combined Sixth and Seventh Reports of the United Kingdom of Great Britain and Northern Ireland*, 2 June 2023, CRC/C/GBR/CO/6–7 [54].

[5] ibid [53].

example, Carr questions the utility of legal mechanisms by probing the disparity in age limits when it comes to youth-regulated activities:

> We don't allow children of 10 to hold a driver's licence or get married or travel on a plane unaccompanied – we don't even allow them to be left at home alone. Yet we treat them as responsible enough for their own actions – and indeed as significantly *au fait* with the law – to face court if they commit a crime.[6]

In fact, the UN Committee rejected the proposition put forward that a MACR at 10 years was justified because 'children aged 10 can differentiate between bad behaviour and serious wrongdoing'.[7] Further, Include Youth, a leading charity in Northern Ireland, notes that other age limits – including the age when a child can vote (18 years) and the age when a child can leave school (16 years) – sit 'incongruously' alongside the MACR at 10 years.[8]

Other important age limits to consider in the context of sexting behaviours specifically are the age of sexual consent at 16 years, and the age at which a person can legally create and send a sexual image of themselves at 18 years. Some academic commentary exists which explores this disparity in age limits. Gillespie comments on the arbitrariness of certain age limits and the notable inconsistencies when it comes to understanding the level of 'risk' a young person may be exposed to:

> … can it really be said that photography is any more serious than exploitative intercourse? As to whether there are permanent risks, the same can be said for sexual intercourse. Yes, photographs have a degree of permanence, but so do pregnancy and sexually transmitted diseases.[9]

A professional within the criminal justice sector echoed these sentiments by noting that the differing age limits were 'ludicrous' and 'just [don't] make sense'.[10] Similarly, when the legal age limit was explained to the young people in the course of the fieldwork conducted for the present study, some were completely shocked: 'What? But I don't understand. I'm struggling to process,'[11] while other young people simply responded 'no'[12] when asked if sending a naked or semi-naked image under 18 years was a criminal offence. While some young people did understand the law and explained they had recently been taught about it in school, a significant proportion of the young people interviewed had a mistaken belief in full sexual autonomy and the freedom and capacity to consent to all sexual activities at 16 years.

---

[6] N Carr, 'Criminalising Ten-Year-Olds is No Way to Run a Justice System' (*The Conversation*, 20 February 2015).

[7] *Concluding Observations* (n 4) [53].

[8] Cited in E Purvis and P Rodgers, 'The Minimum Age of Criminal Responsibility in Northern Ireland' (Eurochild, 17 March 2023).

[9] AA Gillespie, 'Child Pornography' (2018) 27(1) *Information and Communications Technology Law* 33.

[10] Professional Interview 19 (PhD): Criminal Justice Sector.

[11] Young Person Interview (PhD): Male.

[12] Young Person Interview (PhD): Female.

An important question thus arises – why do these age limits exist? It has been argued that current legal responses to sexting among young people in many countries is 'an example of risk governance' that is centred on prevailing anxieties associated with child pornography and 'unregulated' sexuality in childhood.[13] A key tension has thus emerged in relation to fixed age limits, between adult regulations of youth sexual agency on the one hand and child protection and welfare on the other.

Yet, acknowledging young people's agency has been noted within the law, to a certain degree. For example, and discussed previously, although the age of sexual consent is 16 years, the law provides for a certain level of professional judgement and discretion if young people are in consenting relationships between the ages of 13 and 15 years. This means there is no statutory requirement for the police to report cases involving young people aged 13–15 years if there are no concerning features, including evidence of coercion or a lack of consent. Any case involving a young person under 13 years must be reported and the police discretion does not apply to such cases. The courts have recognised that when it comes to young people and sexual activity, a level of caution should be employed as the 'risk of stigmatising' a young person with a sexual offence, if the facts of the case suggest 'mutual sexual activity' and the parties are of a similar age, would not be in the public interest nor in the best interests of the young people involved.[14] Lord Hope notes that 'a heavy responsibility' lies on prosecutors to differentiate between cases which are exploitative and cases where prosecution could cause 'more harm than good'.[15] A careful balancing exercise is therefore required, that being between the welfare model on the one hand and the justice model on the other. As Forde explains, the youth justice system must 'seek to find a balance between the developmental needs of the child, the need to ensure accountability in order to protect victims and society, and to ensure that due process rights are adequately protected'.[16] The following section will now explore whether this balance has been adequately met within the context of bullying and sexting behaviours (with a focus on the latter).

B.   (Cyber)Bullying: The Law

While most contention arises within discourses on sexting among young people, conflicts still exist when legal frameworks are utilised in an attempt to control

---

[13] M Lee et al, '"Let's Get Sexting": Risk, Power, Sex and Criminalisation in the Moral Domain' (2013) 2(1) *International Journal for Crime and Justice* 44.

[14] *R v G* [2008] UKHL 37 [14].

[15] ibid.

[16] L Forde, 'Welfare, Justice and Diverse Models of Youth Justice: A Children's Rights Analysis' (2021) 29 *The International Journal of Children's Rights* 922. See also H Barnett, *Children's Rights and the Law: An Introduction* (Routledge, 2022).

and regulate peer-based cyberbullying behaviours. While there is no legal definition of 'bullying' under criminal law, a legal definition has been provided under
section 1 of the Addressing Bullying in Schools Act (Northern Ireland) 2016:

> the repeated use of (a) any verbal, written or electronic communication, (b) any other
> act, or (c) any combination of those by a pupil or a group of pupils against another pupil
> or group of pupils, with the intention of causing physical or emotional harm to that
> pupil or group of pupils.

Due to the common features of bullying behaviours and other behaviours that
are punishable by law, there are a number of criminal legislative provisions
which can be engaged. The Protection from Harassment (Northern Ireland)
Order 1997[17] and Malicious Communications (Northern Ireland) Order 1988[18]
are some legislative examples of how bullying behaviours can be regulated.
Interestingly, some of the young people described cyberbullying behaviours
as harassment: 'it counts as harassment'[19] and 'harassment online'.[20] In fact, a
'considerable overlap' between cyberbullying and online harassment has also
been raised within the literature.[21] For example, one of the key elements of a
harassment offence is that a person pursues 'a course of conduct'.[22] This has been
defined as meaning 'on at least two occasions',[23] thus linking to the repetitive
nature of the harm (similar to bullying behaviours).

Yet, the use of harassment laws within bullying contexts has raised a number
of challenges in practice. First, the difficulty in securing convictions was noted.
In order to receive a conviction for harassment (or indeed any offence), *all* the
elements of an offence must be satisfied, and this can often be difficult to prove
with online infractions between young people. The complication in collecting the
evidence needed to meet the legal threshold was noted by a forensic psychologist:
'where you're talking about young people and you're talking about offences …
they may have done a bit of this and a lot of that but not altogether what …
they need for the offences'.[24] Moreover, a professional from within the criminal justice sector explained that the legal response to online harmful behaviours
was 'woolly' and that the 'law needs to change'.[25] The challenges for professionals
were therefore twofold: (i) distinguishing the behaviours as criminal or not; and
(ii) deciding which legislative framework (if any) was most suitable in light of the
offence(s) committed. It is important to note here, though, that most professional

---

[17] SI 1997/1180 (NI 9).
[18] SI 1988/1849 (NI 18).
[19] Young Person Focus Group (PhD): Female.
[20] Young Person Focus Group (PhD): Female.
[21] J Wolak et al, 'Does Online Harassment Constitute Bullying? An Exploration of Online Harassment
by Known Peers and Online-Only Contacts' (2007) 41 *Journal of Adolescent Health* 52.
[22] Protection from Harassment (Northern Ireland) Order 1997, Art 3(1).
[23] ibid Art 2(3).
[24] Professional Interview 3 (PhD): Forensic Psychologist.
[25] Professional Interview 4 (PhD): Criminal Justice Sector.

interviewees felt that very few cases were directed to the police, as very often bullying behaviours were dealt with as a pastoral issue, mainly within schools.

Peer-on peer bullying behaviours displayed within a school setting raised a number of notable points – in particular, concerns associated with the extent and remit of regulatory powers given to staff to respond to online bullying behaviours. As explained in the introductory chapter, education is a devolved matter within Northern Ireland. The Addressing Bullying in Schools Act (Northern Ireland) 2016 (2016 Act), requires the Board of Governors in schools to ensure that a prevention policy is in place which explicitly deals with bullying behaviours alongside an effective reporting process. This policy should be reviewed and updated at appropriate intervals (at least every four years).[26] The Department of Education and the Education Authority recommend that 'restorative interventions' are engaged but consideration should be given to the nature, frequency, duration, and perception of the behaviour (from the person being bullied), when determining what type of intervention is most appropriate.[27]

Interventions have been categorised into four levels. Level 1 is a low-risk intervention and is often engaged with the pupils directly involved in the behaviour. Level 2 can include group-focused interventions, either large groups or whole classes (and both Level 1 and 2 interventions can work alongside each other). Level 3 addresses more complex bullying behaviours or group dynamics, perhaps due to the nature of the behaviours being displayed and frequency of occurrence. The designated teacher for child protection may need to be involved at this level (as well as other senior staff). Level 4 would be considered a high-risk intervention. This would include cases where there is deemed to be a significant threat to the wellbeing of one or more pupils. Partner agencies may need to be involved in these types of cases, including the Police Service of Northern Ireland, Education Authority and Child and Adolescent Mental Health Services, depending on the facts of the case.[28]

Yet, individual schools have a wide discretion regarding content and implementation of these policies. What types of interventions are engaged can depend on the schoolteacher tasked with overseeing the case and their level of knowledge of the behaviours being displayed. In addition, while the definition in section 1 of the 2016 Act incorporates the on- and offline elements of bullying, there are limitations. For example, section 2(1)(b) of the 2016 Act sets out the varying situations which place a duty on a school; these are primarily centred on the 'premises of the school during the school day'. Duties extend to include 'travelling to or from school', any situation where the school is in 'lawful control' of the pupil and any 'educational provision' which the school has arranged for the pupil off the school premises. In 2015, The Children's Law Centre and Save the Children

---

[26] Department of Education, *Effective Responses to Bullying Behaviours* (DoE, EA and NIABF, 2022).
[27] ibid 21.
[28] *Effective Responses to Bullying Behaviours* (n 26) 21–25.

Northern Ireland expressly noted concerns that the new legislation proposed (which became the 2016 Act) would not be 'wide enough to address incidents of cyber-bullying'.[29] Section 2(2) of the 2016 Act does seem to impose a discretionary power on schools. The Act states that when reviewing bullying behaviours, if the behaviours displayed are not defined in section 2(1)(b) but involve electronic communications and the behaviours are 'having a detrimental effect on the pupil's education at the school', the school 'may' take 'reasonable' measures to prevent the bullying behaviour. However, the legislative provision makes clear that a school's primary duty does not normally extend beyond the school gates. Further, while section 2(2) of the 2016 Act is a welcome addition, the discretion imposed on schools will inevitably result in a lack of consistency in approach and application.

Concerns were mentioned by professional interviewees about whether current frameworks were providing enough protections for young people:

> The majority of the time [incidents] happen outside of school. However, the impact is felt within the school and it's very difficult for schools to manage that because they don't have the legality, the legal hold to deal with it when it's outside of the school.[30]

> Maybe more assistance given to them [teachers] as to what to do. Because certainly in my dealings they're dealing with stuff that's happening outside school ... but it filters in.[31]

While an objective of the 2016 Act was to eliminate uncertainty among professionals within the education sector in relation to bullying, especially online bullying, and when it is appropriate to intervene, the anti-bullying legislation has failed to consider the complexity of bullying situations among young people. A significant gap and limitation of the legislation is the absence of a more robust provision in relation to the 'filtering' nature of bullying behaviours: bullying can begin online and then transfer into the offline school setting (or vice versa). The blurred boundaries that can exist between on- and offline bullying behaviours and the nature of the discretionary powers are creating confusion among professionals. This can lead to ambiguity and inconsistency in responses and the type and quality of interventions engaged.

C. Sexting: The Law

Sexting is not a specific offence under any piece of legislation and the practice of sharing naked content – including images – is not confined to young people.

---

[29] Northern Ireland NGO Alternative Report, *Submission to the United Nations Committee on the Rights of the Child for Consideration during the Committee's Examination of the United Kingdom of Great Britain and Northern Ireland Government Report* (Children's Law Centre and Save the Children, 2015) 34.

[30] Professional Interview 9 (PhD): Education Sector.

[31] Professional Interview 4 (PhD): Criminal Justice Sector.

Chapter 6 has already provided an analysis of the legislative provision governing indecent image legislation. This section expands on that analysis and explores some of the broader limitations of the law.

Research has explored the practice of sending naked images among adults, including as a form of 'revenge pornography'.[32] Noted previously in Chapter 6, in response to heightened calls for reform in this area a new offence was introduced, 'Disclosing private sexual photographs and films with intent to cause distress'. This offence is codified under section 33 of the Criminal Justice and Courts Act 2015 and section 51 of the Justice Act (Northern Ireland) 2016 respectively. While legislative reform has now categorised 'revenge porn' as an offence, McGlynn et al critiqued the legislation, assessing it as 'piecemeal' and 'largely ad hoc',[33] while Oriola explains that the legislative provisions are 'inherently weak'.[34] A key and important point is that the laws governing the sending of images of young people under 18 years is a much more draconian piece of legislation. The act of either creating/possessing/sending and/or receiving a naked image of a child – ie someone under 18 years of age – automatically falls under the criminal offence of 'indecent photographs of children'. The offence is codified under Article 3 of The Protection of Children (Northern Ireland) Order 1978[35] (as amended by Article 42 of The Sexual Offences (Northern Ireland) Order 2008).[36] Yet, applying this piece of legislation to peer-based sexting has been described as a 'disproportionate' response.[37]

Several concerns associated with the legislative provisions were raised by a number of professional interviewees. A professional working in the criminal justice sector commented on the social labelling that is attached to this particular sexual offence: 'it's all people see it as, paedophilia – you're a paedophile'.[38] A professional working in the education sector also explained that while you want young people 'to recognise the consequences' of their actions, you do not want them to be 'defined' by behaviour they engaged in when they were a child.[39] Concerns regarding over-criminalisation of young people, with what is a particularly stigmatising offence, have thus been raised. As a number of professionals

---

[32] See C McGlynn and E Rackley, 'Image-Based Sexual Violence' (2017) 37(3) *Oxford Journal of Legal Studies* 534.

[33] C McGlynn et al, 'Beyond "Revenge Porn": The Continuum of Image Based Sexual Abuse' (2017) 25(1) *Feminist Legal Studies* 25, 26.

[34] T Oriola, 'Criminalising Revenge Pornography in Northern Ireland: Laws and Lessons from England and Wales and Other Common Law Jurisdictions', Knowledge Exchange Seminar 2017–18 (Northern Ireland Assembly, 2018) 6.

[35] Within England the offence of sending naked images is found under the Protection of Children Act 1978, s 1 (as amended by the Sexual Offences Act 2003, s 45).

[36] Both Art 43 of the Sexual Offences (Northern Ireland) Order 2008 and s 45 of the Sexual Offences Act 2003 raised the age from 16 years to 18 years under the definition of 'children'.

[37] AA Gillespie, 'Adolescents, Sexting and Human Rights' (2013) 13(4) *Human Rights Law Review* 643.

[38] Professional Interview 19 (PhD): Criminal Justice Sector.

[39] Professional Interview 20 (PhD): Education Sector.

explain, 'it sticks with them for life'[40] and 'the stigma of a sexual offence on your record even as a caution, the lifelong consequences of that is really severe'.[41] Indeed, many professionals described the current legislation as being not fit for purpose, as the legislation was originally designed to capture 'a predator who is an adult'.[42] It is evident that the sharing of naked or semi-naked images among young people has 'outstripped the law'[43] with one professional noting, 'as technology advances the law seems to have to catch up, which is a real problem'.[44]

An essential question must be asked and one which was alluded to in Chapter 6: should indecent image legislation – which was designed to prosecute adults who sexually exploit children – *ever* be used when responding to peer-based sexting? In this regard, three main issues of concern can be noted. First, peers engaging in the behaviour with other peers possess different motivations to adults who engage in the sexual behaviour (see Chapter 5 for a more nuanced understanding of the peer-on-peer context – ranging from exploration to more coercive settings). Second, the power differentials between the parties involved are markedly different – ie between two peers or between an adult and a child – particularly in terms of age and stage of development. Third, and interrelated to the previous point, the types and levels of interventions required are different due to power dynamics, for example.[45] Using this particular piece of legislation to criminalise young people who share images therefore seems completely out of line with the intention behind the construction of the legislation.

In relation to the young people, there was a recognition that sending 'sexts' could lead to serious consequences and a potential criminal record. However, there was some confusion around what actual 'offence' sending naked or semi-naked images was categorised under. Some young people thought that within certain contexts it would amount to 'sexual harassment'[46] while others understood that it was a 'child pornography' offence.[47] When questioned on whether legal mechanisms were appropriate in responding to the sending of naked and/or semi-naked images between young people, the young people focused on contextual factors:

> It depends on the circumstances because if it is someone they know and it's like their girlfriend or something like that then I don't see the problem with that. Then obviously the age, I definitely see there's a problem if the age gap between them. And then if the

---

[40] Professional Interview 1 (PDF): Independent Social Work Consultant.
[41] Professional Interview 4 (PDF): Children's Charity.
[42] Professional Interview 1 (PhD): Education Sector.
[43] R Richards and C Calvert, 'When Sex and Cell Phones Collide: Inside the Prosecution of a Teen Sexting Case' (2009) 32(1) *Hastings Communications and Entertainment Law Journal* 3.
[44] Professional Interview 2 (PDF): Sexual Health Charity.
[45] See eg A-M McAlinden, *The Shaming of Sexual Offenders: Risk, Retribution and Reintegration* (Bloomsbury, 2007).
[46] Young Person Focus Group (PhD): Female.
[47] Young Person Focus Group (PhD): Female.

person breaks up and puts it up then yes, they should ... but if you know that's not going to happen then I don't see the point.[48]

It depends on the severity of the situation. If they're being used for, for not right ends ... then yeah by all means.[49]

Some young people believed there was a need for targeted responses if there was a significant age gap or if the pictures were posted out of revenge. However, it was agreed among most youth participants that to criminalise young people who send images within relationships was futile – emphasising the normative nature of the practice.

Indeed, the apparent normative nature of peer-based sexting within youth culture and notable concerns surrounding the over-criminalisation of young people echoed throughout primary research findings. For example, one of the young people said, 'it's not as easy to catch people sexting. It's easy to catch a murderer, well not easy but you know what I mean ... you wouldn't know if someone has sexted.'[50] Some of the professional participants also explained:

That would be like rounding up the entire young population and putting them in jail, you know, because they are all doing it.[51]

The whole sexting thing I think you could end up criminalising half the population.[52]

This analysis is supported by Lunceford, who comments on how utilising criminal law in sexting cases among young people is risky and could result in 'creating an entire generation' of young people being labelled as 'sex offenders'.[53] In other words, using criminal law in an attempt to regulate youth sexual behaviour will not address the underlying social and cultural issues at play when young people engage in sexting.

Peer-based sexting has been described as a contemporary 'teenage risk-taking activity'.[54] In support, several young people interviewed commented on the desire within some teenagers to 'rebel' and challenge boundaries placed on them. For example, 'I use it [sending naked images] as a method to rebel and to say I don't obey the rules. So, I do what I want.'[55] Professional interviewees also commented on the risk-taking dimension to the behaviour:

They see it as something that's, you know, 'risky', but in a safe way as far as they're concerned ... the more 'risky' it is the more adventure it can be, the more they feel they can do it and it's just cameraderie. This idea that a sub-culture has been created ... and to be part of it is more important than the consequences that might happen ... the

---

[48] Young Person Interview (PhD): Male.
[49] Young Person Interview (PhD): Female.
[50] Young Person Interview (PhD): Male.
[51] Professional Interview 16 (PhD): Independent Researcher on Harmful Sexual Behaviours.
[52] Professional Interview 7 (PhD): Children's Voluntary Organisation.
[53] B Lunceford, 'Sex in the Digital Age: Media Ecology and Megan's Law' (2010) 9(4) *Explorations in Media Ecology* 239, 241.
[54] Lee et al (n 13).
[55] Young Person Focus Group (PhD): Male.

risk-taking reward they get from being part of sub-culture it's much more rewarding than the risk-taking consequences. They just feel that the risk is worth it.[56]

As you emerge into adolescence ... the concept of what is appropriate or inappropriate sexual behaviour can be quite fluid depending on the circumstances. But also it is part and parcel of a young person's development ... young people by their very nature have to be and should be risk-takers.[57]

It is well documented within the field of psychology that adolescents are more likely to engage in risk-taking behaviours than any other age group. Hackett et al also explain that 'children and young people are developmentally different to adults and should be responded to as such'.[58] Despite recognition that children *can* and *do* engage 'in various forms of sex-related play',[59] the online dimension attached to sexting behaviours intensifies the perceived threat to the romantic view of the child.[60] In the words of Lunceford, we are 'too invested'[61] in the traditional notion of adolescent sexual innocence and it is not a true reflection of childhood or adolescence. Failing to fully recognise the diversity of peer-based sexual practices can therefore lead to quite invasive regulatory measures being engaged, even where there is no evidence of exploitation or coercion. This is powerfully illustrated in the legislative provisions that can be engaged when young people engage in peer-based sexting. It thus begs the question, has Youth Justice received the correct balance between recognising the developmental needs of the child and ensuring accountability and due process rights are protected? Drawing on empirical findings, it would appear not.

Yet, as more evidence is gathered surrounding this type of sexual behaviour and professionals' and scholars' understanding of the behaviour develops, measures have been put in place to try and limit the unnecessary criminalisation of young people.

II. Sexting and Current Responses: A Brief Analysis

A. Outcome 21

In 2016 the Home Office introduced 'Outcome 21'[62] as a more balanced and formalised response to peer-related sexting behaviours in England and Wales.

---

[56] Professional Interview 20 (PhD): Education Sector.
[57] Professional Interview 10 (PhD): Statutory Sector.
[58] S Hackett et al, 'Harmful Sexual Behaviour Framework: An Evidence-Informed Operational Framework for Children and Young People Displaying Harmful Sexual Behaviours' Project Report (London, NSPCC, 2016) 22.
[59] B Simpson, 'Challenging Childhood: Challenging Children: Children's Rights and Sexting' (2013) 16(5/6) *Sexualities* 691.
[60] See also Chapters 3 and 5.
[61] Lunceford (n 53) 242.
[62] Currently only rolled out in England and Wales.

At the centre of this initiative is the public interest test – is it in the public interest to prosecute? Outcome 21 states:

> Further investigation, resulting from the crime report, which could provide evidence sufficient to support formal action being taken against the suspect is not in the public interest – police decision.[63]

Context is therefore key and the College of Policing in its briefing report stressed that responses to peer-based sexting behaviours should be 'proportionate and necessary'.[64] Case law has also referred to Outcome 21 providing some clarity in terms of its relevance to youth produced sexual imagery cases. For example, in *R (on the application of CL) v The Chief Constable of Greater Manchester Police*, Lord Justice Hickinbottom specifically referenced the National Crime Recording Standard in his judgment, highlighting important sections, including:

> Outcome 21 may be considered the most appropriate resolution in youth produced sexual imagery cases where the making and sharing is considered non-abusive and there is **no evidence** of exploitation, grooming, profit motive, malicious intent (e.g. extensive or inappropriate sharing (e.g. uploading onto a pornographic website) or it being persistent behaviour. Where these factors are present, Outcome 21 would not apply.[65]

This case also noted that the collection and retention of data relating to sexting among young people (that being a minor under law) did not contravene a person's rights under Article 8 of the European Convention of Human Rights (ECHR).[66] The retention of the data in this case was permitted under Article 8(2) for the prevention of crime and protection of others and was therefore in accordance with the law.[67] When looking at the public interest test, it was emphasised that a balancing exercise was required: consideration of the best interests of the claimant (a minor) but also the interests of the other parties involved (also minors) and any 'potential victims of other and further sexting incidents'.[68] The outcome of this case is significant. As previously noted, concerns have been raised regarding a child's criminal record and future enhanced disclosure and barring service (DBS) checks, particularly in relation to peer-based sexting. It has been noted that 'it is possible' for a child who is processed under Outcome 21 to have

---

[63] GD8, 'Youth Produced Sexual Imagery – Guidance for Disclosure' (2016) https://assets.publishing.service.gov.uk/government/uploads/system/uploads/attachment_data/file/578979/GD8_-_Sexting_Guidance.pdf, last accessed 17 July 2023.

[64] College of Policing, *Briefing Note: Police Action in Response to Youth Produced Sexual Imagery* ('Sexting'), Version 1.0 (November 2016) 2.

[65] *R (on the application of CL) v The Chief Constable of Greater Manchester Police* [2018] EWHC 3333 (Admin), 2018 WL 06355511 [24].

[66] ibid [99].

[67] ibid [106].

[68] ibid [112].

this information disclosed under a DBS check (specifically an enhanced criminal records check).[69]

It is also important to note that, at the time of writing this book, Outcome 21 currently does not apply in Northern Ireland. The Northern Irish Public Prosecution Service has issued guidance for prosecutors noting that 'all relevant public interest considerations' must be taken into account before making a prosecutorial decision.[70] The following factors will be particularly important: the age of the parties; the type of relationship the parties shared; the number of images and the nature of such images; and whether consent was present. In Northern Ireland, while the police have discretion to divert cases away from the Public Prosecution Service if it is not in the 'public interest' to pursue them, not having such protections enshrined in law places young people at risk of slipping through the net and/or being criminalised for behaviour when they should not be. Further, Outcome 21 in England and Wales does provide *some* reassurances for young people by providing a more formalised process. This places young people in Northern Ireland at a disadvantage when compared to their peers in England and Wales. This is concerning, given what professionals have noted regarding the inconsistency in approach of some police officers: 'how it's applied and the discretion and that's a bit of a postcode lottery'.[71]

It should be noted that a pilot scheme has been running in Northern Ireland since 2019, the Sexting Referral Scheme. While the scheme was initially only rolled out across three police districts, as of 2020 it is now in place across all of Northern Ireland. The Youth Justice Agency and the Police Service of Northern Ireland have been working together to refer to an awareness and education programme children who have been involved in 'minor' sexting offences.[72] While little information is available to date, it is said that 'minor' cases involve young people who would 'benefit from education rather than a formal justice disposal'.[73] Youth Justice Northern Ireland also reports that in the year 2021–22, 167 sexting awareness programmes were delivered to children alongside their parents/guardians.[74] Further, 98.8 per cent of children said that attending the programmes would minimise the chances of 'further offending'.[75] It will be interesting to see how this

---

[69] *Sharing Nudes and Semi-Nudes: Advice for Education Settings Working with Children and Young People* (UK Council for Internet Safety, 2020) 15.

[70] Public Prosecution Service, *Guidelines for the Prosecution of Young People* (Public Prosecution Service for Northern Ireland, 2021) 29.

[71] Professional Interview 4 (PDF): Children's Charity.

[72] Northern Ireland Audit Office, *Managing Children Who Offend – Report* https://www.niauditoffice.gov.uk/publications/html-document/managing-children-who-offend-report, last accessed 17 July 2023.

[73] Police Service of Northern Ireland, *Chief Constable's End of Year Report to the Northern Ireland Policing Board 2021–2022* (Police Service of Northern Ireland Strategic Communications and Engagement Department, 2022) 55.

[74] T Brown, *Northern Ireland Youth Justice Agency Annual Workload Statistics 2021/22* (Northern Ireland Statistics and Research Agency, 2022) 26.

[75] ibid.

scheme evolves over time and how the referral scheme accounts for the highly complex behaviours children are presenting with.

Concerns about young people engaging in harmful behaviours, in particular peer-on-peer sexting behaviours, is not unique to this jurisdiction. Legal landscapes internationally are also trying to address and manage these complex youth behaviours.

B. International Responses: A Comparison

Indecent image legislation exists internationally and has been activated for peer-based sexting cases, in the absence of an alternative response. In North Carolina (US) for example, it is an offence to create, share or receive a sexually explicit photo of any person under the age of 18 years.[76] These laws can be used to charge and prosecute teenagers who engage in sexting behaviours and have stirred similar debates surrounding the appropriateness of utilising such draconian and stigmatising legislative frameworks.[77] Indeed, a case that received considerable publicity involved two 16-year-old teenagers who were in a relationship and who had consensually and voluntarily sent naked images to each other. The images were only shared with each other (the two parties) and no-one else. Yet, both teenagers were charged for sending sexually explicit photos under North Carolina laws.[78] Many legal scholars and practitioners condemned the treatment of the two young teenagers, arguing that the response was 'ludicrous' and that the case illustrates 'an utter failure to understand the nature of sexual exploitation'.[79] This case thus raises similar questions surrounding getting the correct balance between protecting the welfare of the young people involved, recognising the developmental needs of the young people, accountability and due process.

Other States in America have introduced laws which are specifically drafted and designed to respond to peer-based forms of sexting behaviours. Civil law has been activated as an alternative response to sexting behaviours among young people in Colorado, US. Peer-based sexting can therefore trigger civil rather than criminal proceedings. This essentially gives prosecutors an alternative response route – depending on the individual details of the case. If the facts suggest that the sending of the images was consensual then a civil suit is likely to be sought which

---

[76] NC Gen Stat §§ 14-190.13–14-190.17A.

[77] K O'Connor et al, 'Sexting Legislation in the United States and Abroad: A Call for Uniformity' (2017) 11(2) *International Journal of Cyber Criminology* 219.

[78] ibid 219.

[79] ME Miller, 'NC Just Prosecuted a Teenage Couple for Making Child Porn – of Themselves' (*The Washington Post*, 21 September 2015) https://www.washingtonpost.com/news/morning-mix/wp/2015/09/21/n-c-just-prosecuted-a-teenage-couple-for-making-child-porn-of-themselves/, last accessed 17 July 2023.

can involve the young person having to attend an education programme and/or pay a small fine (approximately $50).[80] Another alternative response framework was introduced in Rhode Island where peer-based sexting is dealt with within the family court and the young person therefore avoids a criminal record and potentially being placed on the sex offender register (which can be a direct consequence of a sexual offence conviction in the criminal court).[81]

A 'similar age defence' for certain consensual sexual activity between peers (including sexual intercourse and sexual touching) has also been introduced by other international jurisdictions, including New South Wales (NSW), Australia. The defence was created in response to the findings from the Royal Commission into Institutional Responses to Child Sexual abuse. This defence was one of a range of laws introduced to better protect children and young people from child sexual abuse and exploitation. The defence is *not* available if one of the parties is under 14 years of age or if there is an age difference of more than two years.[82] While the police in Northern Ireland have a similar discretion (noted above), it is not explicitly noted in law and therefore there can be ambiguities in responses and treatment of young people in these types of cases.

Similar 'defences' or 'exceptions' have also been applied to peer-based sexting behaviours in NSW. A 'limited sexting defence' to peer-based sexting has been introduced.[83] An exception was added to section 91H of the Crimes Act 1900 which outlines the offence to 'produce, disseminate, possess child abuse material'. The key elements of the defence/exception include: (i) that the parties were under 18 years; and (ii) that a reasonable person would consider the possession of the image as acceptable. Factors taken into consideration when determining what 'a reasonable person' would regard as 'acceptable' include: the nature and content of the material; circumstances of production and possession; age, vulnerability and circumstances of the child depicted in the image; the defendant's age, vulnerability and circumstances; and the relationship between the parties.[84] It was said that the new defences/exceptions were introduced to 'reflect current understanding about normal sexual development and experimentation amongst teenagers'.[85]

---

[80] A Bryant, 'Minors Sexting in Colorado: What Does the Law Say?' (The Law Office of Andrew Bryant, 7 July 2021) https://andrewbryantlaw.com/2021/06/05/minors-sexting-in-colorado-what-does-the-law-say/, last accessed 17 July 2023; see also B Bayliss, 'The Kids Are Alright: Teen Sexting, Child Pornography Charges, and the Criminalization of Adolescent Sexuality' (2020) 91(1) *University of Colorado Law Review* 251.

[81] Cyberbullying Research Center, 'Sexting Laws in Rhode Island' https://cyberbullying.org/sexting-laws/rhode-island#:-:text=In%20Rhode%20Island%2C%20a%20minor,of%20the%20sex%20offender%20registry, last accessed 17 July 2023.

[82] Crimes Act 1900, s 80AG.

[83] See M Speakman, 'Landmark Child Sexual Abuse Laws in Force' (NSW Government, 1 December 2018) https://www.justice.nsw.gov.au/Documents/Media%20Releases/2018/landmark-child-sexual-abuse-laws-in-force.pdf, last accessed 17 July 2023.

[84] Crimes Act 1900, s 91HAA.

[85] *New Legislation to Strengthen Child Sexual Abuse Laws: Factsheet for Service Providers* (NSW Government, 2018).

It is clear that Criminal Justice Systems globally are struggling to grabble with the complexity of peer-based sexting behaviours. Legislators are having to play catch-up and attempts to reform laws are often failing to capture the variety of behaviours young people are presenting with alongside the shifting 'norms' within youth culture. While some international jurisdictions are attempting to minimise the unnecessary criminalisation of young people by introducing exceptions into law, there are still significant limitations. For example, as noted in Chapter 7, the breadth of behaviours young people are engaging in alongside the range of motivations displayed, means the behaviours cannot be easily categorised into 'legal' and 'illegal' behaviour. Legislation will only capture a certain group of sexting behaviours – those which neatly fit and meet the criteria noted in law. Further, and importantly, a key concern is that current reforms in law and policy are *still* using legislation which was designed to prosecute adult perpetrators of child exploitation and abuse.

Reflecting on the above analysis, it appears that current failures within regulatory frameworks are due to a primary focus on legal sanctions as the primary solution to peer-based sexting behaviours. Having considered the significant limitations of this approach, it is suggested that we must look beyond the confinement of criminal law. Engaging a rights-based approach, one which places children's rights at the centre of responses, is proposed. Placing peer-based sexting (and bullying) behaviours within a children's rights framework could help construct a more effective response: one which focuses on education and a public health approach, rather than criminalisation. Such an approach would align with the UNCRC recommendations which make clear that early intervention is preferred and that countries should 'actively promote' the use of non-judicial measures.[86]

III. Young People and a Children's Rights Framework

While the recognition of children's rights, in some form, can be dated back to the nineteenth century, primary focus still very much remained on parental rights during this time and institutions were reluctant to interfere in family life.[87] It was not until 1924 that the first Declaration of the Rights of the Child or Geneva Declaration was adopted. The main focus of the declaration was on 'normal development' (materially and spiritually), nurturing the child (the child that is hungry must be fed), providing relief (in times of distress) and protection

---

[86] Committee on the Rights of the Child (2023) *Concluding Observations on the Combined Sixth and Seventh Reports of the United Kingdom of Great Britain and Northern Ireland*, 2 June 2023, CRC/C/GBR/CO/6-7.

[87] See Barnett (n 16) Chapter 2.

(from exploitation).[88] In 1959 the Declaration of the Rights of the Child was modernised. Ten key principles were endorsed, including the right to be protected against all forms of neglect, cruelty and exploitation, the right to a name and the right to free and compulsory education.[89] Principle 2 specifically endorsed that the 'the best interests of the child should be the paramount consideration' – a principle that has continued to be the focus of many legal frameworks.

The most substantial children's rights framework (and the most ratified international treaty in history), did not come until 1989 in the form of the UNCRC. The Convention, which includes 54 articles, provides a range of protections which address the social, cultural, political and economic rights of the child. A notable distinction between the 1989 UNCRC and previous children's rights frameworks was the introduction of participatory rights which moved children from 'passive objects of concern to subjects with their own interests, priorities and rights'.[90] It is important to note also that, although the UK has ratified the Convention (in 1991), it is not part of domestic law. This means that unless an Act of Parliament is passed, the rights enshrined are not legally enforceable within domestic courts and courts *can* and *have* made decisions which are incompatible with the UNCRC.[91] Yet, State Parties *are* required to submit reports regularly on how they are implementing the rights enshrined under the UNCRC and there is a Committee on the Rights of the Child (the Committee) which carefully monitors State Parties obligations under the Convention. There are also legal examples where the UNCRC has been cited and engaged within court judgments, primarily within family court settings.[92] It is also important to note that while the UNCRC is not legally enforceable in domestic courts within the UK, rights enshrined under the ECHR *are* – via the Human Rights Act 1998 (HRA 1998). The rights outlined in the HRA 1998 apply to both children and adults and so provide a level of protection for children also. However, a key distinction is that the rights enshrined under the UNCRC are more wide-ranging, child-specific and focus on the unique vulnerabilities of children.

Children's rights are constantly evolving, and recognition of such rights has gained momentum over recent years. For example, in a ground-breaking move, in March 2021 the Scottish Parliament (a devolved nation within the UK, similar to Northern Ireland) unanimously passed the United Nations Convention on the Rights of the Child (Incorporation) (Scotland) Bill (the Scottish Bill). The Scottish Bill would incorporate the UNCRC into domestic law, making the rights legally

---

[88] Geneva Declaration of the Rights of the Child, adopted 26 September 1924, League of Nations.

[89] UN Declaration on the Rights of the Child (1959), proclaimed by General Assembly Resolution 1386(XIV) of 20 November 1959.

[90] A Cole-Albäck, A Brief History of Children's Rights' https://www.birthto5matters.org.uk/wp-content/uploads/2021/04/Childrens-rights-for-Birth-to-Five-Matters.pdf, last accessed 17 July 2023, 2.

[91] Barnett (n 16).

[92] See S Gilmore, 'Use of the UNCRC in Family Law Cases in England and Wales' (2017) 25 *The International Journal of Children's Rights* 500.

enforceable in court.[93] However, the Scottish Bill was challenged by the UK Government in the Supreme Court. It was held that certain parts of the Scottish Bill were outside the limits of the Scottish Parliament's legislative competence.[94] In May 2022 the Deputy First Minister said, following the Supreme Court decision, they were taking actions to amend the Bill.[95] Beyond this, there have also been pockets of activism within Northern Ireland to ensure the rights of children are upheld. There have been numerous campaigns to try and raise the MACR so it is more in line with international standards, with a public consultation on the MACR being called by the Justice Minister in October 2022.[96] Some 87 per cent of respondents supported raising the MACR from 10 to 14 years, which marks a desire to shift the focus from within the youth justice system to one which concerns itself with rehabilitation.[97]

Yet, with the constant advancement of technology and a lot of anxiety surrounding certain online dimensions, such as a young person's 'digital footprint',[98] a number of challenges have emerged, most specifically ensuring that young people are protected from exploitative online harms on the one hand, and ensuring children's autonomy and right to expression is not being compromised on the other. This tension is most heightened within the context of peer-based sexting behaviours.

A. Sexting and Children's Rights

As noted throughout the book, sexting as a form of sexual behaviour that young people are engaging in ranges from an act of flirtation and a form of sexual expression to more concerning scenarios, including pressurised and coercive settings.[99]

---

[93] Scottish Government, 'United Nations Convention on the Rights of the Child Implementation: Introductory Guidance' (19 November 2021) https://www.gov.scot/publications/implementing-united-nations-convention-rights-child-introductory-guidance/pages/5/, last accessed 17 July 2023.

[94] REFERENCE by the Attorney General and the Advocate General for Scotland – United Nations Convention on the Rights of the Child (Incorporation) (Scotland) Bill REFERENCE by the Attorney General and the Advocate General for Scotland – European Charter of Local Self Government (Incorporation) (Scotland) Bill [2021] UKSC 42.

[95] Together (Scottish Alliance for Children's Rights), 'Deputy First Minister Gives Update on UNCRC Incorporation' (24 May 2022) https://togetherscotland.blog/2022/05/24/deputy-first-minister-gives-update-on-uncrc-incorporation/, last accessed 17 July 2023.

[96] See Department of Justice, 'Long Launches Public Consultation on the Minimum Age of Criminal Responsibility' (NI Direct, Department of Justice, 3 October 2022).

[97] J O'Neill, '"Strong Support" for Raising the NI Minimum Age of Criminal Responsibility, Consultation Finds' (BBC, 2 June 2023).

[98] GS O'Keeffe and K Clarke-Pearson, 'The Impact of Social Media on Children, Adolescents, and Families' (2011) 127(4) *Pediatrics* 802.

[99] See J Ringrose et al, *A Qualitative Study of Children, Young People and 'Sexting': A Report Prepared for the NSPCC* (NSPCC/LSE, 2012); E Agnew, 'Sexting among Young People: Towards a Gender Sensitive Approach' (2021) 29(1) *International Journal of Children's Rights* 3; M Lee and T Crofts, 'Gender, Pressure, Coercion and Pleasure: Untangling Motivations for Sexting between Young People' (2015) 55(3) *British Journal of Criminology* 454.

Given the diverse range of motivations and contexts in which the behaviour is being displayed, two key questions arise. First, what is the most appropriate way to conceptualise peer-based sexting? Illustrated in Chapter 7, given the diversification of sexual behaviours, it has been argued that the behaviour should be viewed as part of a continuum of sexual behaviour. This would account for the sexual behaviour being displayed consensually between peers but also recognise the varied pressures young people can be subjected to alongside the more coercive and exploitative dimensions that can be presented. In this regard, a graduated response would be advocated for. Second, when it comes to appropriate and effective responses, what children's rights should be considered? It is this second question which will be examined now.

B. United Nations Convention on the Rights of the Child

Noted previously, the UNCRC is the most comprehensive international children's rights instrument to date. The UN Committee on the Rights of the Child expressly notes that Northern Ireland (and England) take measures to 'promote a positive image of children as right-holders'.[100] In fact, the most recent report released by the Committee, as noted by Fergal McFerran (Policy and Public Affairs Manager at the Children's Law Centre in Northern Ireland), reflects a 'grim picture' and how the 'gap in children's rights has grown significantly over the last decade'.[101] Therefore, consideration and implementation of rights enshrined within the UNCRC is crucial. There are several articles which could be unpacked, but for the purposes of this book, the author has picked two key articles for consideration below: Articles 12 and 13 UNCRC.

i. Article 12 UNCRC

> States Parties shall assure to the child who is capable of forming his or her own views the right to express those views freely in all matters affecting the child, the views of the child being given due weight in accordance with the age and maturity of the child.

This article refers to a child's participatory rights and, while no definition of 'participation' was originally provided, the UN Committee on the Rights of the Child has since elaborated on what 'participation' means within a children's rights framework. It is a term which has 'evolved' but would include 'ongoing processes, which include information-sharing and dialogue between children and adults based on mutual respect'.[102] The Committee also explains that participation involves children learning how their views and the views of others have helped

---

[100] *Concluding Observations* (n 4).

[101] F McFerran, 'UN Concluding Observations Demonstrate Scale of Failure to Meet Children's Rights Requirements' (Children's Law Centre, 2023).

[102] General Comment No 12 (2009) *The Right of the Child to be Heard*, 1 July 2009, CRC/C/GC/12.

shape certain outcomes. When it comes to bullying, and in particular peer-based sexting behaviours, little has been done to try and incorporate the voices of young people into initiatives that directly impact their lives. In fact, the voices of young people are often missing from any stage of the decision-making process. In broader terms, children are often given 'tokenistic opportunities' to have their voices heard within all areas that impact their lives, including education, health and youth justice.[103]

Article 12 has been labelled by some scholars as the 'most important provision in the Convention'.[104] Yet, it was also an extremely controversial addition with some parts of the world – including the United States – concerned that it would 'annihilate' and 'threaten' parental rights.[105] Further, given that children's participatory rights are often dictated by 'complex environments and multifaceted social identities', applying this article in practice often presents a number of significant challenges.[106] In addition, and at the heart of a lot of the UNCRC rights, is a recognition of a child's developing capacity: 'due weight in accordance with the age and maturity of the child'. Yet, it is an approach which is 'fraught with difficulty'[107] and often dictated by adults.[108]

With these tensions in mind, Lundy proposed four key factors that should be considered if Article 12 is to be successfully implemented: space; voice; audience; and influence.[109] In very simplistic terms, Lundy's model recognises the importance of listening to a representative and diverse group of young people (including those marginalised), and proactively incorporating the views of those young people into initiatives that impact the lives of young people. Using Lundy's model, the young people should be given the space to be involved in the decision-making process. The right to have their voices heard and listened to by an audience who is *actively* listening and will apply 'due weight' to the views expressed. Within the wider context of the decision-making process, Lundy also notes a number of other important rights including Article 3 (best interests of the child) and Article 5 (guidance from adults).

ii. Article 13 UNCRC

> The child shall have the right to freedom of expression; this right shall include freedom
> to seek, receive and impart information and ideas of all kinds, regardless of frontiers,

---

[103] L Lundy, '"Voice" is Not Enough: Conceptualising Article 12 of the United Nations Convention on the Rights of the Child' (2007) 33(6) *British Educational Research Journal* 927, 929.

[104] M Freeman, 'The Future of Children's Rights' (2000) 14 *Children & Society* 288.

[105] S Kilbourne, 'The Wayward Americans – Why the USA Has Not Ratified the UN Convention on the Rights of the Child' (1998) 10(3) *Child and Family Law Quarterly* 243, 244.

[106] P Cuevas-Parra, 'Multi-Dimensional Lens to Article 12 of the UNCRC: A Model to Enhance Children's Participation' (2023) 21(3) *Children's Geographies* 363.

[107] Freeman (n 104) 289.

[108] Lundy (n 103).

[109] ibid.

either orally, in writing or in print, in the form of art, or through any other media of the child's choice.

If consensual sexting is to be considered part of the broader remit of sexually explorative behaviours that young people are engaging in, with some young people viewing the behaviour as 'exciting'[110] and 'flirtatious',[111] questions arise as to whether activating criminal sanctions to regulate the behaviours contravenes Article 13. Yet, as noted in the previous chapter, sexting behaviours can possess problematic and more concerning features; in these cases, appropriate interventions would be necessary. There is also the need to assess whether the behaviour is considered to be appropriate for the child's age and stage of development,[112] noting also that, when determining what is appropriate, due consideration needs to be given to the heightened narrative surrounding peer-based sexting behaviours. In line with Hackett's leading work in the area of HSB among young people, the more concerning facets of sexting behaviours can be dealt with via local therapeutic help and specialist provisions (see also Chapter 7).[113]

It is crucial to ensure that a decision is made in the best interests of the child, rather than from a desire to ensure children conform to adult's expectations of what it means to be a child.[114] What is also important to consider in relation to Article 13 is that it must be read alongside other provisions which are designed to protect children from sexually exploitative behaviours, including Article 34 of UNCRC. Article 34 requires State Parties to protect children from all forms of sexual exploitation and abuse, including exploitative use of children in pornographic materials. A very careful balancing exercise is therefore required.

In addition, the Council of Europe Convention on Protection of Children against Sexual Exploitation and Sexual Abuse, known also as the Lanzarote Convention (signed in 2008 and ratified in the UK in 2018), has referred to peer-based image sharing (sexting). This reference was made within the framework of Article 20, which outlines offences concerning child pornography. Article 20(3) notes that State Parties 'have the right' not to prosecute parties for possession and production of pornographic material if the children involved have reached the age of consent, the material was 'solely for their own private use' and there was no evidence of coercion. Yet, as noted in Chapters 2 and 3, and by scholars such as Gillespie, issues associated with sex and sexuality are 'sensitive moral issues', which is perhaps why the wording of Article 20 indicates that this is a discretionary power.[115]

---

[110] L Karaian, 'Lolita Speaks: "Sexting" Teenage Girls and the Law' (2012) *Crime Media Culture* 10.

[111] Ringrose et al (n 99).

[112] See Chapter 7 of this book and S Hackett, 'Children and Young People with Harmful Sexual Behaviours' in C Barter and B David (eds), *Children Behaving Badly? Peer Violence between Children and Young People* (John Wiley and Sons, 2010).

[113] *Harmful Sexual Behaviour Framework: An Evidence-Informed Operational Framework for Children and Young People Displaying Harmful Sexual Behaviours*, 2nd edn (NSPCC, 2019).

[114] S Angelides, 'Technology, Hormones and Stupidity: The Affective Politics of Teenage Sexting' (2013) 16(5–6) *Sexualities* 665.

[115] Gillespie (n 37).

In light of the above, education therefore becomes a key staple when it comes to active preventative measures, in particular Relationship and Sexuality Education (RSE) programmes, so children can 'be empowered to protect themselves'.[116] Aligning with Articles 12 and 13, such programmes should be drafted *with* young people and reflecting the real issues impacting their lives.

IV. Education: 'Our Best Weapon'

In light of: (i) the complexity of behaviours young people are engaging within bullying and sexting contexts; (ii) consideration of key rights enshrined under the UNCRC; and (iii) the limitations of current legal regulatory frameworks, education was described as 'our best weapon'.[117] Significantly, it was noted within the empirical research that the breadth of peer-on-peer online harmful behaviours displayed and the vastness of the digital space in which young people are operating, is something that parents in particular are struggling to relate to. This is partly because they did not grow up in the technologically-driven world in which we now live. There was a pressing call therefore to not only educate young people but 're-educating us all'.[118]

Professionals commented on parental naivety when it came to the internet and their lack of understanding in relation to the variability of online harmful behaviours young people can engage in. For example, where a child has sent a naked or semi-naked image the teachers are often faced with parents saying, 'my child wouldn't do that'.[119] Many parents fail to understand youth culture and the socio-cultural norms at the heart of certain behaviours, including peer-based sexting. Educating parents and placing a level of responsibility on them to educate their children about online harmful behaviours would also place less strain on school resources. One professional expressed concern that a lot of pressure was being placed on schools: 'There's been a huge pressure I think on the education sector to be the response to this whole thing ... and I'm not sure that's entirely fair'.[120] Further, another professional explained: 'the danger is when it gets shoe-horned into one body's responsibility then they can't actually address the problem fully at all'.[121] What was clear was the need for an *all-inclusive* education framework which includes the participation of key professionals, parents/guardians/carers and young people.

---

[116] Lanzarote Convention, Council of Europe Convention on the Protection of Children against Sexual Exploitation and Sexual Abuse: A Global Tool to Protect Children from Sexual Violence (Council of Europe) https://www.coe.int/en/web/children/lanzarote-convention, last accessed 17 July 2023.
[117] Professional Interview 6 (PhD): Children's Voluntary Organisation.
[118] Professional Interview 11 (PhD): Victim Support Organisation.
[119] Professional Interview 20 (PhD): Education Sector.
[120] Professional Interview 1 (PhD): Education Sector.
[121] Professional Interview 18 (PhD): Children's Voluntary Organisation.

Concerns were expressed by interviewees regarding how information would be disseminated and the apparent saturation of materials available regarding online safety. A number of professionals working within children's voluntary organisations noted how there is 'so much stuff'[122] and 'there needs to be one initial point of core focus'[123] which young people, parents and professionals can all access. Yet, primary data demonstrates a clear lack of consistent messaging, and this confusion is far-reaching, including within public and private sectors. This has resulted in a lack of cohesive responses regarding online harmful behaviours thus causing confusion among professionals in how best to respond to cases of cyber-bullying, especially sexting, among young people.

Regarding actual content, professional participants proposed an 'experiential' education programme. For example, a forensic psychologist noted that such a programme 'needs to be more experiential in the sense of showing them how to deal with it as opposed to just giving them information about what's safe and what's not safe'.[124] This was also echoed by the young people who wanted an RSE programme which recognised the different contexts and changing social attitudes among young people: 'it's less of just going "don't do it. You're not allowed to do it. You're going to get arrested" ... it should be actual education about it'.[125] The young people were also very keen to be educated on serious issues which impact them on a daily basis. As one young person explains: 'You can't just teach children what's been taught over like friggin' over 150 years. You have to realise that ok we can't do this anymore, we need to be more modern'.[126]

The young people noted a range of issues that they wanted to learn more about or had received limited to no information on. A prevalent theme was on healthy relationships and sex positive education. In fact, when asked what topics/content they would like covered in an RSE programme, the young people listed: 'signs of [an] abusive relationship',[127] 'different types of relationships i.e. gay lesbian,'[128] 'contraception',[129] 'that we shouldn't feel pressured to do things that we don't want to do'[130] and 'safety and consent e.g. dangers'.[131]

Professional participants also argued that the age in which RSE needs to be taught in schools should be younger (albeit age appropriate):

> Doing that [education] from a very early age with those P.1's ... you know respecting ... each other right from the outset.[132]

---

[122] Professional Interview 6 (PhD): Children's Voluntary Organisation.
[123] Professional Interview 14 (PhD): Children's Voluntary Organisation.
[124] Professional Interview 3 (PhD): Forensic Psychologist.
[125] Young Person Focus Group (PhD): Female.
[126] Young Person Interview (PhD): Male.
[127] Young Person Survey (PDF): Girl, 16 years.
[128] Young Person Survey (PDF): Boy, 17 years.
[129] Young Person Survey (PDF): Neither, 15 years.
[130] Young Person Survey (PDF): Girl, 15 years.
[131] Young Person Survey (PDF): Girl, 17 years.
[132] Professional Interview 1 (PhD): Education Sector.

> Education is key. But it comes from no age. It's about morals and manners and looking out for each other and having human, you know, sympathy and empathy.[133]

Teaching healthy inter-personal relationships early on in a child's educational journey would help young people navigate more complex relationship dynamics such as those raised in Chapter 4 regarding 'bystander' status. It would also challenge unhealthy narratives, including the misplaced presumption that bullying is simply a part of childhood.

Some measures have been taken to update RSE programmes in Northern Ireland. For example, in June 2023, the Secretary of State said that amendments would include:

> age-appropriate, comprehensive and scientifically accurate education on sexual and reproductive health and rights, a compulsory component of curriculum for adolescents, covering prevention of early pregnancy and access to abortion in Northern Ireland, and monitor its implementation.[134]

In addition, it is important to note that the most recent budget for Northern Ireland (2023–24) stated that the education sector was to receive a huge cut in funding, equating to around £70 million.[135] This amendment to RSE programmes in Northern Ireland followed the UN Committee on the Rights of the Child explicitly referring to the 2023–24 budget and asking the Secretary of State to 'withdraw' the current proposal and to 'fully consider the equality and human rights implications of a new budget'.[136]

There are a few important points to consider. First, in light of ongoing cuts within the education sector in Northern Ireland, it is hoped that there are no setbacks or delays when it comes to implementing this important initiative. Second, how much depth the programme will go into is yet to be seen. Indeed, there is still a fear that children and young people 'might learn too much too soon'.[137] This fear is why there has been a lack of education on these topical issues to date. Rolston and colleagues explain:

> It was evident that sex education was used to reaffirm the dominant sexual and moral values of society, values with strong and often explicit religious overtones. Instead of focusing on advocating responsibility within relationships and the fostering of mutual respect, the emphasis was on what were perceived as negative aspects of sexuality. Within that approach topics such as abortion and homosexuality ... and sex outside marriage (particularly in the Catholic sector) were constructed as 'contentious'.[138]

---

[133] Professional Interview 19 (PhD): Criminal Justice Sector.

[134] C Heaton-Harris, *Northern Ireland Update* (UK Parliament 2023) https://questions-statements.parliament.uk/written-statements/detail/2023-06-06/hcws824, last accessed 17 July 2023.

[135] R. Meredith, 'Northern Ireland Education Cuts "Equivalent to Losing 6,600 Staff" (BBC, 24 May 2023).

[136] *Concluding Observations* (n 4).

[137] S Jackson and S Scott, 'Risk Anxiety and the Social Construction of Childhood' in D Lupton (ed), *Risk and Sociocultural Theory: New Directions and Perspectives* (Cambridge University Press, 1999) 100.

[138] B Rolston et al, 'Sex Education in Northern Ireland Schools: A Critical Evaluation' (2005) 5(3) *Sex Education* 219.

Such concerns have been voiced in several Northern Irish reports. This includes the Marshall Inquiry, which noted 'deficiencies' in sex education,[139] and the Gillen Review, which highlighted the limitations of the current RSE curriculum and advocated for a standardised programme.[140] In addition, Belfast Youth Forum advocated for RSE programmes which are proactive and help young people understand and negotiate sexual rights, sexuality and sexual behaviours.[141]

While significant evidence points towards the incorporation of comprehensive RSE programmes, there are still notable objections. In the wake of the proposed changes noted above by the Secretary of State, a Catholic Bishop in Northern Ireland criticised plans to include education on abortion, saying that the change was focused on rights and 'there is no question of morality involved'.[142] Despite religious contentions, young people should be educated on and engage with a wide range of issues related to sexual health, sex and sexuality. Indeed, the World Health Organisation (WHO) has emphasised that sexual health is 'fundamental to the overall health and wellbeing of individuals' and there should be a 'positive and respectful approach' to sex and sexuality.[143] The range of concerns expressed among professional and youth participants illustrates the prevailing failures of the current RSE education programme within schools in Northern Ireland. Relationship and sexuality education can no longer be influenced by the moral fabric of the school to the detriment of young people.

Third, guidance on the content and delivery of the programme must be submitted by the Department of Education by 1 January 2024 but it has been made clear that parents will have the right to withdraw their child from RSE (similar to England and Wales). This inclusion would be somewhat in line with Article 29(c) of the UNCRC, which notes that the education of a child should also be mindful of the child's parents and 'his or her own cultural identity, language and values'. However, it must be balanced against Article 28 (right to education), Article 24 (right to education on health and wellbeing) and Article 29(a) which notes the 'development of the child's personality, talents and mental and physical abilities to their fullest potential'.

Notably, professional interviewees were reluctant to allow parents to opt their children out of RSE. While there was recognition of the need to be sensitive to 'cultural differences', there was a sense that if RSE is taught properly

---

[139] K Marshall, *Child Sexual Exploitation in Northern Ireland: Report of the Independent Inquiry* (Criminal Justice Inspection Northern Ireland, 2014) 12.

[140] Sir John Gillen, 'Report into the Law and Procedures in Serious Sexual Offences in Northern Ireland' (Gillen Review) (Department of Justice, 2019).

[141] *Any Use? Young People's Opinions on Relationship and Sexuality Education in Belfast* (Belfast Youth Forum 2019).

[142] BBC News, 'Catholic Bishop of Derry Criticises Abortion Access Lessons Plans' (BBC, 7 June 2023).

[143] WHO, *Sexual Health*, https://www.who.int/health-topics/sexual-health#tab=tab_1, last accessed 17 July 2023.

and in accordance with the UNCRC, there would be no reason for a parent to want to withdraw their child from RSE classes:

> It's difficult. If it's going to start at a very, where it has to start, like the very basic level – consent of personal space and personal belongings – I would say I can't imagine. I would feel surely a parent shouldn't, like why would your child be taken out of that? I don't know. I kind of feel no.[144]

> I think it should be compulsory ... people will argue that it's the parents right to choose, but in terms of that young person, how is that going to affect their lives whenever they're older? Within society you put so many pressures on young people, but yet we can pick and choose how we give those young people the capacity to deal with them – I don't think that's a fair exchange.[145]

A comprehensive RSE framework which covers the multi-faceted behaviours young people are participating and engaging in, including cyberbullying and sexting, will therefore provide a proactive response and allow young people to make informed decisions relating to sexual behaviours and inter-personal relationships. It is clear, however, that if the programmes are not comprehensive and not reflective of the lived experiences of young people, the majority of young people will seek information on relationships and sexuality through popular culture. Discussed previously, this manifests typically in blurred boundaries and confusion among young people on what is healthy and unhealthy behaviour.

V. Conclusion

This chapter has considered law and policy in the area of bullying and sexting behaviours between young people. A range of legislative provisions have been critiqued and comparisons with international jurisdictions made. A range of challenges and tensions emerge – in particular, when (if ever) should the law be engaged as a regulatory response to peer-based sexting? I see some merit in formalising a legislative exception or defence, similar to NSW, in the context of peer-based sexting behaviours. The introduction of an exception or defence would (or should) protect young people from being unnecessarily prosecuted. However, paying close attention to the stigma attached to indecent image legislation (also referred to as child pornography laws within international contexts), the original intention behind the drafting of the laws, alongside the complexity of identifying consent or non-consent in a legal setting (see Chapter 6), I would argue that engaging indecent image legislation *at all* is inappropriate when dealing with peer-based sexting behaviours. Distinguishing between young people who engage in peer-on-peer sexting behaviours (even within coercive contexts) and adults who

---

[144] Professional Focus Group (PDF): Education Sector.
[145] Professional Interview 2 (PDF): Sexual Health Charity.

coerce and exploit young people for sexual images is essential and criminal law must account for this important distinction.

As noted previously, adult perpetrators present very distinct harms due to heightened power differentials – they therefore require different interventions to be engaged. Further and interrelated to the previous point, the Law Reform Committee of Victoria notes that children who engage in peer-on-peer sexting are often young people 'experiencing a phase of normal development'.[146] With this in mind, to prosecute children under indecent image or child pornography legislation: (i) is to ignore the complexity of the behaviours young people are displaying; (ii) fails to recognise the significant differences in motivations between the two types of behaviours (the peer-on-peer and adult-child dichotomy); and (iii) takes no account of the stigma and life-long consequences of having, even a caution, on a child's record for an indecent image or child pornography offence. All things considered, it may be more appropriate to utilise laws designed to specifically deal with image-based abuse – such as 'Disclosing private sexual photographs and films with intent to cause distress' codified under section 33 of the Criminal Justice and Courts Act 2015 – in more serious peer-on-peer cases. Yet, as noted above, even this legislative framework has its limitations.

Beyond the legal landscape, the main recommendation, and one which should be prioritised, is responding to sexting among young people as an education and health issue rather than a criminal one. In this vein, a comprehensive RSE programme would be promoted: a programme which: (i) involves young people from the outset in designing its content and structure (considering Article 12 UNCRC and Lundy's model of participation); and (ii) accounts for a child's right to receive information which impacts their lives (Article 13 UNCRC).[147] Further, in line with the Northern Ireland's Executive *Children and Young People's Strategy 2020–2030*, if children are to 'grow to become resilient, confident young people who are well equipped to take on the challenges and opportunities that adulthood brings',[148] comprehensive and gender-sensitive education programmes are essential.

Yet, activating non-legal responses, or even to engage other legislative provisions (as noted above), would require a significant shift in socio-political thinking around young people, criminalisation and youth sexuality (see Chapters 2 and 3). In the interim, and to ensure that young people are offered maximum protection from over-criminalisation, formalising measures such as Outcome 21 in Northern Ireland would provide greater protections for young people who engage in consensual peer-based sexting behaviours. While not an ideal solution, in the absence of

---

[146] Cited in T Crofts and E Lievens, 'Sexting and the Law' in M Walrave et al (eds), *Sexting: Motives and Risk in Online Sexual Self-Representation* (Palgrave, 2018) 125.

[147] See Lundy (n 103); *Concluding Observations* (n 4).

[148] *Children and Young People's Strategy 2020–2030* (Northern Ireland Executive, 2020) https://www.education-ni.gov.uk/publications/children-and-young-peoples-strategy-2020-2030, last accessed 17 July 2023.

a timely alternative – noting the range of concerns discussed earlier in this book around childhood sexuality – formalising this measure could be a quick way to ensure that young people are protected from draconian regulatory frameworks.

In relation to bullying behaviours, greater clarity is required when it comes to a school's position on bullying behaviours that occur outside the school grounds but nevertheless infiltrate the classroom. Very often the behaviours can be displayed both on- and offline, inside and outside the school gates. While many schools are proactive in this regard, to ensure consistency in responses, the 2016 Act should be amended to provide: (i) greater clarity surrounding the scope and remit of powers; and (ii) a more robust response to dealing with the complex range of bullying cases. In addition, similar to sexting behaviours, professional interviewees were keen for bullying to be responded to via pastoral practices and non-legal methods.[149] Many voiced concerns that legal frameworks were not suitable when it came to responding to bullying behaviours among young people. As one professional interviewee explains: 'I don't think the law … is geared for young people under 18 and I think … we have to be more sensitive and I don't think it's a legislation issue I think it is an education issue'.[150] In a similar vein, a professional within the education sector also noted, 'It's not seen as a discipline issue. It's seen as a pastoral issue'.[151] Comprehensive education programmes would therefore be fitting and could address the more complex dimensions to bullying behaviours, including bystander status.

---

[149] Although there is little evidence to suggest that criminal law is activated within peer-based bullying contexts.
[150] Professional Interview 5 (PhD): Safeguarding Organisation.
[151] Professional Interview 20 (PhD): Education Sector.

9

Conclusion

Taking social media from a young person is like taking their arm off ... When I worked in the Trust if there were issues about a 16-year-old and how vulnerable she was and the use of social media, it was remove her phone. Then when I came to work here it was like, that just heightens it even more because if they don't have a phone they're more at risk because they're going to go and find another way to do that and place themselves in a riskier situation.[1]

This book has illustrated how over simplistic accounts of bullying and sexting behaviours have resulted in significant gaps and limitations within key theoretical and regulatory frameworks. In particular, a failure to account for the complexity of peer-on-peer sexting behaviours and the normative dimension attached, has led to theoretical tensions associated with childhood sexuality and the criminalisation of young people (Chapters 2 and 3). It has been a central argument of this book that the breadth and variety of behaviours young people are engaging in must be recognised to ensure that proportionate and effective interventions are activated (Chapters 4 and 5). Yet, prevailing societal reluctance to accept that young people can and do engage in sexual behaviours has presented a number of regulatory difficulties. I argue that there is a need to recognise certain forms of peer-on-peer sexting behaviours as a representation of sexual expression within the technologically advanced age in which we are living. While there are elements of risk involved in the practice – risks young people may not be fully aware of – education must be promoted over criminalisation. More intensive or higher-level interventions should be focused on those cases which involve more problematic or harmful dimensions to the behaviour.

It is for this reason that I argue that the behaviours are better placed on a continuum of sexual behaviour (Chapter 7), recognising the diverse range of motivations and contexts in which the behaviours are displayed. Key to distinguishing between the different behaviours are issues of consent. Yet, as Chapter 6 illustrates, conceptualising and framing consent within highly complex youth interactions is not easy. Consideration must be given to the prevailing socio-cultural pressures young people are exposed to and how these pressures impact and influence young people's understanding of consent. While the law can play an important role in targeting and responding to adults who perpetrate sexual harms,

---

[1] Professional Interview 4 (PDF): Children's Charity.

Chapter 8 reinforces the limitations in using current legislative frameworks to respond to *peer-on-peer* sexting behaviours. In the absence of an effective regulatory framework which captures the diversification of practices young people are engaging in, legal responses to date have been inadequate. This is primarily due to engaging a piece of legislation that was not in fact designed to respond to youth sexting (indecent image legislation).[2] I argue that different interventions must be activated, with a focus on gender-sensitive education programmes over punitive legal sanctions. Such measures would more readily align with important rights found under the UNCRC.

A key contribution of this book is adding to the small body of literature available in Northern Ireland which explores online peer-on-peer harmful behaviours, in particular sexting behaviours. In addition, incorporating both professional and youth voices provided a valuable and unique opportunity to: (i) identify key tensions between both groups of interviewees – something that is often lacking in literature to date; and (ii) engage with a wide range of voices across various key sectors, including criminal justice, education and safeguarding organisations. Yet, noted in Chapter 1 and below, it is important to recognise the unique political landscape of this jurisdiction which adds unique dimensions to certain debates, in particular those relating to relationships and sexuality education. Despite the history of Northern Ireland adding a unique perspective, discussions relate to and resonate with both national and international debates in the area. In particular, the pervasive culture of sexism and misogyny that unfortunately permeates beyond the Irish border.

This concluding chapter therefore provides an overview of the key findings and themes outlined in preceding chapters, deconstructs the main challenges facing legal and other professionals in terms of regulating sexting and cyberbullying among young people, and concludes with the key recommendations moving forward.

I. Deconstructing 'Cyberbullying' Among Young People

A. Theoretical Tensions

My research demonstrates the need to challenge misplaced presumptions that bullying behaviours among young people are simply 'a bit of fun'.[3] The impact of bullying behaviours can vary from minor to more serious, including physical, emotional and psychological harms. Empirical research has also shown

---

[2] Section 3 of The Protection of Children (Northern Ireland) Order 1978 (as amended by s 42 of The Sexual Offences (Northern Ireland) Order 2008).
[3] Professional Interview 14 (PhD): Children's Voluntary Organisation.

how bullying behaviours can have a detrimental impact on a child's educational journey, resulting in school absences and a lack of concentration. This is also reflected in the literature.[4] Trivialising the behaviours as simply 'a part of child-hood' therefore minimises the harm caused and can result in young people not coming forward for help or dismissing the behaviour as 'normal'. This book reinforces the importance of education programmes, from a young age, which focus on healthy inter-personal relationships. In doing so, troubling narratives which suggest that peer-on-peer bullying is innocuous childhood behaviour will be challenged.

Also noted within the research study was the need to challenge gendered stereotypes surrounding expressions of anger and harm. While professionals did indicate that girls were more likely to engage in online harmful behaviours, others noted having to respond to incidents involving organised fights among girls. Important, therefore, is the need to recognise that boys *and* girls can engage in *any* form of harmful activity (on- and offline). This can be done while still being aware of the gendered dimensions attached to certain *types* of behaviours and exposure to 'risk', such as gaming sites and boys being groomed, for example. If effective safeguarding measures are to be put in place, the more nuanced features of these behaviours must be acknowledged.

B. On- and Offline Bullying

The diverse range of bullying behaviours regularly displayed online was noted in Chapter 4; this section will identify some of the main themes discussed. A key finding was an unwillingness among some professionals and practitioners interviewed to suggest that bullying online was more severe or damaging to children and young people than offline bullying. While those professionals interviewed challenged the supposedly 'unique' and distinctive aspects of cyberbullying including the 24/7 dimension (this was especially in relation to children in care), there was a clear understanding among most professionals interviewed that cyberbullying behaviours can and do present a very different set of 'risks'. For example, the ability to quickly disseminate harmful material to a far-reaching audience may simultaneously enhance opportunities for bullying behaviours to be displayed as well as augment the harm caused and thus activate more serious legal ramifications. Primary and secondary data analysis also demonstrates, in contrast to offline bullying, the permanent nature of a young person's 'digital footprint'. In fact, this has been described as being one of the most significant 'threats' online, as risk-taking behaviours are documented and shared on a worldwide network.[5]

---

[4] V Brown et al, *Estimating the Prevalence of Young People Absent from School Due to Bullying* (Red Balloon Learner Centre Group, 2011).

[5] GS O'Keeffe and K Clarke-Pearson, 'The Impact of Social Media on Children, Adolescents, and Families' (2011) 127(4) *Pediatrics* 802.

It was also noted that the current understanding of bullying online does not account for the more subtle aspects of harmful behaviours among peers. Considering bullying online in its broadest terms, the behaviour has been described as intentional harmful behaviour that is displayed between two or more parties, where there is an imbalance of power, and the behaviour is repeated.[6] Yet, as noted in Chapter 4, a significant concern was current understandings of what the term 'repeated' means within a definition of cyberbullying specifically. The primary research highlights the importance of rethinking the repetitive element when analysing bullying behaviours online. While scholarly works, including Kowalski et al, observe the significance of repetition (to separate it from other forms of harmful behaviour),[7] the unique nature of the World Wide Web can make it challenging to conceptualise this important feature. For example, one harmful comment may have been posted online by one person but the repeated hurt and humiliation that the young person can be exposed to via screenshots, retweets, shares, adding comments or simply reacting to the post by other persons must be considered.[8] Indeed, the build-up of hurt can span over days, weeks and even months as the harmful content is continually shared. This example therefore speaks directly to the onion analogy and the layers of harm to which a young person may be exposed.[9] This argument challenges how the term 'repeated' is understood within an online bullying context by recognising the unique medium through which the behaviour is displayed and the extent of injury that can be inflicted. This nuanced understanding of cyberbullying behaviours – stemming from a one-off incident with repeated or longer-term consequences – reinforces the need to properly identify the 'harmful' and 'risky' behaviours children and young people are subjected to online. Properly identifying the extent of harm caused will help ensure that a more robust and consistent response framework is put in place.

C. Bystander

Another notable theme was that relating to bystander status. The role of the bystander was noted within the literature as significant, as their presence (whether active or passive) can contribute to the harm caused, depending on the context of the interaction. It was clear that the young people interviewed wanted to intervene in certain situations but were reluctant to do so – due to a fear of themselves being subjected to bullying. Given the complexity of peer-based relationships and the constantly evolving digital landscape, exploring the unique role of the

---

[6] See RM Kowalski et al, *Cyberbullying: Bullying in the Digital Age*, 2nd edn (Oxford, Wiley-Blackwell, 2012).

[7] ibid.

[8] For example, on Facebook users can 'react' by clicking on icons which symbolise different emotions including love, laughter and anger.

[9] Noted by a professional interviewee in Chapter 4.

bystander within an online bullying context would provide a nuanced under-standing of the behaviour. In addition, the breadth of potential injury caused would also be examined, acknowledging that those who witness the behaviour can also be harmed.

D. Regulation

In terms of regulating harmful behaviours online, professionals were often perplexed by the legal sanctions, describing them as confusing. This underlines the need to ensure that any policy or legal development in this area accounts for the complexity and diversity of behaviours that young people are presenting with. For example, as noted in the primary research, bullying online does not appear in isolation and often there is a level of overlap between bullying on- and offline. A wider acknowledgement of the limits of the law in regulating harmful behaviours among young people will also assist in promoting more effective child safeguard-ing and welfare measures.

Significantly, the primary research also illustrates some novel behaviours young people are exposed to which must be more carefully considered when examining 'risk' and comprehensive regulatory frameworks. Such behaviours include 'catfishing' and illicit behaviours carried out as part of the Dark Web. Most noteworthy was the limited research and professional understanding surrounding these harmful behaviours and interactions online. Further, while young people demonstrate a certain degree of awareness about a range of online risks, it was concerning how little education young people receive on sexual risks. This was significant in relation to sexual bullying and sexting behaviours among young people.

II. Deconstructing 'Sexting' Among Young People

While it is clear that sexting among young people has understandably unnerved child welfare professionals and practitioners, the need to move beyond a narrow and purely 'harmful' framework has been identified. Indeed, a socio-legal focus on conceptualising sexting among young people purely within a 'risk' and 'harmful' context has hindered effective regulatory reform in the area. The circumstances surrounding sexting cases are variable and can range from explorative, coercive, manipulative or part of a wider remit of harmful sexual behaviour, for example, grooming. Therefore, to label *all* forms of 'sexting' behaviour as 'harmful' ignores the complexity of the practice. A balance, therefore, needs to be struck between child protection and welfare on the one hand and a young person's right to sexual autonomy and sexual expression on the other. In this section, I briefly draw together some of the key findings, noting how the research has contributed to the broader debates in the area.

A. Theoretical Tensions

Theoretical tensions were noted surrounding childhood, youth sexuality and sexting.[10] Examining theory across a range of disciplines brought to the fore how sexting among young people as a possible form of sexual expression contradicts popular discourses on childhood sexuality. Due to a prevailing discomfort with youth expressions of sexuality, young people who engage in sexting behaviours are often exposed to labelling, shaming and stigma (often gendered in nature). In addition, out of date laws are being used to regulate sexting – a youth behaviour that was not anticipated by the legislator. Yet, as Albury and Crawford state:

> Young people should not be universally prohibited from producing images or texts that reflect their experiences of sexual experience or imagination; and that these self-representations should not be interpreted solely through the lens of adult anxieties around technology and sexuality.[11]

While differentiating between what is 'normal' and 'abnormal' sexual development is 'a formidable challenge',[12] my research emphasises an urgent need to address the gaps, especially in relation to sexting among young people. This is to ensure an end to the unnecessary criminalisation of young people and exposure to harmful shaming and labelling narratives.

This book therefore contributes to the broader literature on childhood sexuality and criminalisation. The book highlights how oversimplified accounts of key issues, including consent, as well as significant limitations of criminal law as an effective regulatory tool in this area, are placing young people at risk of being unnecessarily processed through the criminal justice system. Positive steps must be taken to differentiate between *consensual* and *non-consensual* sexting practices. Yet, as discussed below, in order for true and effective change to happen, comprehensive education programmes must be implemented which challenge the traditional notions of childhood sexuality and raise awareness around the more problematic dimensions to sexting behaviours. Only then will we begin to see a socio-cultural shift in how we understand and regulate peer-on-peer sexting behaviours.

B. Complexity of Sexting Behaviours

First, given the complexity of behaviours young people are presenting with, ranging from consensual to more harmful, a continuum was proposed to better

---

[10] Chapters 2 and 3.

[11] K Albury and K Crawford 'Sexting, Consent and Young People's Ethics: Beyond Megan's Story' (2012) 26(3) *Continuum: Journal of Media and Cultural Studies* 471.

[12] J Bancroft, 'Normal Sexual Development' in HE Barbaree and WL Marshall (eds), *The Juvenile Sex Offender*, 2nd edn (Guilford Press, 2008) 39.

capture the range of behaviours displayed. While the majority of professional interviewees referred to different levels of pressure within the context of peer-based sexting, the research also emphasised the need to appropriately differentiate between consensual and non-consensual sexting. In addition, recognising that behaviours can shift over time adds a further dimension to the issue: what was once consensual can become more harmful and this is most obvious when relationships break down. Within this context, acknowledging the different pressures young people can be exposed to and how these can influence understanding of what is healthy and unhealthy sexual behaviour, is crucial. Sexual behaviours do not develop and evolve in a vacuum but are shaped by the social, legal and political environment in which the human interactions are displayed.[13] Important socio-cultural factors influencing sexual behaviours between children include easy access to sexual material online such as pornography and the sexualisation of pop culture.

Second and interrelated to the previous point, problematic social norms within youth culture, in particular misplaced understandings around consent, must be challenged. For example, the presence of a sexual double standard and a gendered expectation of receiving sexual images was noted – primarily boys making requests to girls.[14] This directly links to broader discourses on power dynamics, consent and sexual behaviours. Indeed, Powell states that consent cannot be analysed in isolation but must take account of 'gendered norms and discourse regarding expectations of men's sexuality as active/pursuant and women's as passive/submissive, much of this remains unarticulated and not readily open to conscious reflection'.[15] This was especially pertinent when distinguishing between sexting as respectively explorative, problematic or harmful. Examining the social rules children engage with will reveal more clearly whether coercion or manipulation is present. Yet, while sexting practices have been described as a gendered form of harmful sexual behaviour,[16] there was also evidence to suggest that there is a notable pressure on boys to conform to a hyper-masculine 'macho' image. Therefore, while it is clear that a gender imbalance exists within the context of peer-based sexting behaviours, a more careful examination and understanding of the pressures on boys within this context is required.[17]

---

[13] See eg A-M McAlinden, *Children as 'Risk': Sexual Exploitation and Abuse by Children and Young People* (Cambridge, Cambridge University Press, 2018).

[14] Chapter 5.

[15] A Powell, *Sex, Power and Consent: Youth Culture and the Unwritten Rules* (Cambridge University Press, 2010) 99.

[16] See J Ringrose et al, *A Qualitative Study of Children, Young People and 'Sexting': A Report Prepared for the NSPCC* (London, NSPCC, 2012); E Agnew, 'Sexting among Young People: Towards a Gender Sensitive Approach' (2021) 29(1) *International Journal of Children's Rights* 3.

[17] See E Setty, '"Confident" and "Hot" or "Desperate" and "Cowardly"? Meanings of Young Men's Sexting Practices in Youth Sexting Culture' (2020) 23(5) *Journal of Youth Studies* 561; see also Agnew (n 16).

Inevitably there will be complex cases where differentiating the behaviour is extremely challenging and problematic. Indeed, the significant gaps in knowledge surrounding the varied contexts in which sexting can occur, including the potential for young people to groom their peers for images, need to be closed. Research demonstrates how each case brings different mitigating and aggravating factors in determining the extent of harm caused. In fact, Wolak and Finkelhor posit that there are many issues that must be taken into consideration when determining whether there was criminal intent behind a youth-generated image:

> The ages of the minors involved and the developmental appropriateness of their actions … their backgrounds, including factors such as history of sexual abuse and prior involvement with the criminal justice system … whether there was a sexual or social relationship that was coercive … the nature of the images and … the extent of any dissemination that occurred.[18]

Therefore, interventions require adjustment according to where the behaviour falls along the continuum of peer-based sexual behaviour. Failure to acknowledge the multi-faceted and complex nature of the practice only results in young people being neglected – both as victims and as those perpetrating the harmful behaviour. Accordingly, young people can fall through the gaps when it comes to appropriate interventions.

C. Gendered Dimensions

Already discussed above, my research reinforced how socio-cultural messages surrounding gender, female sexuality and identity are blurred and convoluted. This can leave young people vulnerable to coercive and harmful sexting behaviours. This was most prevalent when discussing the normative nature of sexism, the conflicting messaging surrounding gender roles and the 'damned if you do, damned if you don't' maxim. While literature has explored the important role of gender and the prevalence of a sexual double standard among young people,[19] this book provides a deeper insight into the nuanced nature of sexting behaviours and the complexity of gender roles.

First, research demonstrates the powerful influence that peer pressure has on young people and their participation in sexting, including the more subtle forms of pressure. Indeed, a gendered dimension attached to peer pressure was noted and stemmed from the existing and prevalent sexualised culture young people live in and the socio-cultural pressures they are under to conform to a particular body image and sexual identity. Further, the gendered dimension attached to victim

---

[18] J Wolak and D Finkelhor, 'Sexting: A Typology' (Durham NH, Crimes against Children Research Centre, 2011) 8.

[19] Powell (n 15); S Shariff, *Sexting and Cyberbullying: Defining the Line for Digitally Empowered Kids* (Cambridge University Press. 2015).

blaming and shaming was also noted throughout the primary research. This gendered discourse attached to the wider sexting debate highlights how gender stereotypes and power are influencing young relationships and youth participation in sexting behaviours. Future response frameworks would therefore need to be sensitive to the complex role gender plays in negotiating sexual behaviours among young people.

All in all, there is a pressing need to ensure that the wide range of behaviours young people are engaging in, and the varied contexts in which the behaviours are being displayed, are better understood within socio-legal frameworks. The next section, therefore, will explain why research findings point towards a need to move beyond legal frameworks, noting in particular the 'vacuum in gender responsive justice'.[20]

III. Regulatory Frameworks: Education Over Criminalisation

A crucial argument presented in this book is the limitation of criminal law as a regulatory framework for dealing with sexting cases among young people. In the absence of an alternative response, while there *may* be a place for criminal law in cases which fall into more harmful sexting behaviour categories, educational frameworks were proposed as a more effective prevention tool. As illustrated in Chapter 8, sending naked or semi-naked images has surpassed any existing criminal legislation and is therefore covered under a sexual offence which was designed to prosecute adult perpetrators who create, possess or distribute child abuse images. Consequently, sexting has inadvertently been categorised under an offence presumed to be perpetrated exclusively by adults.[21] An analysis of the primary research highlights that criminal law fails to consider the wide and complex societal influences lying at the heart of sexting behaviours practised by young people. As noted above, these include cultural influences, the gendered dimension often associated with the sexual behaviour, consent issues and the underlying power dynamics.

My research demonstrates that clearer guidelines are required for police officers, teachers and other professionals who work with children on how best to respond to the wide-ranging sexting cases young people are involved in. While police have discretionary powers to divert cases away from the Public Prosecution Service and thus prevent young people being unnecessarily prosecuted, discretionary powers can lead to case anomalies. Further, and noted in

---

[20] G McNaull, 'Contextualising Violence: An Anti-Carceral Feminist Approach' in R Killean et al (eds), *Sexual Violence on Trial* (Routledge, 2021) 225.
[21] See eg AA Gillespie, 'Adolescents, Sexting and Human Rights' (2013) 13(4) *Human Rights Law Review* 623.

Chapter 8, Outcome 21 is a more formalised process by which the police can determine whether it is in the public interest to prosecute. Currently, Outcome 21 only applies to England and Wales. While concerns have been noted regarding children's criminal records (and this should be more carefully considered), I would argue that the current discretionary powers bestowed on police officers in Northern Ireland be formalised, similar to England and Wales. In addition, up-to-date training on effectively differentiating between the different types of behaviours young people are displaying is required. This would ensure a greater level of consistency in applying Outcome 21 to individual cases and thus provide a greater level of protection for young people who engage in consensual peer-based sexting. Further, and importantly, a more formalised process would provide clarity for the young people themselves. As one professional explains:

> If you're saying to a young person, listen, you're under the age of consent, I need to report this through to the police and when you do the police aren't doing anything … that is confusing.[22]

The book also examined some international responses to peer-based sexting, such as exceptions/defences in law to prevent young people from being criminalised.[23] In New South Wales, Australia, for example, an 'exception' exists which considers whether a 'reasonable person' would consider possession of the image to be 'acceptable'. A range of factors are examined in determining whether this threshold has been met, including the ages of and relationship between the parties. While there was merit in introducing these exceptions (mainly reducing the potential for young people to be criminalised), notable concerns were expressed surrounding the use of indecent image legislation *at all*. A number of professional interviewees voiced concerns that a young person even being charged with such a stigmatising offence could have detrimental and life-long consequences. Further, indecent image legislation was not meant to capture peer-based sexual behaviours, even those behaviours which possess more coercive and manipulative dimensions. Despite noting the legislative limitations and gaps, some interviewees did not completely dismiss the law as there was no effective alternative being proposed. There was therefore still a level of uncertainty as to *when* and *if* the law should be activated in cases involving young people who share sexual images under more coercive circumstances. This ambivalence resonates globally as the range and varied responses, both nationally and internationally, demonstrate how the sexual behaviour has perplexed legal professionals.

Noting the limitations and failings with utilising a criminal law framework, I propose that education could be an effective alternative to legal sanctions (and

---

[22] Professional Interview 4 (PDF): Children's Charity.
[23] Chapter 8.

indeed more in line with the UNCRC). As poignantly noted in the opening quotation to this chapter, the Internet is not going away, and it is an integral – and indeed essential – part of young people's lives today. It is therefore not about removing the technology; this will not work. It is about helping young people navigate the online world in a safe and healthy way. Education is the best way to do this. Significantly, young people asked for more education on healthy inter-personal and social relationships as well as key concepts including consent. The primary research therefore strongly advocates for comprehensive and gender-sensitive education programmes and schemes which align with key rights enshrined under the UNCRC, in particular Articles 12, 13, 28 and 29.

This would involve a programme which: (i) engages with Lundy's model of participation and thus involves young people in designing the content and structure of the programme; (ii) is inclusive and engages all youth voices, including those currently marginalised from RSE content, including LGBTQ+ young people; and (iii) uses the UN Convention on the Rights of the Child as its guiding framework during implementation.[24] Comprehensive education programmes which *directly* address the key needs of young people means including content which reflects the lived experiences of young people within contemporary youth culture in a digital era. Drawing on my research, this would include: (i) the range of pressures, mostly gendered in nature, that young people are exposed to and how these can influence the *giving* and *receiving* of consent; (ii) the wide-ranging and complex sexual practices young people are participating in and; (iii) the socio-cultural context in which the behaviours manifest – in particular, problematic notions of masculinity and femininity.[25] Such a response, if activated properly, could be a powerful tool in challenging the prevailing patriarchal culture of misogyny and sexism within youth culture – and indeed within broader socio-cultural contexts.

Finally, wider public education is required. Primary research illustrates how the family setting as well as the morally conservative Northern Irish context are sending confusing and conflicting messages to young people on what are healthy relationships and expressions of sexuality. Introducing campaigns which focus on 'withdrawing consent' and which speak specifically to the range of sexual behaviours young people are engaging in and exposed to, is essential. As noted in Chapter 6, awareness campaigns have the potential to help aid understanding on the more complex and nuanced features of human interactions as well as drawing attention to problematic and harmful sexual behaviours.

To be blunt, if we fail to enact such changes, then in the words of one young person, 'you've lost this generation.'[26]

---

[24] See L Lundy, '"Voice" is Not Enough: Conceptualising Article 12 of the United Nations Convention on the Rights of the Child' (2007) 33(6) *British Educational Research Journal* 927; Committee on the Rights of the Child (2023) *Concluding Observations on the Combined Sixth and Seventh Reports of the United Kingdom of Great Britain and Northern Ireland*, 2 June 2023, CRC/C/GBR/CO/6–7.

[25] See Agnew (n 16).

[26] Young Person Interview (PhD): Male.

IV. Northern Ireland and Beyond

As noted throughout the book, for effective and consistent education programmes to be initiated on relationships and sex, a social and cultural shift is required regarding young people, sexual agency and sexual relationships. This is especially pertinent within Northern Ireland's education system. As noted in Chapter 1, the tight regulation of youth sexuality and the promotion of heteronormativity as the 'norm' within schools is shaping how young people understand sex and sexuality.[27] As one professional remarks:

> [there] is still … a culture within our society that's still struggling with sexuality, and that, therefore, we tend to separate it out and see it as very difficult and very shameful and something that's not the norm. So, I think that's part of the difficulty. We still struggle.[28]

This was also felt by the young people, who noted that in relation to RSE, they wanted a programme which helped 'get rid of the shame of sex'.[29]

Indeed, laws relating to same-sex marriage and abortion access have all vividly highlighted the conservative strain throughout law and policy in Northern Ireland. Further, the gendered discourse, in particular the complex role of gender and pressure attached to the behaviour, was highlighted. In the context of Northern Ireland, the research speaks to the broader literature which brings to light the limitations placed on female sexual identity and agency. Indeed, scholars including McNaull comment on 'patriarchal privilege', noting how in Northern Ireland there is a 'distinct religious cultural gendering of women within particular ideals of heteronormative womanhood'.[30] There is, therefore, a clear need to contest the heteronormative dimension to RSE programmes and further challenge institutionalised myths surrounding masculinity and femininity.

Similar debates have been had internationally, for example, when the US Supreme Court overturned abortion rights set down in *Roe v Wade* in 2022. This move by the Supreme Court ended safe abortion access for many women in America – access that had been a constitutional right since 1973.[31] In addition, a lack of consistency in how RSE is delivered and the moral framework that is often a point of contention within the framing of such programmes, has been noted in Australia.[32] Consequently, while the focus of this book was exploring online

---

[27] See B Rolston et al, 'Sex Education in Northern Ireland Schools: A Critical Evaluation' (2005) 5(3) *Sex Education* 217.

[28] Professional Interview 3 (PDF): Independent Social Work Consultant.

[29] Young Person Survey (PDF): Girl, 16 years.

[30] McNaull (n 20) 215.

[31] See J Glenza et al, 'US Supreme Court Overturns Abortion Rights, Upending Roe v Wade' (*The Guardian*, 24 June 2022).

[32] A Waling et al, '"Please Teach Students that Sex is a Healthy Part of Growing Up": Australian Students' Desires for Relationships and Sexuality Education' (2021) 18 *Sexuality Research and Social Policy* 1113.

bullying and sexting behaviours within the context of Northern Ireland, as alluded to throughout the book, the core discussions resonate with broader childhood and youth sexuality debates. The book in this sense speaks to the unique legal and policy challenges faced in Northern Ireland, while also contributing to an analysis of the wider tensions surrounding law and policy within international contexts.

V. Conclusion

While there is a plethora of evidence-based research on bullying behaviours and a growing literature base on sexting behaviours, limited academic material is available within Northern Ireland on the nature, impact and regulation of the online harmful behaviours among young people. The current gaps in knowledge and the ongoing social, political and legal interest in relation to these online behaviours is why 'cyberbullying' and 'sexting' were the focus of this book.

Drawing on both empirical studies, the analysis presented in this book has explored a range of issues ranging from conceptualising the behaviours, examining the prevailing presence of sexism, myths and stereotypes surrounding gender roles and identity, the limitations of regulatory frameworks and the need for more effective and comprehensive gender-sensitive education programmes. In particular, this book has provided a more developed conceptual understanding of sexting behaviours among young people by viewing the behaviour as part of a continuum. Priority was placed on young people who fall within the grey area of age limits, 13–17 years inclusive. To implement practical and efficient policies, the idea that young people can and do express 'explorative', 'problematic' and/or 'harmful' sexting behaviour must be accepted within social and political discourses. Failure to be inclusive risks reinforcing current stereotypes and myths surrounding sex offending behaviours and augmenting misconceptions and narrow constructions surrounding childhood, sexuality and youth agency.

The book not only presents new insights regarding young people, cyberbullying and sexting but also reinforces the need to consider interventions beyond the law and in line with UNCRC recommendations,[33] ie accepting the limits of criminal law as an appropriate regulatory measure and considering the benefits of non-legal responses. In the main, this would include a comprehensive education programme which identifies the specific and different needs of the parties involved: young people (the victims and those young people displaying the harmful behaviour) and parents/guardians and professionals/practitioners who work with the young people. Yet, education should not reinforce and affirm a 'moral panic' regarding cyberbullying and sexting behaviours among young people. What is important is that young people, parents and guardians are made aware of what

---

[33] See *Concluding Observations* (n 24).

is 'healthy' behaviour in the digital era, including healthy sexual expression, while also being mindful of the range of online risks. In doing so, all parties should be able to make informed decisions, thus minimising exposure to potential harms. As one young person explains, 'maybe if parents themselves seemed a bit more understanding … young people would be able to open up more'.[34] In addition, effective and creative guidelines which are well-informed and respond to the voices and experiences of young people are required. Adults will never be able to keep abreast of developments within youth culture without constant engagement with young people themselves.

Finally, the research brought to light a number of significant scholarly gaps. First, there is little research which focuses on exploring peer-on-peer sexting practices and the experiences of LGBTQ+ young people. Understanding the motivations and intentions of LGBTQ+ young people when they engage in the behaviour requires further research. Second, it is recommended that further research be undertaken which targets other vulnerable or marginalised groups, including children in care: for example, the unique setting children in care are exposed to and how this can augment harms, particularly within a bullying context. Third, further examination of behaviours such as 'catfishing' and the risks young people are exposed to when they access the Dark Web is required. While the Internet is constantly evolving, and law and policy in the area seems to be always one step behind, up-to-date research is needed if we are to even scratch the surface when it comes to understanding some of the more complex digital settings and networks young people are accessing. Fourth, noting the uncertainty and confusion most young people felt surrounding bystander status, more research examining the tensions and challenges with the key parties ('victim', 'offender' and 'bystander') is needed. While some research has started to explore this relationship,[35] more needs to be done to understand this complex relationship dynamic within a peer setting.

One significant theme that emerged constantly throughout the research, and one which I want to leave you with, is that the voices of young people are *imperative* if real and effective change is to be made. As one young person poignantly explains: 'You have to understand that things have changed in the last 50 years. Things are happening … this is a serious topic.'[36]

---

[34] Young Person Focus Group (PhD): Male.
[35] See A-M McAlinden et al, 'Sexual Violence in the Digital Age: Replicating and Augmenting Harm, Victimhood and Blame' (2022) 31(6) *Social and Legal Studies* 871.
[36] Young Person Interview (PhD): Male.

Appendix 1

Professional Interviews (PhD)

Interview	No of Participants	Sector/Organisation
1	4	Education Sector
2	1	Children's Voluntary Organisation
3	1	Forensic Psychologist
4	1	Criminal Justice Sector
5	1	Safeguarding Organisation
6	1	Children's Voluntary Organisation
7	1	Children's Voluntary Organisation
8	1	Anti-Bullying Organisation
9	1	Education Sector
10	1	Statutory Sector
11	1	Victim Support Organisation
12	1	Education Sector
13	3	Safeguarding Sector
14	2	Children's Voluntary Organisation
15	1	Criminal Justice Sector
16	1	Independent Researcher on HSB
17	1	Children's Voluntary Organisation
18	2	Children's Voluntary Organisation
19	1	Criminal Justice Sector
20	1	Education Sector
21	1	Safeguarding Sector

Total = 28 Participants

Appendix 2

Interviews and Focus Groups with Young People (PhD)

Interview/Focus Group	No of Participants	Age range	Gender
Interview	1	17 years	F
Interview	2	13–14 years	F
Interview	2	15–17 years	M
Focus Group	6	15–17 years	F
Focus Group	4	15–17 years	M

Total = 15 Participants

Appendix 3

Professional Interviews (PDF)[1]

Interview	No of Participants	Sector/Organisation
1	1	Independent Social Work Consultant
2	1	Sexual Health Charity
3	1	Independent Social Work Consultant
4	2	Children's Charity
5 (Focus Group)	5	Education Sector

Total = 10 Participants

[1] Due to time constraints on the part of some participants, a number of group interviews were arranged (see interviews 4 and 5).

Appendix 4

Young People (Survey – PDF)

Gender	Age	Number
Boy	18	5
	17	9
	16	13
Girl	18	4
	17	9
	16	12
	15	5
	14	1
Neither	15	1
Did not say	Did not say	2

Total = 61 Participants

BIBLIOGRAPHY

Aalsma, MC and Brown, JR, 'What is Bullying' (2008) 43 *Journal of Adolescent Health* 101

Agnew, E, 'Sexting among Young People: Towards a Gender Sensitive Approach' (2021) 29(1) *International Journal of Children's Rights* 3

—— 'Sexting, Consent and Young People: Regulatory Challenges' (2021) 9 *Queen's Policy Engagement* 1

Agnew, E and McAlinden, A-M, 'Harmful Sexual Behaviour among Children and Young People Online: Cultural and Regulatory Challenges' in R Killean et al (eds), *Sexual Violence on Trial: Local and Comparative Perspectives* (Routledge, 2021)

—— 'Addressing Harmful Sexual Behaviours among Children and Young People: Definitional and Regulatory Tensions' in AK Gill and H Begum (eds), *Child Sexual Abuse in Black and Minoritised Communities* (Palgrave Macmillan, 2023)

Ahmed Zaky, E, 'Adolescence: A Crucial Transitional Stage in Human Life' (2017) 4(6) *Journal of Child and Adolescent Behavior* 1

Albury, K. and Crawford, K, 'Sexting, Consent and Young People's Ethics: Beyond Megan's Story' (2012) 26(3) *Continuum: Journal of Media and Cultural Studies* 463

Albury, K, Crawford, K, Byron, P and Mathews, B, 'Young People and Sexting in Australia: Ethics, Representation and the Law', *ARC Centre for Creative Industries and Innovation/Journalism and Media Research Centre* (The University of New South Wales, 2013)

Andersson, W and Bladini, M, 'Autonomy and Beyond – Voluntariness in the Light of Lived Autonomy' (2021) (3 & 4 /170) *Retfærd. Nordic Legal Journal* 35

Angelides, S, 'Technology, Hormones and Stupidity: The Affective Politics of Teenage Sexting' (2013) 16(5–6) *Sexualities* 665

Antoniadou, N and Kokkinos, CM, 'Cyber and School Bullying: Same or Different Phenomena?' (2015) 25 *Aggression and Violent Behaviour* 363

Anti-Bullying Alliance, *Bullying and Care-Experienced Young People* https://anti-bullyingalliance.org.uk/tools-information/all-about-bullying/at-risk-groups/looked-after-children/bullying-and-care, accessed 17 July 2023

Any Use? Young People's Opinions on Relationship and Sexuality Education in Belfast (Belfast Youth Forum, 2019)

APPG on Social Media and UK Safer Internet Centre, *Selfie Generation: What's Behind the Rise of Self-Generated Indecent Images of Children Online?* (APPG on Social Media, 2021)

Ariés, P, *Centuries of Childhood*, translated from the French by Robert Baldick (London, Cape, 1962)

Ashurst, L and McAlinden, A-M, 'Young People, Peer-to-Peer Grooming and Sexual Offending' (2015) 62(4) *Probation Journal* 374

Bailey, R, *Letting Children be Children: Report of an Independent Review of the Commercialisation and Sexualisation of Childhood* (Department for Education, 2011)

Bancroft, J, 'Normal Sexual Development' in HE Barbaree and WL Marshall (eds), *The Juvenile Sex Offender*, 2nd edn (The Guilford Press, 2008)

Bandalli, S, 'Children, Responsibility, and the New Youth Justice' in B Goldson (ed), *The New Youth Justice* (Russell House Publishing, 2000)

Barnett, H, *Children's Rights and the Law: An Introduction* (Routledge, 2022)

Barter, C, 'Attitudes and Behaviour in Teenage Intimate Relationships' in *Premature Sexualisation: Understanding the Risks: Outcomes of the NSPCC's Expert Seminar Series* (NSPCC, 2011)

Bayliss, B, 'The Kids Are Alright: Teen Sexting, Child Pornography Charges, and the Criminalization of Adolescent Sexuality' (2020) 91(1) *University of Colorado Law Review* 251

BBC News, 'Woman Dies after Abortion Request "Refused" at Galway Hospital' (BBC, 14 November 2012)

—— 'Starved Boy Daniel Pelka "Invisible" to Professionals' (BBC, 17 September 2013)

—— 'Amanda Hutton Guilty of Starving Hamzah Khan to Death' (BBC, 3 October 2013)

—— 'Timeline of Baby P Case' (BBC, 8 October 2013)

—— 'Police "Sorry" over Rochdale Child Sex Abuse Failures' (BBC, 13 March 2015)

—— 'Riley Siswick Murder: Pair Jailed over Boy's Death' (BBC, 13 June 2019)

—— 'Keigan O'Brien: Doncaster Couple Jailed over Boy's Death' (BBC, 11 November 2020)

—— 'Catholic Bishop of Derry Criticises Abortion Access Lessons Plans' (BBC, 7 June 2023)

Becker, HS, *Outsiders: Studies in the Sociology of Deviance* (The Free Press, 1963)

Beckett, H, 'Sexual Exploitation and Sexual Violence in Adolescence' in D Schubotz and P Devine (eds), *Not So Different: Teenage Attitudes across a Decade of Change in Northern Ireland* (Russell House Publishing, 2014)

Beckett, H, Brodie I, Factor F, Melrose M, Pearce, J, Pitts, J, Shuker, L and Warrington, C, '"It's Wrong … But You Get Used to It" A Qualitative Study of Gang-Associated Sexual Violence towards, and Exploitation of, Young People in England', A Report commissioned by the Office of the Children's Commissioner's Inquiry into Child Sexual Exploitation in Gangs and Groups (University of Bedfordshire and Children's Commissioner, 2013)

Beckett, H and Walker, J, 'Words Matter: Reconceptualising the Conceptualisation of Child Sexual Exploitation' in H Beckett and J Pearce. (eds), *Understanding and Responding to Child Sexual Exploitation* (Routledge, 2018)

Bentley, H, Fellowes, A, Glenister, S et al, *How Safe Are Our Children? 2020* (NSPCC, 2020)

Berelowitz, S, Clifton, J, Firimin, C, Gulyurtlu, S and Edwards, G, *If Only Someone Had Listened*, final report (London, Office of the Children's Commissioner Inquiry, 2013)

Besag, V, *Understanding Girls' Friendships, Fights and Feuds: A Practical Approach to Girls' Bullying* (Open University Press, 2006)

Bindel, J, 'Rochdale Victim: 'I Was Groomed at 14, Then the Courts Came for my Children' (*The Guardian*, 17 April 2022)

Bingham, J, 'Nine out of 10 Teenage Girls Digitally Enhance Their Own Facebook Pictures, Claim' (*The Telegraph*, 19 September 2015)

Bohner, G, Eyssel, F, Pina, A, Siebler, F and Viki, GT, 'Rape Myth Acceptance: Cognitive, Affective, and Behavioral Effects of Beliefs that Blame the Victim and Exonerate the Perpetrator' in M Horvath and J Brown (eds), *Rape: Challenging Contemporary Thinking* (Cullompton, Willan, 2009)

Boyle, K, 'What's in a Name? Theorising the Inter-Relationships of Gender and Violence' (2019) 20(1) *Feminist Theory* 19

Brown, J and Saied-Tesser, A, *Preventing Child Sexual Abuse: Towards a National Strategy for England* (NSPCC, 2015)

Brown, T, *Northern Ireland Youth Justice Agency Annual Workload Statistics 2021/22* (Northern Ireland Statistics and Research Agency, 2022)

Brown, V, Clery, E and Ferguson, C, *Estimating the Prevalence of Young People Absent from School Due to Bullying* (Red Balloon Learner Centre Group, 2011)

Bryant, A, 'Minors Sexting in Colorado: What Does the Law Say?' (The Law Office of Andrew Bryant, 7 July 2021) https://andrewbryantlaw.com/2021/06/05/minors-sexting-in-colorado-what-does-the-law-say/ accessed 17 July 2023

Buckingham, D, *After the Death of Childhood* (Polity Press, 2000)

Bunting, L, McCartan, C, Davidson, G, Grant, A, McBride, O, Mulholland, C, Murphy, J, Schubotz, D, Cameron, J and Shevlin, M, *The Mental Health of Parents and Children in Northern Ireland* (Youth Wellbeing NI, 2020)

Burgin, R, 'Persistent Narratives of Force and Resistance: Affirmative Consent as Law Reform' (2019) 59 *British Journal of Criminology* 296

Burkett, M and Hamilton, K, 'Postfeminist Sexual Agency: Young Women's Negotiations of Sexual Consent' (2012) 15(7) *Sexualities* 815

Burr, V and Dick, P, 'Social Constructionism' in B Gough (ed), *The Palgrave Handbook of Critical Social Psychology* (Palgrave Macmillan, 2017)

Byron Review, *Safer Children in a Digital World: The Report of the Byron Review* (DCSF Publications, 2008)

Calogero, RM, 'Objectification Theory, Self-Objectification, and Body Image' in T Cash (ed), *Encyclopedia of Body Image and Human Appearance* (Academic Press, 2012)

Care Quality Commission, 'GP Mythbuster 8: Gillick Competency and Fraser Guidelines' (23 December 2022) https://www.cqc.org.uk/guidance-providers/gps/gp-mythbusters/gp-mythbuster-8-gillick-competency-fraser-guidelines accessed 17 July 2023

Carrabine, E, Cox, P, Lee, M, Plummer, K and South, N, *Criminology: A Sociological Introduction*, 2nd edn (Routledge, 2009)

Carr, N, 'Criminalising Ten-Year-Olds is No Way to Run a Justice System' (*The Conversation*, 20 February 2015)

Casey, BJ, Duhoux, S and Cohen, MM, 'Adolescence: What do Transmission, Transition and Translation Have to Do with It?' (2010) 67(5) *Neuron* 749

Chandra, J, 'Celebrities Open up About Shocking Sexual Harassment and Assault Experiences' (*Elle Australia*, 18 October 2017)

Chester West and Chester Council, 'Young People and Consent: Guidance Notes' https://www.cheshirewestandchester.gov.uk/documents/social-care-and-health/children/team-around-the-family/young-people-and-consent-guidance-notes-130219.pdf accessed 17 July 2023

Chi En Kwan, G and Skoric, MM, 'Facebook Bullying: An Extension of Battles in School' (2012) 29 *Computers in Human Behavior* 16

Child Exploitation and Online Protection Centre, *Out of Mind, Out of Sight: Breaking Down the Barriers to Understanding Child Sexual Exploitation* (CEOP, 2011)

Children and Young People's Strategy 2020–2030 (Northern Ireland Executive, 2020) https://www.education-ni.gov.uk/publications/children-and-young-peoples-strategy-2020-2030 accessed 17 July 2023

Children's Commissioner, *Interim Findings on Government's Commission on Online Peer-on-Peer Abuse* (Children's Commissioner for England, 2021)

Children's Experiences of Legal but Harmful Content Online, Helplines Insight Briefings (NSPCC, 2022)

Ching Yang, S, 'Paths to Bullying in Online Gaming: The Effects of Gender, Preference for Playing Violent Games, Hostility, and Aggressive Behaviour on Bullying' (2012) 47(3) *Journal of Educational Computing Research* 235

Choi, H, Van Ouytsel, J and Temple, JR, 'Association between Sexting and Sexual Coercion among Female Adolescents' (2016) 53 *Journal of Adolescence* 164

Christie, N, 'The Ideal Victim' in EA Fattah (ed), *From Crime Policy to Victim Policy* (Palgrave Macmillan, 1986)

Christopherson, KM, 'The Positive and Negative Implications of Anonymity in Internet Social Interactions: "On the Internet, Nobody Knows you're a Dog"' (2007) 23(6) *Computers in Human Behaviour* 3038

Cipriani, D, *Children's Rights and the Minimum Age of Criminal Responsibility: A Global Perspective* (Routledge, 2009)

Clark Mane, R, 'Transmuting Grammars of Whiteness in Third-Wave Feminism: Interrogating Postrace Histories, Postmodern Abstraction, and the Proliferation of Difference in Third-Wave Texts' (2012) 38(1) *The University of Chicago Press* 71

Cloete, A, 'Youth Culture, Media and Sexuality: What Could Faith Communities Contribute?' (2012) 68(2) *HTS Teologiese Studies/ Theological Studies* 1

Cochrane, K, *All the Rebel Women: The Rise of the Fourth Wave of Feminism* (Guardian Book, 2013)

Cockbain, E, and Tufail, W, 'Failing Victims, Fuelling Hate: Challenging the Harms of the "Muslim Grooming Gangs" Narrative' (2020) 61(3) *Race and Class* 3

Cohen, S, *Folk Devils and Moral Panics*, 3rd edn (Routledge, 2002)

College of Policing, *Briefing Note: Police Action in Response to Youth Produced Sexual Imagery ('Sexting')*, Version 1.0 (November 2016)

Committee on the Rights of the Child, *Concluding Observations on the Combined Sixth and Seventh Reports of the United Kingdom of Great Britain and Northern Ireland*, 2 June 2023, CRC/C/GBR/CO/6–7

Commission to Inquire into Child Abuse, *Report of the Commission to Inquire into Child Abuse (The Ryan Report)* (Dublin, Government Publications, 2009)

Cole-Albäck, A, 'A Brief History of Children's Rights' https://www.birthto5matters.org.uk/wp-content/uploads/2021/04/Childrens-rights-for-Birth-to-Five-Matters.pdf accessed 17 July 2023

Coppock, V, Haydon, D and Richter, I, *The Illusions of 'Post-Feminism': New Women, Old Myths* (Routledge, 1995)

Corteen, K. and Scraton, P, 'Prolonging "Childhood", Manufacturing Innocence and Regulating Sexuality' in P Scraton (ed), *'Childhood' in 'Crisis'?* (UCL Press, 1997)

Cowan, R, 'Asking for It' in R Killean, E Dowds and A-M McAlinden, *Sexual Violence on Trial* (Routledge, 2020)

Cowan, S, 'Freedom and Capacity to Make a Choice: A Feminist Analysis of Consent in the Criminal Law of Rape' in VE Munro and CF Stychin (eds), *Sexuality and the Law: Feminist Engagements* (Taylor and Francis, 2007)

Coy, M, 'Milkshakes, Lady Lumps and Growing up to Want Boobies: How the Sexualisation of Popular Culture Limits Girls' Horizons' (2009) 18(6) *Child Abuse Review* 372

—— 'The Impact of the Sexualisation on Young People's Attitudes and Relationships' in *Premature Sexualisation: Understanding the Risks: Outcomes of the NSPCC's Expert Seminar Series* (NSPCC, 2011) 5

Crofts, T and Lievens, E, 'Sexting and the Law' in M Walrave, J Ouytsel, K Ponnet and J Temple (eds), *Sexting: Motives and Risk in Online Sexual Self-Representation* (Palgrave, 2018)

Cross, EJ, Piggin, R, Douglas, T and Vonkaenel-Flatt, J, *Virtual Violence II: Progress and Challenges in the Fight against Cyberbullying* (Beatbullying, 2012)

Crossey Malone, E, 'The Ulster Rugby Rape Trial: No to Victim-Blaming & Rape Culture' *Socialist Party* (7 March 2018)

Crown Prosecution Service, 'Upskirting: Public Urged to Report Offenders As Prosecutions Double' (CPS, 3 December 2021) https://www.cps.gov.uk/cps/news/upskirting-public-urged-report-offenders-prosecutions-double accessed 17 July 2023

Cuevas-Parra, P, 'Multi-Dimensional Lens to Article 12 of the UNCRC: A Model to Enhance Children's Participation' (2023) 21(3) *Children's Geographies* 363

Cuna, JP, 'What Are the Three Stages of Adolescence?' (Childrens Health Centre, 2021) https://www.emedicinehealth.com/what_are_the_three_stages_of_adolescence/article_em.htm accessed 17 July 2023

Cunningham, H, *Children and Childhood in Western Society Since 1500*, 2nd edn (Pearson Education, 2005)

Cyberbullying Research Center, 'Sexting Laws in Rhode Island' https://cyberbullying.org/sexting-laws/rhode-island#:~:text=In%20Rhode%20Island%2C%20a%20minor,of%20the%20sex%20offender%20registry accessed 17 July 2023

Da Costa Nunes, J, 'The Naughty Child in Nineteenth-Century American Art' (1987) 21(2) *Journal of American Studies* 225

Davidson, J, Aiken, MP, Farr, R and Philips, K, *European Youth Cybercrime, Online Harm and Online Risk Taking: 2022 Research Report* (London, United Kingdom Institute for Connected Communities, University of East London, 2022)

Davis, H and Bourhill, M, '"Crisis": The Demonization of Children and Young People' in P Scraton (ed), *'Childhood' in 'Crisis'?* (UCL Press, 1997)

Day, T, 'The New Digital Dating Behaviour – Sexting: Teens' Explicit Love Letters: Criminal Justice or Civil Liability' (2010) 33(1) *Hastings Communications and Entertainment Law Journal* 69

DeLamater, J and Hyde, J, 'Essentialism vs Social Constructionism in the Study of Human Sexuality' (1998) 35(1) *The Journal of Sex Research* 10

Delmage, E, 'The Minimum Age of Criminal Responsibility: A Medico-Legal Perspective' (2013) 13(2) *Youth Justice* 102

Denzin, NK, *Childhood Socialization*, 2nd edn (New York, Routledge, 2010)

Department for Children, Schools and Families, *Safe from Bullying in Children's Homes* (DCSF Publications, 2009)

Department of Education, *Effective Responses to Bullying Behaviours* (DoE, EA and NIABF, 2022)

Department of Health, *Publication of 'Children's Social Care Statistics for Northern Ireland 2021/22'* (3 November 2022)

Department of Justice, 'Long Launches Public Consultation on the Minimum Age of Criminal Responsibility' (NI Direct, Department of Justice, 3 October 2022)

Devlin, A, 'Where is Robert Thompson Now, When Did the James Bulger Killer Come Out as Gay and Was He the Ringleader in the Murder?' (*The Sun*, 19 March 2018)

Dickson, B, *Law in Northern Ireland*, 3rd edn (Oxford, Hart Publishing, 2018)

Doherty, S, 'Exhibition Review: A Reflection on Ruth Maxwell's Not Consent Exhibition as a Method of Challenging Rape Myths in Ireland' (2020) 14(2) *Law and Humanities* 273

Dowds, E, 'Sexual Consent in Northern Ireland: The Social and Legal Dimensions' (2020) *Queens Policy Engagement* 1

—— 'Consent, Autonomy and Coercion: A Response to Robin West' (2020) *The Modern Law Review* 1

—— 'Rethinking Affirmative Approaches to Consent: A Step in the Right Direction' in R Killeen, R Dowds and A-M McAlinden (eds), *Sexual Violence on Trial* (Routledge, 2020)

—— 'I Presume She Wanted It to Happen': Rape and Reasonable Belief in Consent, and Law Reform in Northern Ireland' (2022) 73(1) *Northern Ireland Legal Quarterly* 74

—— 'Refining Consent: Rape Law Reform, Reasonable Belief, and Communicative Responsibility' (2022) 49(4) *Journal of Law and Society* 824

Dowds, E and Agnew, E, 'Rape Law and Policy: Persistent Challenges and Future Directions' in M Horvath and J Brown (eds), *Rape: Challenging Contemporary Thinking – 10 Years On* (Routledge, 2022)

Drouin, M, Ross, J and Tobin, E, 'Sexting: A New, Digital Vehicle for Intimate Partner Aggression' (2015) 50 *Computers in Human Behaviour* 197

Dufour, K, 'Amanda Todd Case Highlights Issue of Online Bullying' (*The Telegraph*, 16 October 2012)

Dutta, K, 'Charlotte Church Slams "Hyper-Sexualised" Music Industry and "Unattainable Sexbots" Rihanna and Miley Cyrus' (*The Independent*, 14 October 2013)

Dworkin, A, 'Pornography: The New Terrorism' (1977) 8 *Review of Law and Social Change* 217

Egan, RD and Hawkes, G, 'Sexuality, Youth and the Perils of Endangered Innocence: How History Can Help Us Get Past the Panic' (2012) 24(3) *Gender and Education* 269

Elgot, J, 'DUP Will "Vigorously Oppose" UK Intervention to Speed up NI Abortion Services' (*The Guardian*, 18 March 2021)

Ellison, G, 'Criminalizing the Payment for Sex in Northern Ireland: Sketching the Contours of a Moral Panic' (2017) 57(1) *The British Journal of Criminology* 194

Ellison, G, Ni Dhónaill, C and Early, E, *A Review of the Criminalisation of Paying for Sexual Services in Northern Ireland* (Department of Justice, 2019)

Estimating the Prevalence of Young People Absent from School Due to Bullying (Red Balloon Learner Centre Group, 2011)

Family Lives, *Sexual Bullying* https://www.familylives.org.uk/advice/bullying/general-advice/what-is-sexual-bullying accessed 17 July 2023

Faure-Walker, D and Hunt, N, 'The Prevalence of Adverse Childhood Experiences among Children and Adolescents Who Display Harmful Sexual Behaviour: A Review of the Existing Research' (2022) 15 *Journal of Child and Adolescent Trauma* 1051

Finkelhor, D, Baron, L, Browne, A, Peters, SP and Wyatt, GE, *A Sourcebook on Child Sexual Abuse* (SAGE, 1986)

Firmin, C, *Abuse between Young People* (Routledge, 2018)

—— 'Contextual Safeguarding: Theorising the Contexts of Child Protection and Peer Abuse' in J Pearce (ed), *Child Sexual Exploitation: Why Theory Matters* (Policy Press, 2019)

Fishman, S, 'The History of Childhood Sexuality' (1982) 17(2) *Journal of Contemporary History* 269

Flood, M, 'The Harms of Pornography Exposure among Children and Young People' (2009) 18(6) *Child Abuse Review* 384

Forde, L, 'Welfare, Justice and Diverse Models of Youth Justice: A Children's Rights Analysis' (2021) 29 *The International Journal of Children's Rights* 920

Franklin, B, *The New Handbook of Children's Rights: Comparative Policy and Practice* (London, Routledge, 2022)

Franklin, B and Horwath, J, 'The Media Abuse of Children: Jake's Progress from Demonic Icon to Restored Childhood Innocent' (1996) 5 *Child Abuse Review* 310

Fredrickson, BL and Roberts, T, 'Objectification Theory: Toward Understanding Women's Lived Experiences and Mental Health Risks' (1997) 21(2) *Psychology of Women Quarterly* 173

Freeman, H, 'What Does the Belfast Rape Trial Tell Women? Make a Complaint and You'll be Vilified' (*The Guardian*, 4 April 2018)

Freeman, M, 'The Future of Children's Rights' (2000) 14 *Children & Society* 277

Frith, H, 'Sexual Scripts, Sexual Refusals and Rape' in M Horvath and J Brown (eds), *Rape: Challenging Contemporary Thinking* (Willan Publishing, 2009)

Furedi, F, *Culture of Fear Revisited: Risk-Taking and the Morality of Low Expectation* (London, Continuum, 2006)

—— *Moral Crusades in an Age of Mistrust: The Jimmy Savile Scandal* (Palgrave Macmillan, 2013)

GD8, 'Youth Produced Sexual Imagery – Guidance for Disclosure' (2016) https://assets.publishing. service.gov.uk/government/uploads/system/uploads/attachment_data/file/578979/GD8_-_ Sexting_Guidance.pdf accessed 17 July 2023

Gerassi, L, 'A Heated Debate: Theoretical Perspectives of Sexual Exploitation and Sex Work' (2015) 42(4) *Journal of Sociology and Social Welfare* 79

Geldard, K, Geldard, D and Yin Foo, R, *Counselling Adolescents: The Proactive Approach for Young People*, 4th edn (SAGE, 2016)

Gerrard, N, 'Holly and Jessica – We'll Never Know' (*The Guardian*, 21 December 2003)

Giles, J, 'Social Constructionism and Sexual Desire' (2006) 36(3) *Journal for the Theory of Social Behaviour* 225

Gill, AK and Harrison, K, 'Child Grooming and Sexual Exploitation: Are South Asian Men the UK Media's Folk Devils?' (2015) 4(2) *International Journal for Crime, Justice and Social Democracy* 34

Gill, R, 'Empowerment/Sexism: Figuring Female Sexual Agency in Contemporary Advertising' (2008) 18(1) *Feminism and Psychology* 35

Gillen, Sir J, 'Report into the Law and Procedures in Serious Sexual Offences in Northern Ireland' (Gillen Review) (Department of Justice, 2019)

Gillespie, AA, 'Adolescents, Sexting and Human Rights' (2013) 13(4) *Human Rights Law Review* 623

—— 'Child Pornography' (2018) 27(1) *Information and Communications Technology Law* 30

Gilmore, S, 'Use of the UNCRC in Family Law Cases in England and Wales' (2017) 25 *The International Journal of Children's Rights* 500

Glenza, J, Pengelly M and Levin, S, 'US Supreme Court Overturns Abortion Rights, Upending Roe v Wade' (*The Guardian*, 24 June 2022)

Goffman, E, *Stigma: Notes on the Management of Spoiled Identity* (Penguin, 1963)

Goldson, B, '"Childhood": An Introduction to Historical and Theoretical Analyses' in P Scraton (ed), *'Childhood' in 'Crisis'* (UCL Press, 1997)

Gotell, L, 'Rethinking Affirmative Consent in Canadian Sexual Assault Law: Neoliberal Sexual Subjects and Risky Women' (2008) 41 *Akron Law Review* 865

Graham, R, 'Male Rape and the Careful Construction of the Male Victim' (2006) 15(2) *Social and Legal Studies* 187

Green, S, *Criminalizing Sex: A Unified Liberal Theory* (Oxford University Press, 2020)

Greer, C, *Sex, Crime and the Media: Sex Offending and the Press in a Divided Society* (Routledge, 2003)

Grierson, J, 'Bulger Killer Jailed over Indecent Images of Children' (*The Guardian*, 7 February 2018)

Grisafi, P, 'Natalie Portman Says That Sexualised Roles as a Teen Harmed Her. When Will Hollywood Listen?' (Think Opinion, Analysis, Essays, 13 December 2020)

Hackett, S, 'Children and Young People with Harmful Sexual Behaviours' in C Barter and B David (eds), *Children Behaving Badly? Peer Violence between Children and Young People* (John Wiley and Sons, 2010)

—— *Children and Young People with Harmful Sexual Behaviours* (Research in Practice, 2014)

Hackett, S, Holmes, D, and Branigan, P, 'Harmful Sexual Behaviour Framework: an Evidence-Informed Operational Framework for Children and Young People Displaying Harmful Sexual Hehaviours' Project Report (London, NSPCC, 2016)

Hackett, S, Masson, H and Philips, S, *Services for Young People Who Sexually Abuse. A Report on Mapping and Exploring Services for Young People Who Have Sexually Abused Others* (NSPCC/Youth Justice Board for England and Wales, 2005)

Harmful Sexual Behaviour Framework: An Evidence-Informed Operational Framework for Children and Young People Displaying Harmful Sexual Behaviours, 2nd edn (NSPCC, 2019)

Harvey, L and Ringrose, J, 'Sexting, Ratings and (Mis)Recognition: Teen Boys Performing Classed and Racialized Masculinities in Digitally Networked Publics' in E Renold, J Ringrose and RD Egan (eds), *Children, Sexuality and Sexualisation* (Palgrave Macmillan, 2015)

Haydon, D and Scraton, P, '"Condemn a Little More, Understand a Little Less": The Political Context and Rights' Implications of the Domestic and European Rulings in the Venables-Thompson Case' (2000) 27(3) *Journal of Law and Society* 416

Haydon, D, Scraton, P and McAlister, S, 'Young People, Conflict and Regulation' (2012) 51(5) *The Howard Journal* 503

Heaton-Harris, C, *Northern Ireland Update* (UK Parliament, 2023) https://questions-statements.parliament.uk/written-statements/detail/2023-06-06/hcws824 accessed 17 July 2023

Heilmann, A, *New Woman Fiction: Women Writing First-Wave Feminism* (Macmillan Press, 2000)

Henniker, J, Print, B and Morrison, T, 'An Inter-Agency Assessment Framework for Young People Who Sexually Abuse: Principles, Processes and Practicalities' (2002) 8(2) *Child Care in Practice* 114

Henry, N, Flynn, A and Powell, A, 'Technology-Facilitated Domestic and Sexual Violence: A Review' (2020) 26(15–16) *Violence against Women* 1828

Henry, N and Powell, A, 'Beyond the "Sext": Technology-Facilitated Sexual Violence and Harassment against Adult Women' (2015) 48(1) *Australian and New Zealand Journal of Criminology* 104

Henry, N and Powell, A, 'Sexual Violence in the Digital Age: The Scope and Limits of Criminal Law' (2016) 25(4) *Social and Legal Studies* 397

Herring, J, *Criminal Law Text, Cases, and Materials*, 10th edn (Oxford University Press, 2022)

Heywood, C, *A History of Childhood: Children and Childhood in the West from Medieval to Modern Times* (Polity Press, 2001)

Hill, M, 'The Manifest and Latent Lessons of Child Abuse Inquiries' (1990) 20(3) *The British Journal of Social Work* 197

Hird, MJ and Jackson, S, 'Where "Angels" and "Wusses" Fear to Tread: Sexual Coercion in Adolescent Dating Relationships' (2001) 37(1) *Journal of Sociology* 27

Hollis, V and Belton, E, *Children and Young People Who Engage in Technology-Assisted Harmful Sexual Behaviour: A Study of Their Behaviours, Backgrounds and Characteristics* (NSPCC, 2017)

Holt, JC, *Escape from Childhood: The Needs and Rights of Children* (Medford, HoltGWS LLC, 2013)

Horeck, T and Negra, D, 'Reconsidering True Crime and Gendered Authority in Allen v Farrow' (2022) 22(6) *Feminist Media Studies* 1564

Horvath, M, Alys, L, Massey, K, Pina, A, Scally, M and Adler, J, '*Basically ... Porn Is Everywhere*': *A Rapid Evidence Assessment on the Effects That Access and Exposure to Pornography Has on Children and Young People* (London, Office for the Children's Commissioner, 2013)

Hinduja, S, 'Sexting, the Jesse Logan Case, and What Schools Can Do' (Cyberbullying Research Centre, 2009)

Ibbetson, C, *How Many Children Have Their Own Tech?* (YouGov UK, 2020)

James A. and James A, *Constructing Childhood Theory, Policy and Social Practice* (Palgrave Macmillan, 2004)

James A and Jenks, C, 'Public Perceptions of Childhood Criminality' (1996) 47(2) *The British Journal of Sociology* 315

James A and Prout, A (eds), *Constructing and Reconstructing Childhood: Contemporary Issues in the Sociological Study of Childhood* (Falmer Press, 1997)

Jackson, S, *Childhood and Sexuality* (Oxford, Basil Blackwell, 1982)

Jackson, S and Scott, S, 'Risk Anxiety and the Social Construction of Childhood' in D Lupton (ed), *Risk and Sociocultural Theory: New Directions and Perspectives* (Cambridge University Press, 1999)

Javier, RA, Dillon, J, DaBreo, C and De Mucci, J, 'Bullying and its Consequences: In Search of Solutions – Part II' (2013) 22(2) Journal *of Social Distress and the Homeless* 59

Jenks, C, *Childhood* (London, Routledge, 1996)

Jewkes, Y, *Media and Crime*, 2nd edn (SAGE, 2010)

—— *Media and Crime*, 3rd edn (SAGE, 2015)

Kao, Y, Coster, W, Cohn, ES and Orsmond, GI, 'Preparation for Adulthood: Shifting Responsibility for Management of Daily Tasks from Parents to Their Children' (2021) 75(2) *The American Journal of Occupational Therapy* 1

Karaian, L, 'Lolita Speaks: "Sexting" Teenage Girls and the Law' (2012) *Crime Media Culture* 1

Karaian, L, 'Policing "Sexting": Responsibilization, Respectability and Sexual Subjectivity in Child Protection/Crime Prevention Responses to Teenagers' Digital Sexual Expression' (2013) 18(3) *Theoretical Criminology* 282

Kelly, L, *Surviving Sexual Violence* (Cambridge, Polity Press, 1988)

Kempe, CH, Silverman, FN, Steele, BF, Droegemueller, W and Silver, HK, 'The Battered-Child Syndrome' (1985) 9 *Child Abuse and Neglect* 143

Khomami, N, 'James Bulger Killer Back in Jail after Being Caught with Abuse Images Again' (*The Guardian*, 23 November 2017)

Kilbourne, S, 'The Wayward Americans – Why the USA Has Not Ratified the UN Convention on the Rights of the Child' (1998) 10(3) *Child and Family Law Quarterly* 243

Killean, R, Dowds, E and McAlinden, A-M (eds), *Sexual Violence on Trial* (Routledge, 2020)

Killean, R, McAlinden, A-M and Dowds, E, 'Sexual Violence in the Digital Age: Replicating and Augmenting Harm, Victimhood and Blame' (2022) 31(6) *Social & Legal Studies* 871

Kitzinger, J, 'Who are you Kidding? Children, Power and the Struggle against Sexual Abuse' in A James and A Prout (eds), *Constructing and Reconstructing Childhood* (Falmer Press, 1997)

Kota, R, Schoohs, S, Benson, M and Moreno, M, 'Characterizing Cyberbullying among College Students: Hacking, Dirty Laundry, and Mocking' (2014) 4(4) *Societies* 549

Kowalski, RM, Limber, SP and Agatston, PW, *Cyberbullying: Bullying in the Digital Age*, 2nd edn (Oxford, Wiley-Blackwell, 2012)

Lagaay, M and Courtney, L, 'Time to Listen: Independent Advocacy within the Child Protection Process' (London, The National Children's Bureau, 2013)

Lanzarote Convention, *Council of Europe Convention on the Protection of Children against Sexual Exploitation and Sexual Abuse: A Global Tool to Protect Children from sexual violence* (Council of Europe) https://www.coe.int/en/web/children/lanzarote-convention accessed 17 July 2023

Lee, M and Crofts, T, 'Gender, Pressure, Coercion and Pleasure: Untangling Motivations for Sexting between Young People' (2015) 55(3) *British Journal of Criminology* 454

Lee, M, Crofts, T, Salter, M, Milivojevic, S and McGovern, A, '"Let's Get Sexting": Risk, Power, Sex and Criminalisation in the Moral Domain' (2013) 2(1) *International Journal for Crime and Justice* 35

Lenhart, A, *Teens and Sexting: How and Why Minor Teens are Sending Sexually Suggestive Nude or Nearly Nude Images via Text Messaging* (Pew Research Center Report, 2009)

Lesko, N, *Act Your Age!: A Cultural Construction of Adolescence* (New York, Routledge Farmer, 2001)

Lewis, R and Anitha, S, 'Upskirting: A Systematic Literature Review' (2023) 24(3) *Trauma, Violence and Abuse* 1

Lewis, R, Tanton, C, Mercer, C, Mitchell, K, Palmer, M, Macdowall, W and Wellings, K, 'Heterosexual Practices among Young People in Britain: Evidence from Three National Surveys of Sexual Attitudes and Lifestyles' (2017) 61 *Journal of Adolescent Health* 694

Lipmann, J and Campbell, S, 'Damned If You Do, Damned If You Don't … If You're a Girl: Relational and Normative Contexts of Adolescent Sexting in the United States' (2014) 8(4) *Journal of Children and Media* 371

Livingstone, S, *Young People and New Media: Childhood and the Changing Media Environment* (SAGE, 2002)

Livingstone, S, Haddon, L, Görzig, A and Ólafsson, K, *EU Kids Online: Final Report* (EU Kids Online, London School of Economics & Political Science, 2011)

Lóóf, L, 'Sexual Behaviour, Adolescents and Problematic Content' in E Quayle and K Ribisl (eds), *Understanding and Preventing Online Sexual Exploitation of Children* (London, Routledge, 2012)

Lunceford, B, 'Sex in the Digital Age: Media Ecology and Megan's Law' (2010) 9(4) *Explorations in Media Ecology* 239

Lundy, L, '"Voice" is Not Enough: Conceptualising Article 12 of the United Nations Convention on the Rights of the Child' (2007) 33(6) *British Educational Research Journal* 927

Lusher, A, 'James Bulger Murder: How Failure to Deal with Killer Jon Venables Became Latest Episode in Tragedy That Shames a Nation' (*Independent*, 9 February 2018)

Lykens, J, Pilloton, M, Silva, C, Schlamm, E, Wilburn, K and Pence, E, 'Google for Sexual Relationships: Mixed-Methods Study on Digital Flirting and Online Dating Among Adolescent Youth and Young Adults' (2019) 5(2) *JMIR Public Health and Surveillance* 1

MacKinnon, C, 'Sexuality, Pornography and Method: Pleasure under Patriarchy' (1989) 99(2) *Ethics* 314

MacKinnon, C, 'Rape Redefined' (2016) 10 *Harvard Law and Policy Review* 431

Malvaso, CG, Cale, J, Whitten, T, Day, A, Singh, S, Hackett, L, Delfabbro, PH and Ross, S, 'Associations between Adverse Childhood Experiences and Trauma among Young People Who Offend: A Systematic Literature Review' (2022) 23(5) *Trauma, Violence and Abuse* 1677

Marshall, K, *Child Sexual Exploitation in Northern Ireland: Report of the Independent Inquiry* (Criminal Justice Inspection Northern Ireland, 2014)

Marston, C and Lewis, R, 'Anal Heterosex among Young People and Implications for Health Promotion: A Qualitative Study in the UK' (2014) 4 *British Medical Journal Open* 1

Martellozzo, E, Monaghan, A, Adler, JR, Davidson, J, Leyva, R and Horvath, M, '… I Wasn't Sure It Was OK to Watch It …' A Quantitative and Qualitative Examination of the Impact of Online Pornography on the Values, Attitudes, Beliefs and Behaviours of Children and Young People (NSPCC and Children's Commissioner for England, 2016)

McAlinden, A-M, '"Setting' Em Up": Personal, Familial and Institutional Grooming in the Sexual Abuse of Children' (2006) 15(3) *Social and Legal Studies* 339

—— *The Shaming of Sexual Offenders: Risk, Retribution and Reintegration* (Bloomsbury, 2007)

—— '*Grooming' and the Sexual Abuse of Children* (Clarendon Studies in Criminology, 2012)

—— 'Sexting and Cyberbullying' in R Atkinson (ed), *Shades of Deviance: A Primer on Crime, Deviance and Social Harm* (London, Routledge, 2014)

—— 'Deconstructing Victim and Offender Identities in discourses on Child Sexual Abuse: Hierarchies, Blame and the Good/Evil Dialectic' (2014) 54(2) *British Journal of Criminology* 180

—— *Children as 'Risk': Sexual Exploitation and Abuse by Children and Young People* (Cambridge University Press, 2018)

McAlinden, A-M, Killean, R and Dowds, E, 'Sexual Violence in the Digital Age: Replicating and Augmenting Harm, Victimhood and Blame' (2022) 31(6) *Social and Legal Studies* 871

McAlister, S, Scraton, P and Haydon, D, 'Childhood in Transition: Growing up in "Post-Conflict" Northern Ireland' (2014) 12(3) *Children's Geographies* 297

McEvoy, K and McConnachie, K, 'Victimology in Transitional Justice: Victimhood, Innocence and Hierarchy' (2012) 9(5) *European Journal of Criminology* 527

McFerran, F, 'UN Concluding Observations Demonstrate Scale of Failure to Meet Children's Rights Requirements' (Children's Law Centre, 2023)

McGlynn, C. and Rackley, E, 'Image-Based Sexual Violence' (2017) 37(3) *Oxford Journal of Legal Studies* 534

McGlynn, C, Rackley, E and Houghton, R (2017) 'Beyond "Revenge Porn": The Continuum of Image Based Sexual Abuse' (2017) 25(1) *Feminist Legal Studies* 25

McGlynn, C, Rackley, E, Johnson, K, Henry, N, Flynn, A, Powell, A, Gavey, N and Scott, A, *Shattering Lives and Myths: A Report on Image-Based Sexual Abuse* (Durham University/University of Kent, 2019)

McKay, S, 'How the "Rugby Rape Trial" Divided Ireland' (*The Guardian*, 4 December 2018)

McNaull, G, 'Contextualising Violence: An Anti-Carceral Feminist Approach' in R Killean, E Dowds and A-M McAlinden (eds), *Sexual Violence on Trial* (Routledge, 2021)

Melrose, M, 'Twenty-First Century Party People: Young People and Sexual Exploitation in the New Millennium' (2013) 22(3) *Child Abuse Review* 155

Meredith, R, 'Northern Ireland Education Cuts "Equivalent to Losing 6,600 Staff"' (BBC, 24 May 2023)

Miller, ME, 'NC Just Prosecuted a Teenage Couple for Making Child Porn – of Themselves' (The Washington Post, 21 September 2015) https://www.washingtonpost.com/news/morning-mix/wp/2015/09/21/n-c-just-prosecuted-a-teenage-couple-for-making-child-porn-of-themselves/ accessed 17 July 2023

Milton, AC, Gill, BA, Davenport, TA, Dowling, M, Burns, JM and Hickie, IB, 'Sexting, Web-Based Risks, and Safety in Two Representative National Samples of Young Australians: Prevalence, Perspectives, and Predictors' (2019) 6(6) *JMIR Mental Health* 1

Miriam, K, 'Stopping the Traffic in Women: Power, Agency and Abolition in Feminist Debates over Sex-Rafficking' (2005) 36(1) *Journal of Social Philosophy* 1

Mitchell, KJ, Finkelhor, D, Jones, LM and Wolak, J, 'Prevalence and Characteristics of Youth Sexting: A National Study' (2012) 129(1) *Pediatrics* 13

Montgomery-Devlin, J, 'The Sexual Exploitation of Children and Young People in Northern Ireland: Overview from the Barnardo's Beyond the Shadows Service' (2008) 14(4) *Child Care in Practice* 381

Moore, A, 'I Couldn't Save My Child from Being Killed by an Online Predator' (*The Guardian*, 13 January 2016)

Mori, C, Park, J, Temple, JR and Madigan, S, 'Are Youth Sexting Rates Still on the Rise? A Meta-Analytic Update' (2022) 70 *Journal of Adolescent Health* 531

Moss, P, 'Northern Ireland: A Year without Devolved Government' (BBC, 9 January 2018) https://www.bbc.co.uk/news/uk-northern-ireland-politics-42608322 accessed 17 July 2023

Muncie, J, *Youth and Crime*, 3rd edn (SAGE, 2009)

Munro, E, 'Feminism: A Fourth Wave?' (2013) 4(2) *Political Insight* 22

Munro, V, 'Constructing Consent: Legislating Freedom and Legitimising Constraint in the Expression of Sexual Autonomy' (2008) 41 *Akron Law Review* 923

National Union of Teachers (NUT), *NUT Policy Statement on Preventing Sexual Harassment and Bullying* (NUT, 2014)

New Legislation to Strengthen Child Sexual Abuse Laws: Factsheet for Service Providers (NSW Government, 2018)

Newburn, T, 'Tackling Youth Grime and Reforming Youth Justice: The Origins and Nature of "New Labour" Policy' (1998) 19(3–4) *Policy Studies* 199

Newburn, T and Stanko, E, 'When Men Are Victims: The Failure of Victimology' in T Newburn and E Stanko (eds), *Men, Masculinities and Crime: Just Boys Doing Boy's Business?* (London, Routledge, 1994)

Northamptonshire Police, 'Breck's Last Game' (Northamptonshire Police, 2019)

Northern Ireland Audit Office, *Managing Children Who Offend – Report* https://www.niauditoffice.gov.uk/publications/html-document/managing-children-who-offend-report accessed 17 July 2023

Northern Ireland NGO Alternative Report, *Submission to the United Nations Committee on the Rights of the Child for Consideration during the Committee's Examination of the United Kingdom of Great Britain and Northern Ireland Government Report* (Children's Law Centre and Save the Children, 2015)

NSPCC, 'Child Sexual Exploitation Crimes up 10% in the Last Year' https://www.nspcc.org.uk/about-us/news-opinion/2022/child-sexual-exploitation-crimes-up-10-in-the-last-year/ accessed 17 July 2023

NSPCC, *Statistics Briefing: Child Sexual Abuse* (NSPCC, 2021)

NSPCC, *Sexual Development and Behaviour in Children* (NSPCC, 5 August 2022) https://learning.nspcc.org.uk/child-health-development/sexual-behaviour accessed 17 July 2023

Oakley, A, *Sex, Gender and Society* (Maurice Temple Smith Ltd, 1972)

Obermann, M-L, 'Moral Disengagement among Bystanders to School Bullying' (2011) 10(3) *Journal of School Violence* 239

Obermaier, M, Fawzi, N and Koch, T, 'Bystanding or Standing By? How the Number of Bystanders Affects the Intention to Intervene in Cyberbullying' (2016) 18(8) *New Media & Society* 1491

O'Connor, K, Drouin, M, Yergens, N and Newsham, G, 'Sexting Legislation in the United States and Abroad: A Call for Uniformity' (2017) 11(2) *International Journal of Cyber Criminology* 218

Office for National Statistics, *Online Bullying in England and Wales: Year Ending in March 2020* (ONS, 2020)

O'Keeffe, GS and Clarke-Pearson, K, 'The Impact of Social Media on Children, Adolescents, and Families' (2011) 127(4) *Pediatrics* 800

Oliver, M, 'Whiting Found Guilty of Sarah Payne Murder' (*The Guardian*, 12 December 2001)

Olweus, D, 'Annotation: Bullying at School: Basic Facts and Effects of a School Based Intervention Program' (1994) 35(7) *The Journal of Child Psychology and Psychiatry* 1171

Olweus, D, 'Bully/Victim Problems among School Children: Basic Facts and Effects of a School-Based Intervention Program' in D Pepler and K Rubin (eds), *The Development and Treatment of Childhood Aggression* (Lawrence Erlbaum Associates Inc, 1991)

O'Neill, J, '"Strong Support" for Raising the NI Minimum Age of Criminal Responsibility, Consultation Finds' (BBC, 2 June 2023)

Oriola, T, 'Criminalising Revenge Pornography in Northern Ireland: Laws and Lessons from England and Wales and other Common Law Jurisdictions', Knowledge Exchange Seminar 2017–18 (Northern Ireland Assembly, 2018)

Ortega, R, Elipe, P, Mora-Merchan, JA, Genta, ML, Brighi, A, Guarani, A, Smith, PK, Thompson, F and Tippett, N, 'The Emotional Impact of Bullying and Cyberbullying on Victims: A European Cross-National Study' (2012) 38(5) *Aggressive Behaviour* 342

Paine, ML and Hansen, DJ, 'Factors Influencing Children to Self-Disclose Sexual Abuse' (2002) 22 *Clinical Psychology Review* 271

Palmer, MJ, Clarke, L, Ploubidis, G and Wellings, K, 'Prevalence and Correlates of "Sexual Competence" at First Heterosexual Intercourse among Young People in Britain' (2019) 45 *BMJ Sex Reproductive Health* 127

Papadopoulos, L, *Sexualisation of Young People Review* (Home Office, 2010)

Pearce, J, 'A Social Model of "Abused Consent"' in M Melrose and J Pearce (eds), *Critical Perspectives on Child Sexual Exploitation and Related Trafficking* (Palgrave Macmillan, 2013)

Penney, R, 'The Rhetoric of the Mistake in Adult Narratives of Youth Sexuality: The Case of Amanda Todd' (2016) 16(4) *Feminist Media Studies* 710

Perraudin, F, 'Offenders in Rochdale Child Sexual Abuse Scandal "Remain at Large"' (*The Guardian*, 16 May 2017)

Perry, C, *Independent Inquiry into Online Child Protection* (London, 2012)

Perry, R, 'Revising Irish History: The Northern Ireland Conflict and the War of Ideas' (2010) 40(4) Journal of European Studies 329

Pesa, JA, Syre, TR and Jones, E, 'Psychosocial Differences Associated with Body Weight among Female Adolescents: The Importance of Body Image' (2000) 26(5) *Journal of Adolescent Health* 335

Phippen, A, *Sexting: An Exploration of Practices, Attitudes and Influences* (London, UK Safer Internet Centre and NSPCC, 2012)

——— *Children's Online Behaviour and Safety: Policy and Rights Challenges* (Palgrave Macmillan, 2017)

Phippen, A and Wright, D, *Sharing Personal Images and Videos among Young People* (UKCCIS, 2011)

Phoenix, J, 'Child Sexual Exploitation, Discourse Analysis and Why We Still Need to Talk about Prostitution' in J Pearce (ed), *Child Sexual Exploitation: Why Theory Matters* (Policy Press, 2019)

Pineau, L, 'Date Rape: A Feminist Analysis' (1989) 8(2) *Law and Philosophy* 217

Police Service of Northern Ireland, *Chief Constable's End of Year Report to the Northern Ireland Policing Board 2021–2022* (Police Service of Northern Ireland Strategic Communications and Engagement Department, 2022)

Powell, A, 'Sexual Pressure and Young People's Negotiation of Consent' ACSSA Newsletter No 14 (Australian Institute of Family Studies, 2007)

Powell, A, *Sex, Power and Consent: Youth Culture and the Unwritten Rules* (Cambridge University Press, 2010)

Powell, A and Henry, N, 'Blurred Lines? Responding to "Sexting" and Gender-Based Violence among Young People' (2014) 39(2) *Children Australia* 119

Public Prosecution Service, *Guidelines for the Prosecution of Young People* (Public Prosecution Service for Northern Ireland, 2021)

Purvis, E and Rodgers, P, 'The Minimum Age of Criminal Responsibility in Northern Ireland' (*Eurochild*, 17 March 2023)

Qvortrup, J, 'Childhood Matters: An Introduction' in J Qvortrup, M Bardy, G Sgritta and H Wintersberger (eds), *Childhood Matters: Social Theory, Practice and Politics* (Vienna, Avebury, 1994)

Radford, L, Corral, S, Bradley, C, Fisher, H, Bassett, C, Howat, N and Collishaw, S, 'Child Abuse and Neglect in the UK Today' (NSPCC, 2011)

Rallings, J, *Youth and the Internet: A Guide for Policy Makers* (Barnardo's, 2015)

Rape and Sexual Assault Statistics https://rapecrisis.org.uk/get-informed/statistics-sexual-violence/ accessed 17 July 2023

Richards, R and Calvert, C, 'When Sex and Cell Phones Collide: Inside the Prosecution of a Teen Sexting Case' (2009) 32(1) *Hastings Communications and Entertainment Law Journal* 1

Rigby, K, 'Consequences of Bullying in Schools' (2003) 48(9) *The Canadian Journal of Psychiatry* 583

Ringrose, J, 'Are you Sexy, Flirty or a Slut? Exploring Sexualization and How Teen Girls Perform/ Negotiate Digital Sexual Identity on Social Networking Sites' in R Gill and C Scharff (eds), *New Femininities: Postfeminism, Neoliberalism and Subjectivity* (Palgrave Macmillan, 2011)

Ringrose, J and Renold, E, 'Slut-Shaming, Girl Power and "Sexualisation": Thinking through the Politics of the International SlutWalks with Teen Girls' (2012) 24(3) *Gender and Education* 333

Ringrose, J, Gill, R, Livingstone, S and Harvey, L, *A Qualitative Study of Children, Young People and 'Sexting': A Report Prepared for the NSPCC* (NSPCC/LSE, 2012)

Ringrose, J, Harvey, L, Gill, R and Livingstone, S, 'Teen Girls, Sexual Double Standards and "Sexting": Gendered Value in Digital Image Exchange' (2013) 14(3) *Feminist Theory* 305

Rolston, B, Schubotz, D and Simpson, A, 'Sex Education in Northern Ireland Schools: A Critical Evaluation' (2005) 5(3) *Sex Education* 217

Rumney, P and Fenton, R, 'Intoxicated Consent in Rape: Bree and Juror Decision-Making' (2008) 71(2) *Modern Law Review* 279

Rubin, GS, 'Thinking Sex: Notes for a Radical Theory of the Politics of Sexuality' in K Plummer (ed), *Sexualities: Critical Concepts in Sociology* (first published 1984, Routledge, 2002)

Sabella, RA, Patchin, JW and Hinduja, S, 'Cyberbullying Myths and Realities' (2013) 29(6) *Computers in Human Behavior* 2703

Salter, M, Crofts, T and Lee, M, 'Beyond Criminalisation and Responsibilation: Sexting, Gender and Young People' (2013) 24(3) *Current Issues in Criminal Justice* 301

Sargeant, J, 'Northern Ireland: Functioning of Government without Ministers' (Institute for Government, 14 November 2022) https://www.instituteforgovernment.org.uk/article/explainer/northern-ireland-functioning-government-without-ministers accessed 17 July 2023

Schubotz, D and Devine, P, *Not So Different: Teenage Attitudes across a Decade of Change in Northern Ireland* (Russell House Publishing, 2014)

Scraton, P, '*Childhood' in 'Crisis'?* (UCL Press, 1997)

Scott, S, Jackson, S and Beckett-Milburn, K, 'Swings and Roundabouts: Risk Anxiety and the Everyday Worlds of Children' (1998) 32(4) *Sociology* 689

Scottish Government, 'United Nations Convention on the Rights of the Child Implementation: Introductory Guidance' (19 November 2021) https://www.gov.scot/publications/implementing-united-nations-convention-rights-child-introductory-guidance/pages/5/ accessed 17 July 2023

Setty, E, '"Confident" and "Hot" or "Desperate" and "Cowardly"? Meanings of Young Men's Sexting Practices in Youth Sexting Culture' (2020) 23(5) *Journal of Youth Studies* 561

Schobert, K, Cooper, S, Fries, N and Chervilllil, M, '"I Thought We Were Vibin'": A Qualitative Exploration of Sexual Agency and Consent in Young People' (2021) 24(7) *Sexualities* 906

Shariff, S, *Sexting and Cyberbullying: Defining the Line for Digitally Empowered Kids* (Cambridge University Press, 2015)

Sharing Nudes and Semi-Nudes: Advice for Education Settings Working with Children and Young People (UK Council for Internet Safety, 2020)

Simpson, B, 'Challenging Childhood: Challenging Children: Children's Rights and Sexting' (2013) 16(5/6) *Sexualities* 690

Sjolin, C, 'Ten Years On: Consent under the Sexual Offences Act 2003' (2015) 79(1) *The Journal of Criminal Law* 20

Smahel, D, Machackova, H, Mascheroni, G, Dedkova, L, Staksrud, E, Olafsson, K, Livingstone, S and Hashbrink, U, *EU Kids Online 2020: Survey Results from 19 Countries* (EU Kids Online, 2020)

Smith, C, Allardyce, S, Hackett, S, Bradbury-Jones, C, Lazenbatt, A and Taylor, J, 'Practice and Policy in the UK with Children and Young People Who Display Harmful Sexual Behaviours: An Analysis and Critical Review' (2014) 20(3) *Journal of Sexual Aggression* 267

Snyder, R, 'What is Third-Wave Feminism? A New Directions Essay' (2008) 34(1) *Journal of Women and Culture in Society* 175

SooHoo, S, 'Examining the Invisibility of Girl-to-Girl Bullying in the Schools: A Call to Action' (2009) 13(6) *International Electronic Journal for Leadership in Learning* 1

Soothill, K, and Walby, S, *Sex Crime in the News* (London, Routledge, 1991)

Speakman, M, 'Landmark Child Sexual Abuse Laws in Force' (NSW Government, 1 December 2018) https://www.justice.nsw.gov.au/Documents/Media%20Releases/2018/landmark-child-sexual-abuse-laws-in-force.pdf accessed 17 July 2023

Specia, M, 'How Savita Halappanavar's Death Spurred Ireland's Abortion Rights Campaign' (*The New York Times*, 27 May 2018)

Spencer, D, 'Sex Offender as Homo Sacer' (2009) 11(2) *Punishment and Society* 219

Staffordshire Commissioner, 'Young People Urged to Say No to Sexting in New Campaign' (9 February 2016) https://staffordshire-pfcc.gov.uk/young-people-urged-to-say-no-to-sexting-in-new-campaign/ accessed 17 July 2023

Stanko, E, *Intimate Intrusions: Women's Experience of Male Violence* (London, Routledge, 1985)

Stanko, E and Hobdell, K, 'Assault on Men: Masculinity and Male Victimisation' (1993) 33(3) *British Journal of Criminology* 400

Sticca, F and Perren, S, 'Is Cyberbullying Worse Than Traditional Bullying? Examining the Differential Roles of Medium, Publicity, and Anonymity for the Perceived Severity of Bullying' (2013) 42 *Journal of Youth and Adolescence* 739

Suler, J, 'The Online Disinhibition Effect' (2004) 7(3) *CyberPsychology and Behaviour* 321

Suzuki, LK and Calzo, JP, 'The Search for Peer Advice in Cyberspace: An Examination of Online Teen Bulletin Boards about Health and Sexuality' (2004) 25(6) *Journal of Applied Developmental Psychology* 685

Tadros, V, 'Rape without Consent' (2006) 26(3) *Oxford Journal of Legal Studies* 515

Taylor, A, 'Troubling Childhood Innocence: Reframing the Debate over the Media Sexualisation of Children' (2010) 35(1) *Australasian Journal of Early Childhood* 48

—— 'Reconceptualising the "Nature" of Childhood' (2011) 18(4) *Childhood* 420

Temple, JR, Lee, VD, van den Berg, P, Ling, Y, Paul, JA and Temple, BW, 'Brief Report: Teen Sexting and Psychological Health' (2014) 37(1) *Journal of Adolescence* 33

Thelen, E, '"Keep It Quiet": The Family That Covered Up Sex Abuse' (BBC, 10 April 2012)

Thornberg, R, '"She's Weird!" – The Social Construction of Bullying in School: A Review of Qualitative Research' (2011) 25(4) *Children and Society* 258

Together (Scottish Alliance for Children's Rights), 'Deputy First Minister Gives Update on UNCRC Incorporation' (24 May 2022) https://togetherscotland.blog/2022/05/24/deputy-first-minister-gives-update-on-uncrc-incorporation/ accessed 17 July 2023

Turbert, K, 'Faceless Bullies: Legislative and Judicial Responses to Cyberbullying' (2009) 33(2) *Seton Hall Legislative Journal* 651

Vandebosch, H and Van Cleemput, K, 'Defining Cyberbullying: A Qualitative Research into the Perceptions of Youngsters' (2008) 11(4) *CyberPsychology and Behaviour* 499

Vizard, E, 'Adolescent Sexual Offenders' (2007) 6(10) *Psychiatry* 433

Waling, A, Fisher, C, Ezer, P, Kerr, L, Bellamy, R and Lucke, J, '"Please Teach Students that Sex is a Healthy Part of Growing Up": Australian Students' Desires for Relationships and Sexuality Education' (2021) 18 *Sexuality Research and Social Policy* 1113

Walklate, S, 'Reframing Criminal Vicitmisation: Finding a Place for Vulnerability and Resilience' (2011) 15(2) *Theoretical Criminology* 179

Weiderud, E and Gillum, K, 'The Meaning and Impact of International Solidarity for Abortion Rights in NI' in F Bloomer and E Campbell (eds), *Decriminalising Abortion in Northern Ireland* (Bloomsbury, 2022)

West, R, 'Consent, Legitimation, and Dysphoria' (2020) 83(1) *The Modern Law Review* 1

WHO, *Sexual Health*, https://www.who.int/health-topics/sexual-health#tab=tab_1 accessed 17 July 2023

WHO Team, *Violence against Children Online: What Health Systems and Health Care Providers Can Do* (WHO, 2022)

Wilkinson, DC, 'Sex and Relationships Education: A Comparison of Variation in Northern Ireland's and England's Policy-Making Processes' (2017) 17(6) *Sex Education* 605

Williams, R, 'Annie Lennox "Disturbed and Dismayed" by "Overtly Sexualised" Pop Performances' (*The Telegraph*, 6 October 2013)

Wolak, J and Finkelhor, D, 'Sexting: A Typology' (Durham NH, Crimes against Children Research Centre, 2011)

Wolak, J, Finkelhor, D, Mitchell, KJ and Ybarra, ML, 'Online "Predators" and Their Victims: Myths, Realities, and Implications for Prevention and Treatment' (2008) 63(2) *American Psychologist* 111

Wolak, J, Mitchell, K and Finkelhor, D, 'Does Online Harassment Constitute Bullying? An Exploration of Online Harassment by Known Peers and Online-Only Contacts' (2007) 41 *Journal of Adolescent Health* 51

Wood, M, Barter, C and Berridge, D, '*Standing on My Own Two Feet*': *Disadvantaged Teenagers, Intimate Partner Violence and Coercive Control* (NSPCC, 2011)

Woodiwiss, J, 'Dramatising a Contemporary Childhood Sexual Abuse Narrative: Reinforcing a Hierarchy of Victims' (2022) *Feminist Media Studies* 1

Wood, M, Barter, C, Stanley, N, Aghtaie, N and Larkins, C, 'Images across Europe: The Sending and Receiving of Sexual Images and Associations with Interpersonal Violence in Young People's Relationships' (2015) 59 *Children and Youth Services Review* 149

Wyn, J and White, R, *Rethinking Youth* (London, SAGE, 1997) 22

Ybarra, ML and Mitchell, KJ, 'How Risky Are Social Networking Sites? A Comparison of Places Online Where Youth Sexual Solicitation and Harassment Occurs' (2008) 121(2) *Pediatrics* 350

Young, H, Burke, L and Nic Gabhainn, S, 'Sexual Intercourse, Age of Initiation and Contraception among Adolescents in Ireland: Findings from the Health Behaviour in School-Aged Children (HBSC) Ireland Study' (2018) 18(362) *BMC Public Health* 1

INDEX

Milton Keynes UK
Ingram Content Group UK Ltd.
UKHW031540160224
437875UK00003BA/46